*Managing by Design . . .*
*for Maximum*
*Executive Effectiveness*

# Managing by Design . . . for Maximum Executive Effectiveness

*Ray A. Killian*

American Management Association, Inc.

To
Ray Jr.
and the unlimited potential in management
for contribution and personal fulfillment

# ⊡ Preface

THE purpose of this book is to provide a guide for improved management performance and, in turn, for the profitable growth of individual executives and companies. The book seeks both to show and to convince the reader that successful management can be deliberately designed and attained, thus increasing the benefits to all who are concerned with the results achieved by the enterprise.

*Managing by Design* is based on the premise that an enterprise's most critical need today is for more dynamic executives and improved managerial leadership. The demand is for executives who can manage total resources to maximize asset value—for *management capable of designing and achieving favorable results.* Opportunities have never been more numerous nor rewards greater for the individual capable of this type of management. Yet leading companies list the lack of such individuals as their most serious deterrent to growth and expansion.

Although the criticism is often heard that there are too many chiefs and not enough Indians, the facts prove otherwise. *Newsweek* magazine recently reported that one professional recruiter had 62 positions to fill above the $20,000 level, including three presidencies; that professional recruiters in New York alone handle some 25,000 jobs annually at levels above $15,000; and that at one time International Telephone and Telegraph Corporation had 40 openings at salary levels above $20,000. Confirming the need for more "chiefs" have been the heads of such national concerns as Carrier Corporation,

Columbia Broadcasting System, and Carson Pirie Scott & Company, all of which have cited the scarcity of productive executives as their most pressing problem.

This book is directed to the executive in command and to those of his subordinates who, together with him, are responsible for running the company. As indicated by the table of contents, it focuses on today's demand for a new type of manager who is dedicated to improving company operations; who is capable of efficiently organizing and directing the company's most expensive and vital resource—its people; who can successfully blueprint plans and follow through with purposeful action; who is capable of effectively practicing the highly specialized art of human leadership; who can build individual and group effort through realistic patterns of total involvement; and who believes that maximum contribution is based on professional performance.

A cross-pollination of company types, illustrations based on actual experience, and a generous supply of proven "success stories" testify to the validity of the material and support the fact that a sufficient body of knowledge and guidance is available regarding the successful practice of management. But the emphasis is on the gap between potential and actual management performance. The book suggests specific leadership tools that managers can utilize to close this gap. These include programs to promote higher standards of executive job performance; to establish bench marks against which to measure progress; to create a more productive climate; to better organize people and activities for the achievement of improved results; to foster a total commitment to the pursuit of common goals; and to meet the unique challenge of professional management today and tomorrow.

The text particularly stresses management as a profession, the anatomy of corporate command, and the skills and techniques necessary for managerial success. Recognition is given to the key contribution being made by administrative management both to the continuing rise of our high standard of living and to the continuing growth of the productive free enterprise system. Appropriate attention is also focused on the executive's obligation to the stockholders, as well as his responsibilities to the many people who make up the enterprise and its publics. The approach is not overly technical in that the book does not propose to make EDP experts out of managers or put them in key positions as full-time, long-range planners. But it does recognize that managers must be concerned with these and the other specialized skills and functions of modern professional management. It therefore seeks to make the manager more knowledgeable in these areas and to stimulate him to integrate these contributory functions within his area of responsibility.

There is no advocacy here of naïve notions that management performance can be improved with either magic wands or elaborately contrived programs. However, this book does supply the nutrients capable of producing executive performance of Olympian caliber, provided the reader is willing to follow the guides presented and to live by the disciplines demanded for competitive superiority.

—Ray A. Killian

# ⊞ Contents

## PART I
### FOUNDATION FOR MANAGEMENT

## PART II
### THE SKILLS OF PROFESSIONAL MANAGEMENT

## PART III
## MAXIMIZING MANAGERIAL PERFORMANCE

## PART IV
## KEYS TO HUMAN UNDERSTANDING AND RESPONSE

## PART V
## MANAGEMENT'S UNIQUE CHALLENGES:
## TODAY AND TOMORROW

# PART VI
## CONCLUSION: IMPACTS AND IMPERATIVES

*Part I*

*Foundation for Management*

# I

# Management: The Decisive
# Ingredient of Enterprise

W<small>HAT</small>'s the name of the game? What is the role of management in the free enterprise system? The college graduate writes on his employment application that he wants an "administrative, executive, or management" position with the company. Yet he, along with many presently employed managers and executives, has an inadequate understanding of the functions, characteristics, disciplines, purposes, skills, and responsibilities of management.

Since it is the purpose of this book to provide a guide to management by deliberate design, this first chapter will address itself to an identification and description of the purposes and characteristics of management. It is essential that every individual preparing for, seeking, or pursuing a career in management have a thorough understanding not only of the "name of the game," but, more importantly, of the game itself, the nature of its ball park, and its rules.

3

Management: Servant of Man—Master of Resources

To quote the late President John F. Kennedy, "The role of management in our society is critical in human progress. It serves to identify a great need of our time: to improve the standards of living of all peoples through effective utilization of human and material resources." (1) *

Management thus becomes the servant of mankind in assuming its role as master of resources for the benefit of the employee, the enterprise, the owner, and society. It serves its own personal and professional goals only insofar as its contribution serves the objectives of all those touched by the activity and influence of the company. Management is the most decisive ingredient in the success or failure of any enterprise. This is especially true in the industrial and business community, where management procures and controls the human resource, makes decisions regarding the activities of the company, and, in the final analysis, both shapes and determines the actual destiny of the company. As management goes, so goes the company!

The Significance of Management

The full importance of management becomes evident with the recognition that on its competence depend not only profits, but the attitude of investors and bankers and the confidence with which prospective executives and employees view the company; and its competence also determines whether the company will become a more important factor in the industrial community or will gradually fade into oblivion. Entire companies have been merged or purchased for the sole purpose of acquiring their management talent. Owners of family enterprises, partnerships, and even corporations have deliberately sought to acquire such professional competence.

This search for competent professional leadership is indicative of the competitive challenge inherent in an enterprise system that provides for the survival and growth of only the best-managed companies. The incompetent, the unimaginative, the disorganized, and those unwilling to change are left behind in the race for profitable business. Customers, regardless of who or where they are, eventually determine who will remain in business and who will not. They have demonstrated that they will decide in favor of the company that provides the product and service of the best quality at the fairest

* Numbers in parentheses indicate references listed at the end of each chapter.

price. To do this faster and better than the competition requires a caliber of management that can make the right things happen at the right time.

During recent years, emphasis has been correctly placed on management as the critical factor in the activities of a company. Analysis of business failures and losses, on the one hand, and successes and growth, on the other, has identified management influence as decisive in every case. It is management that ultimately determines the success of an enterprise.

## Management Defined

Lawrence A. Appley, president of the American Management Association, has defined management as "the guiding of human and physical resources into dynamic organization units which attain their objectives to the satisfaction of those served and with a high degree of morale and sense of attainment on the part of those rendering the service." (2) This guidance is manifested in a deliberate, calculated, planned process that blends the rights and needs of all concerned with those of the enterprise as it seeks to serve the maximum interests of all.

Management has also been defined as that group of people responsible for accomplishing results through the efforts of other people. The criteria for successful management, then, include, not just the individual manager's personal diligence and effort, but also his effectiveness in utilizing the total potential of all others subject to his leadership. The only valid test of that leadership is its effectiveness in influencing others, as shown in organizational performance and final results. "Hard work" alone will not guarantee success.

## The Individuality of Management

Managers and management techniques, like the clouds of summer, come in a variety of sizes and shapes. Although the body of management studies has attempted to construct a rigid mold or profile of the "ideal manager," many real-life successes bear little resemblance to that ideal. However, management experts have been able to identify which patterns, tools, and techniques are more likely to lead to the effective practice of management. As guides, these tend to become operating models for the executive who seeks to increase his own contribution to the management process.

The reams of published management materials, as well as the findings of human psychology, business economics, and technology, can contribute substantially to the effective practice of management; but they cannot become a do-it-yourself kit where each step is clearly spelled out from start to finish. If this were possible, any neophyte could simply read the instructions and function successfully in a management capacity. However, the dedicated manager does take full advantage of all information available, while recognizing that its value is in direct proportion to the amount of mature judgment and skill used in putting it into actual practice.

## Management as a Process

The actual practice of management is not carried on in ivory towers or through the medium of fanciful dreams. Rather, it is a dynamic process of making things happen. It constantly involves the selection of activities to be included and increased, the rejection of the undesirable and unsuitable, the fitting of various functions together like building blocks, timing as precise as in a rocket launching, and coordination worthy of an army commander. In one sense, management produces nothing concrete, and yet it is responsible for everything concrete produced by the company. Management serves as a catalyst which causes action; it determines the course to be followed and then leads the way. It ignites the energy, both physical and mental, of other people. It insists on action that leads forward to predetermined goals.

Management, based on accumulated knowledge, moves purposefully along through recognized channels of effectiveness and utilizes tested skills to make the most of every opportunity afforded by the company environment. Most significantly, management consists not of passive maintenance but of goal-oriented activity, which is both accelerated and guided by executive involvement.

## Measuring the Cost of Management

How many dollars could be saved in salaries if all executives were eliminated from the payroll? Is the cost of good management too high? Company owners, those in a position to know, would answer with a resounding no! The only management that is too costly is bad management; good management pays for itself. If management contributes to the business to the limit of its potential, then the profit, or increased return, will be in proportion to the investment.

An electrical manufacturer had four different but identical factories, all producing the same item, yet the cost of operations in one consistently ran from 10 to 15 percent higher than in the other three. The company president concluded that the cost of management was too high only where managers were operating unsuccessfully. The experience of others reinforces that conclusion—the most expensive management is the management that loses money for the company or fails to make a profit. The unit that is operating below its potential is paying for a type of management service that it is not receiving.

It has been said that employees can put in a certain number of hours per day going through the motions of working and get by with it. This may be possible when an assembly line or a flow of customers keeps the momentum rolling. Not so with executives. Instead of waiting for something to happen, they must take the initiative and make certain not only that it happens but that it happens in the manner most beneficial to the company. The executive must clearly understand this, and he must recognize also that his compensation and advancement will be based not on his physical presence but rather on the results of his leadership.

## The Evolution of Management

Business activities and industrial processes have changed more during the past generation than in the entire previous history of mankind. The spread of automation, the installation of computers, and the acceptance of new techniques have caused many to realize that executives must periodically return to school throughout their careers in order to keep up with technology and the dynamics of change.

Not only is technology changing, but changes are also occurring in the human relationships within the management process. As Lawrence A. Appley puts it,

> The most significant development in business and industrial management in the last 40 years is the evolution from master-servant relationship to enlightened leadership of free people. This has required recog-

nition and rapid development of management as a profession. Professional management is the scientific establishment of specific objectives and the intelligent guidance of human effort toward their attainment. (3)

## Dangers of Management Obsolescence

Concepts of management have evolved progressively from the earliest trusteeship ideas through various styles of paternalism, the heroic Horatio Alger image, and scientific planning and control to the high standards of professionalism demanded today. Shortsightedly, many individual managers have retained attitudes and practices that are more characteristic of one of these outmoded styles than of the enlightened, full-development, planned approach that has proved most beneficial to human needs and to profitable return on investment.

Capitalism, in its unique American manifestation, not only provides for change but decrees obsolescence for those who fail to do so. Unlike conditions in many societies, which restrict or prohibit any deviation from prescribed ways of doing things, the climate of capitalism demands change for survival.

Management, like the dodo bird or the blacksmith, can become completely out of step with the challenges and demands of its current environment. Television and radio announcements advise, "You can't meet tomorrow's job demands with yesterday's skills." The worker must constantly train up to stay up with new skills and technological changes. This updating is even more important for the manager. The future of the company cannot be entrusted to those who have failed to prepare for tomorrow's demands and opportunities. Consider these facts:

- Over one-half of the technical information printed during the past hundred years has been printed during the past ten.
- Information in quantities previously unimaginable is now being made readily available.
- National manufacturers report that up to 60 percent of their sales come from products discovered and developed within the past five years.
- Foreign competition is having a dramatic impact on such products as textiles, toys, automobiles, steel, and electronic equipment.

- Acquisitions, mergers, and consolidations have resulted in acute dislocations.
- Organizational structures and management patterns have undergone rapid change.

Management becomes obsolete because of its inability or failure to recognize and properly appraise, adapt, and exploit changes in the environment. Management obsolescence is a form of decay that is caused by a fatal combination of negative attitudes, outworn philosophies, and outmoded procedures that block response to current opportunities. It stems from complacency, fear of change, autocratic management practices, and insensitivity to human needs, both inside and outside the organization. The prescription for curing this otherwise terminal affliction is management capable of understanding and responding to the environment in a manner that develops the personal ability of the individual and encourages healthy growth throughout the company. Its characteristics are enlightened leadership, innovation, and a total organizational development that is geared to maximize the human and material resources of the company.

Today's fast, high-risk, computerized business world is the oyster of the manager with brains, judgment, imagination, education, ambition—and the wisdom of a late 20th century Solomon capable of blending all components together in precisely the right proportions. The strategic work of the manager is analogous to gambling with hundred-sided dice. The stakes of the game are high, and it often takes the finesse and daring of a riverboat gambler to stay in until the "pot" is won.

The aspirant who seeks to star on the management team must accept change as a way of life. Yesterday's home runs will not win today's ball game. Outmoded management techniques served their day well, but they are out of tune both with the needs and expectations of today's workers and with the technological systems and expertise required to compete in the mainstream of modern business society.

## Management as a Profession

Is management a profession? Can it qualify on a basis similar to other, more traditional professions? Managing, supervising, or influencing the behavior of others is one of the oldest activities known to man. It has been experiencing a period of transition and growth, but it still has few professional trappings. It awards no medals, wears no uniform, demands no academic degree, and does not require the passing of a test for legal qualification. It does have a jargon, but even this is not as incomprehensible to the laity as medical or legal terminology. And, in contrast to the lawyer, clergyman, or physician, who often guides and comforts on an individual basis, the professional manager may "minister" to thousands in relative obscurity, working to provide jobs, personal satisfaction, income, and profits.

AMA, however, contends that management is a valid profession, since it meets the following five basic qualifications:

1. It has a body of knowledge that is transferable. There are basic principles of management which can be identified, mastered, and practiced.
2. It follows a scientific approach. There are prescribed patterns for management action and leadership.
3. It involves specific skills and tools. These become the manager's tool kit, or the resources which he uses to carry out his duties and responsibilities.
4. It adheres to a code of ethics. Enlightened professional management responds conscientiously to accepted attitudes, philosophies, and creeds.
5. It has a required discipline. As in the case of other professional careers, managing requires a discipline for effective performance.

Few managers themselves would question whether professional approaches and skills are necessary to carry out the functions of management. The challenge of channeling and sparking maximum human effort calls for "pro" management performance—amateurish management simply will not win the ball game. Management is a profession in that managers, like doctors and lawyers, must be lifelong students, keeping abreast of the latest developments and techniques in their professional area.

In 1963, celebrating 40 years of progress in management, AMA stated:

As an institution, an activity, a philosophy, an art, management is so indispensable to our society that it is all the more astonishing that our concepts were practically unintelligible prior to World War I. Management, however, is more than a human institution. It is rapidly evolving as a true profession, with definable principles and with a body of reference points strong enough to differentiate managers from non-managers and to correlate basic goals for its members, regardless of the nature of their business, their geographical location, or the activity with which they are affiliated. (4)

Many factors have been responsible for the additional demands on management that must be met by performance of a professional caliber. A significant influence has been the diffusion of ownership. When ownership and active management were no longer vested in the same person or small group, management's responsibilities began to change. The ancestral owner-manager was held accountable only to a minimum degree for his management stewardship and faced an almost nonexistent threat of replacement if he failed to meet production, sales, or profit expectations. But, when the nonowner assumed command, he was held accountable by the hundreds of individual and institutional shareholders for a return on investment in the form of profit. If he failed to produce in accordance with expected results, he often found the company board of directors looking for a "more capable manager."

The rapid expansion of the economy, the increasing complexity of the socio-economic business environment, the involvement of government, and the growing complexities of management itself demanded a more professional performance. This, in turn, demanded an individual of more statesmanlike perspective, not just a skilled technician but a leader with the conceptual facility for directing and coordinating a variety of activities. In addition, the quantitative methods of mathematics and statistics are likely to loom larger as the basis of standards for evaluating management.

## A Concept of Excellence

Professionalism, in sports or management, requires the acceptance of those attitudes and practices that hold the greatest potential for both the individual and the group. This involves a concept of excellence based on the premise that the mental image constitutes a standard that controls the subsequent action. This concept, once identified and clarified, must be understood by everyone involved to the degree that all who share and accept it are thereby enabled to work harmoniously within a prescribed system.

This concept should be embodied in a dynamic process that reflects the validity and necessity of change—especially within management itself. Professional management responds to the truism that the most decisive influence on the enterprise and its activity is the kind of competence that is evidenced in constant, diligent, dedicated search for better methods, greater effectiveness, and higher achievements. Competent management has a built-in antenna that sends out and receives evaluations of new techniques and ideas; it both accepts and applies systems and techniques judged to be beneficial; and it is willing at all times to make decisions on the basis of factual evidence of contribution rather than outmoded traditions or personal prejudices.

This type of professional management remains free and unencumbered at all times to accept and apply those new ideas that will contribute most to the established goals of the company. And change is effected with a minimum of delay and a maximum of completeness.

## The Elements of Management

The process of managing involves two basic areas: what the individual executive does himself—his personal job activity—and the management of others. It is characterized not by blind groping, hunch, or impulse but by a deliberately planned approach. The manager knows what will happen because he contrives to make it happen. He makes it his business to predict the future environment and requirements of the enterprise. He then constructs and implements the organization and set of activities that will best meet the challenges of future opportunity as it relates to the operating and profit goals of the company.

The process involves such functions of professional management as planning, organizing, administering, and controlling; it is guided by standards of performance and continually seeks improvement. (These functions will be considered in other parts of this book and integrated into the management process.) The process also takes into account the laws of cause and effect, but on an anticipatory, projected, and compensated-for basis. A key to management by design is that it is not negligent in anticipating causes and effects, but plans for them on a basis that will maximize their advantage to the company. It recognizes and utilizes past experiences so as to channel resources in those directions expected to be most beneficial for the future.

In addition to those areas previously mentioned, the process of management usually includes the following:

- Determining exactly what each member of the group is to do.
- Communicating each member's responsibilities and expected results to him and motivating him to perform satisfactorily.

- Keeping all operations moving forward through the maze of decision making and problem solving.
- Utilizing resources and potential for increased results through appropriate delegation.
- Identifying, anticipating, and making tactical use of all influences for goal-oriented achievement.
- Integrating, meshing, and coordinating all influences, resources, and activities in such an effective manner that performance in one area or function serves to reinforce that in another.

The management process reflects a "take charge" approach to opportunities and resources afforded by the company environment. It is an assault on the beaches designed to produce conscious activity and the best possible results.

## How Management Spends Its Time

The production worker tends the machines; he engages in specific, identifiable activities. The salesman calls on prospects and writes orders. But what about the manager, the executive, the chief executive officer—what are the activities that occupy his time? What contribution do these activities make to other people and to the company?

David F. Linowes, writing in *Management Services*, lists the chief executive's concerns and activities as follows:

1. Communicating with operating personnel and the company's various publics;
2. Watching trends of operations;
3. Looking after the future or long-term interests;
4. Providing for the harmonious, constructive functioning of the organization;
5. Establishing a creative environment; and
6. Accepting the position of chief executive as a position of trust. (5)

The Management Development Laboratory of the University of Minnesota Industrial Relations Center once conducted a research study on "The Job(s) of Management." It found the functional activities of management centered principally in the areas of planning, investigating, coordinating, evaluating, supervising, staffing, negotiating, and representing. A second set of dimensions focused attention on areas of technical competence or knowledge. These included employees, finances, materials and goods, purchases and sales, methods and procedures, and facilities and equipment.

The accompanying table gives some indication of the time spent on various activities and areas of competence that concern management.

It is significant that the amount of time spent on the various functions and activities varied considerably from higher to lower management levels. For example, lower management spent 15 percent of its time planning, while higher management spent 28 percent; lower management spent 51 percent of its time supervising, while higher management spent only 22 percent; and lower management was concerned with being a generalist only 9 percent of the time, while this occupied higher management 20 percent of the time.

In brief, the major duties and responsibilities of management can be generally categorized under three headings:

1. *Planning* in all its various aspects, implications, and interactions.
2. *Organization* of all resources for maximum effectiveness and results.
3. *Execution* of plans so as to attain established objectives.

*Percentage of Work Day Spent by Managers on Various Functions and Areas of Competence*

[Source: Thomas A. Mahoney, Thomas H. Jerdee, and Stephen J. Carroll, "The Job(s) of Management," *Industrial Relations*, Vol. 4, No. 2, February 1965, p. 103.]

| Performance Function | | Area of Competence | |
|---|---|---|---|
| Planning | 19.5% | Employees | 27% |
| Investigating | 12.6 | Money and Finances | 9 |
| Coordinating | 15.0 | Materials and Goods | 15 |
| Evaluating | 12.7 | Purchases and Sales | 10 |
| Supervising | 28.4 | Methods and Procedures | 26 |
| Staffing | 4.1 | Facilities and Equipment | 11 |
| Negotiating | 6.0 | | |
| Representing | 1.8 | | |
| Totals * | 100.1% | | 98% |

* Totals do not add to 100 percent because of rounding.

## Defining the Individual Manager's Job

Although it is more difficult to define the job of the manager than that of the factory worker or the bank clerk, it is being done with a high degree of validity, with resulting benefit to the manager and those affected by his performance. AMA's *Defining the Manager's Job* (6) not only lists the duties and responsibilities of a variety of executives in several different fields, but also includes a large number of actual position descriptions from leading American corporations. This research study clarifies many of the functions of management as well as its relationships with other individuals and groups and its contributions to meeting company goals.

Managing by deliberate design is dependent on a clear identification of the activities in which each manager engages and for which he is accountable. It is accurate, of course, to state that he is responsible for everything that happens or fails to happen within his jurisdiction that affects the company, but this falls short of identifying and describing the specifics of what he does. Although the coach is responsible for the team's performance, he is not responsible for personally throwing the football or blocking a would-be tackler. However, the coach, the players, the college administration, and the fans should understand the types of things for which the coach *is* responsible. Analogously, everyone concerned is better informed and can interact more cooperatively and effectively if the manager-coach's functions have been clearly identified. This should result in a minimum of misunderstanding, overlap, and gaps in both the manager's job performance and his relationships with others.

Virgil K. Rowland suggests that a procedure for determining what the individual manager ought to be doing might well begin with the compilation of a list of the things with which management must be concerned. This can be done through group discussion, during which each item mentioned is listed. Subsequently, the list should be evaluated and agreement reached as to which of the items should be included in the job description as part of the "what" of the job. (7)

## Management's Contribution to Overall Goals

We have said that the only valid test for the existence of any company-related activity or cost is its contribution to the goals of the enterprise. No other test need be used to justify the presence or continuation of management or any executive.

In actual practice, the effective operation of the company depends upon management's skill and success in formulating overall jobs, communicating them, and motivating others to achieve them. Thus:

- Management provides the coaching leadership that converts individual component parts into a coordinated, smoothly functioning, winning team.
- It devises the system that constitutes the operating framework for the company and its people.
- It obtains the capital, the financing, and ultimately the physical plant and resources required.
- It energizes the enterprise that is the company—guiding and directing it into channels that assure maximum productive returns.
- It appraises, controls, and corrects activity for improved performance.
- It sets the pace and the tone; generates the climate, the *esprit de corps* and the attitudes; and thereby determines both effort and result.
- It supplies the necessary human resources through its responsibility to recruit, employ, develop, organize, and direct in a manner most beneficial to the individual and the enterprise.
- It initiates, determines, and directs all activities through its problem-solving responsibility and its decision-making prerogative.
- It selects and reinforces all activity that contributes, and it eliminates all activity that fails to contribute or is detrimental to company goals.
- It is responsible for profits and for control of expenses and is, therefore, accountable for the continued existence of the company, its future growth, and its ability to provide useful products and services to customers and monetary benefits and promotional opportunities to its employees.
- It contributes to the company and to society the benefits of corporate citizenship—its enlightened leadership, its material rewards, and its opportunities for a better way of life for all concerned.

Management, in short, bears a heavy responsibility to people both within the company and outside it who are influenced by its activities. It serves the best interests of its own people through skill and effectiveness in providing employment, a positive work environment, and opportunity for self-realization. It serves the interests of the public by providing products and services that represent dependable quality at fair prices. Its responsibility to the stockholders is served when the operation is profitable and provides a reasonable return on investment.

This broad-gauge responsibility of management fully justifies the attention and recognition it receives in the form of compensation and status. Management that does not manage, or management that provides ineffective leadership, does not merit these benefits because it has not made the contribution traditional to its role.

## The Mission to Manage

Management is the specific instrument of business enterprise that determines the economic performance of the company. When we talk of a company deciding to build a new plant, employ more people, or market a new product, we are talking about management decisions and management action. The enterprise cannot exist and function without management, and management has no excuse for existing except as it successfully manages the affairs of the company. It justifies its presence and cost through its economic performance. This is not to say that people and concepts of service and human welfare are unimportant. However, management's every activity, every decision, every expenditure must take economic considerations into account.

Management's first job is to manage the business. Its success in this mission cannot be measured in terms of knowledge, personality, or good intentions; rather, it rests in proof of achievement. Managing is not limited to passive, adaptive behavior but demands creative action—the action necessary to bring about the desired results. Obviously, managing is adaptation to economic environment, but it also implies active leadership in shaping that environment. Managers manage work, manage people, and manage the operating climate. Although these are separated for purposes of identification and improvement, in practice they must be integrated as one function. Blocking is an important element in a football game, but unless it is coordinated and integrated into the team activity, it serves no useful purpose. When management is managing, it functions as a multipurpose influence that initiates, directs, and controls the activities of the company in such a manner that maximum results are achieved.

## Managers Must Manage!

When there is a task to be performed, someone must be designated to perform it. When a message is to be delivered, a messenger is called. When the task is management, it is the premise of this book that someone must be found who can manage.

The quarterback takes charge, the squad leader assumes control, the teacher manages the class, the captain is in full command of the ship at all times. What of the business manager? Is he managing or just going along for the ride? What would we think of the skipper who failed to assume responsibility for the safety, direction, speed, and satisfactory progress of his ship toward its intended port? He must manage every activity on the ship in the way most conducive to a safe and profitable journey. His decisions are oriented toward the results expected of him; but, most importantly, he is in charge—he is making the right things happen. He is avoiding the wrong courses, steering clear of the icebergs, the severe storms, and the hazardous shoals.

Managers must *manage!* They must manage individual tasks and group tasks so as to best serve the long- and short-range goals of the company. Perhaps the most significant distinction between a "dead" and a "growing" management is the difference between just letting things happen and managing aggressively in a planned, anticipatory, take-charge manner that insures that the right things will happen.

## What Direction? The Future Role of Management

The fantastic rate of change, rising costs, ethical responsibilities, the growing need for technical sophistication, and the increasing complexity of the operating environment foretell a future of almost unbelievable demands on management. Today a manager who has been retired for ten years would feel as though he were in a strange world if he should participate in a management seminar. It is doubtful whether any other profession is more constantly challenged than management to be informed, to make the right responses in a changing world, and to manage effectively in a competitive environment.

Although the concept of management as a profession is relatively new, it contains much of promise and hope for the future of our system of capitalism and free enterprise. Legislative action will undoubtedly contrive to reduce the machinations of the unscrupulous individual or company that would distort the system or live as a parasite upon it. In the final analysis, however, it is the approbation of one's fellow men that is far more persuasive as a regulatory force and that distinguishes a civilized business society and the type of professional management advocated by this book. Philosophies, creeds, and motivations—whether stated or merely evidenced by practice—contain either the germs of death or the seeds of growth.

Management's role in a changing society must at all times be dynamic. Both now and in the future, it will be required to adapt constantly to altered economic conditions, social mores, and noneconomic influences in fields such as education and government. The role, the knowledge requirements, the skills, the systems, and the techniques of management will also be continually changing under the influence of such factors as the following:

1. *New data processing and informational systems.* There will be fantastic changes in the whole electronic-computer world that will drastically influence management and its functions.
2. *Demands for employees, skills, and specialized education* far in excess of supply in the foreseeable future.
3. *Government regulations, restrictions, involvement, and influences* of a magnitude that could very well shape and determine the operation of the company and the practice of management. Management already requires staffs of attorneys, accountants, tax experts, personnel specialists, and a host of others, primarily for the purpose of dealing with various governmental agencies.
4. *Increasing cost of doing business.* The cost of human time, raw materials, financing, services, and every resource required by the company will probably increase. Since economic performance is the primary responsibility of management, this will certainly be one of the most decisive areas.
5. *A world marketplace instead of a localized or national one.* There will be increased opportunity to invest, produce, and sell abroad; and, at the same time, domestic companies will be confronted with competition from foreign-produced goods.

6. *Increased mobility and more rapid communication.* The greater mobility of customers, services, and products will create a changing competitive environment. Instantaneous communication—audible, visual, and graphic—will create an "all at once" awareness of and demand for new products and services. This will also accelerate the rate of obsolescence and the demise of those items being replaced.

7. *Innovation both inside and outside the company.* It will be a rare situation where new products, new techniques, new ideas, new systems, and new services fail to constitute a "sink or swim" influence on the total affairs of the company. Survival demands research and development, deliberately created changes where the end purpose is improvement, and the appropriate management of newness and change.

8. A *dynamic climate best characterized by the term "revolution of rising expectations."* This will take the form of higher salaries and benefits for employees; vastly improved working conditions; opportunities for greater self-realization and participation in shaping future influences; customers who will demand greater conveniences, more service and services, less inferior merchandise, and greater integrity in both advertising and selling.

9. A *total approach to management and enlightened leadership.* This will involve new visions and dimensions of management—planning for long-range profit as well as short-term gains. It will mean greatly enlarged scope and influence for corporate policies and practices. It will demand that management recognize and fulfill its role beyond the economic shoreline, provide a kind of community and social leadership that will minimize the need for government coercion and regulation. Management's own self-interest and sense of ethical morality will motivate it to use its initiative, leadership talents, and financial resources for programming a better standard of living and fulfillment for every individual.

## A New Breed of Managers

Perhaps not a new breed of managers but certainly a new caliber of management performance will be demanded in the future. The manager will be expected to assume broad responsibilities, design and execute management policies with a minimum margin for error, and conduct the enterprise as both a social and an economic institution. The manager of the future must be better educated and more professionally trained for his role. He must be humanist, economist, engineer, salesman, psychologist, sociologist, politician, long-range planner, and field commander. His will be an uncommon challenge offering uncommon rewards for the star performer who masters the job of management to the degree that achieves results superior to those of the competition and in conformity with established objectives.

In summary: Management is a profession which, though at times overwhelming, can be exciting, filled with a sense of achievement, and rewarding for the successful practitioner. It is also one of the fastest-growing professional fields. At no time in the foreseeable future will there be an oversupply of professional managers who can make the right things happen in such a way as to fulfill the maximum expectations of all concerned.

### NOTES

[1] *The New York Times*, September 15, 1963.

[2] Lawrence A. Appley, "The Management Process," speech presented before various meetings of the American Management Association, 1965.

[3] *Ibid.*

[4] *The New York Times, op. cit.*

[5] David F. Linowes, "What Today's Chief Executive Does," *Management Services*, May–June 1966.

[6] C. L. Bennet, *Defining the Manager's Job*, American Management Association, New York, 1958.

[7] Virgil K. Rowland, *Managerial Performance Standards*, American Management Association, New York, 1960, p. 46.

# 2

# Company Philosophy:
# Framework for Policies and Action

C$_{AN}$ a company operate without a basic philosophy? Does your company have such a philosophy? Do you understand it? Do you agree with it? Has your company been operating for too long without subjecting its philosophy to review and re-evaluation? Are you willing to re-examine it and change it if necessary?

## A Starting Point: Defining the Nature of the Business

Before a company can evolve or change its philosophy, it must know what it wants to do and why it wants to do it. In the words of Frederick R. Kappel, when president of American Telephone and Telegraph Company:

A business—any business—is first of all an idea. The nature and shape and character of the business will necessarily grow out of the fundamental thought that drives it. And there must be such a driving thought—some germinal, inspiriting, action-compelling concept—if the business is to really live and grow. (1)

It was more than 50 years ago that Theodore N. Vail of AT&T voiced the idea that gives these words particular pertinence. "Our business," he stated flatly, "is public service." Not the manufacture of telephones. Not the sale of telephones. Not the installation of telephones. But public service as a form of business, with all other activities subordinate thereto.

Suppose the railroads had decided 50 years ago that they were in the "transportation business." Had they done so, they might be operating the trucking and airline companies today instead of competing with them.

Too many old-line retail establishments which decided 50 years ago that their business was to operate a downtown department store waited almost too long to reassess their purpose and decide that it was really their business to supply goods and services for the entire community—where, when, and in the manner that best suited the convenience of customers.

Before a company can establish a philosophy to guide it, it must determine the nature of its business. Does it manufacture motors, transport freight, sell shoes, lend money, operate a baseball team, or publish a paper? In the answer to this seemingly simple question lies the key to a company's operating philosophy and future success.

What is the nature of your company's business? To be valid, the answer should be restrictive enough to allow the business to fulfill the demands of excellence and broad enough to allow it to grow and change without succumbing to obsolescence at the first turn in technology or shift in consumer demand. It should permit the addition of new products and services and the dropping of the unprofitable or outmoded—the birth of a Mustang and the quiet demise of an Edsel.

## Philosophy: The Basis for Action

Closely interwoven and often indistinguishable from the nature of the business is its philosophy or reason for being what it is. A. W. Shaw, publisher of *Magazine of Business,* has said: "Every successful business is based on a philosophy which represents its reason for being. Out of this philosophy its principles are developed. Out of these principles its policies are evolved. To serve these policies, methods are provided." (2)

The expressed philosophy becomes the North Star by which the company proposes to navigate. It states in understandable and communicable form the character of the company, which in essence is thus saying, "By these words and the deeds they give meaning to, we are willing that all men know us—employees, customers, suppliers, and publics." This basic philosophy, once expressed, becomes sacrosanct and should be changed only by the individual or group charged with the direction of the company.

Every company philosophy begins with individual beliefs, finds its expression and implementation within the enlarged company framework, is related to the entire industry of which the company is a part, and supports and is supported by the economic system and environment in which the company operates. Thus a philosophy must encompass and operate on four different levels:

1. *Individual.* Each individual executive should be able to grasp and accept what the company represents itself to be and do. Company philosophy should be in accord with individual beliefs in order to promote harmony and link individual potential to that of the enterprise.

2. *Company.* Company philosophy must be reflected in policies and their influence on operations, and a sound philosophy should promote harmony, success, and profit. How to employ a philosophy to these pragmatic ends is the main thrust of this chapter.

3. *Industry.* Every company's reason for being should be equally applicable to the entire industry of which it is a part. Its executives and employees must believe they are involved in an industry as well as a company that renders a service to society. Thus any company philosophy should promote favorable acceptance and support of the whole industry.

4. *Society.* A sound business philosophy must recognize the social responsibility inherent in the corporate free enterprise system—a responsibility the company discharges not only by producing desired goods and services of high quality but also by assuming its obligations as a corporate citizen. Only by doing so can it continue to maintain and extend the validity of such words as these:

   The corporation as it exists in the United States today has enabled this country to achieve spectacular economic and technological development. In fact, our national affluence is a tribute to its success as a socio-economic institution, for the corporation's record of high achievement has resulted not only from its role as a producer of goods and services but equally from its ability to adapt to changing environment. (3)

As a company seeks to establish or to clarify its beliefs, it is asking and answering questions regarding basic values. It is searching for those culturally established standards that will prove acceptable to all people concerned with its affairs. These standards are often expressed in creeds that set forth the ethics of the profession, the industry, or the individual company. They stem from a value system grounded on Judeo-Christian ethics and beliefs. This base provides a frame of reference and a criterion for acceptable conduct. By linking its own purposes, principles, and methods of operation to this base, a company is able to gain acceptance and active support.

If company philosophy is basically wrong from a moral or ethical standpoint, then the individual executive should work within accepted company procedures toward desired change. Many executives, however, elect the other alternative, that of changing jobs. They say, "I was required to make statements about the product that weren't true." "The practices of the company were against my principles." "I just couldn't stomach what was going on in the company."

Principles translated into policies also serve to

- Perpetuate the continuity and stability of management.
- Integrate functions and activities and encourage teamwork.
- Promote consistency of management decisions and improve relations.
- Permit executives to handle problems more quickly and with greater freedom.
- Enable executives to fulfill their responsibilities by defining constraints within which they must operate. (4)

The Northern Illinois Gas Company has stated what it believes to be its purposes succinctly in this manner: "The basic purpose of Northern Illinois Gas Company is to perpetuate an investor-owned free enterprise company, rendering a needed, satisfactory service and earning optimum, long-range profit." (5)

The company then describes "what we do, where we do it, and how we do it." The purposes and principles are spelled out in detail in statements of what the company will do with regard to investors, customers, employees, the public, suppliers, competitors, government, and the gas industry. Each statement explains what the interested parties can expect from Northern Illinois Gas Company.

Significant benefits from the soul searching that results in this type of articulated statement will accrue to any company willing to examine its purpose, its beliefs, its policies, its procedures, and its relationships with all concerned people. Such an examination becomes necessary from time to time and should result in an evaluation and adjustment of those areas where change will better serve the total purposes of the company.

## Translating Philosophy into Policies and Rules

Expressions of company beliefs that are developed for pretense or for dusty files should be chucked into the wastebasket as quickly as possible. The company should not pretend that it is or represents something that it is not or does not. It should not attempt to stand on an anemic "ho hum, everyone else has one" arrangement of words. This is both false and misleading. The mere spouting or printing of high-sounding principles serves no useful function unless they have become practical guidelines for the strategy and activity of the business. Ask any customer about the philosophy of Macy's, and the reply will reflect an experience at the glove counter or the credit desk or the refund window. Talk with any automobile dealer about the quality control of the manufacturer, and the reply will be in terms of how many complaints and call-backs he has because of defective parts.

Chase Manhattan Bank states that policy, when used actively and positively as a factor in administration, has the following effect:

- It secures consistency of action throughout the undertaking.
- It acts as a basis for future action and decision.
- It insures coordination of plans.
- It requires control of performance in terms of the corresponding plan.
- It provides a means by which authority can be delegated, thus contributing directly to one of the most important principles of organization.

- It preserves the morale of employees when they know the declared policy of the undertaking, particularly if the policy is ethically sound and strictly enforced.
- It stimulates the staff to greater efforts and sustains loyalty in difficult times, with beneficial effect upon labor turnover.
- It maintains sound relations with customers and agents.
- It enhances prestige and reputation in the eyes of the public. (6)

IBM chairman Thomas J. Watson, Jr., summarized the importance of philosophy translated into action policies with this statement:

> . . . The basic philosophy, spirit, and drive of an organization have more to do with its relative achievements than do technological or economic resources, organizational structure, innovation, and timing. All these things weigh heavily on success. But they are, I think, transcended by how strongly the people in the organization believe in its basic precepts and how faithfully they carry them out. (7)

Our fastest-growing, largest, and most profitable corporations believe that their best interests, both long- and short-range, are served by a sound philosophy translated into policies for action. Although the success of such policies is more obvious in the larger, more formally organized companies, the same needs exist in smaller companies, although more informal statements and communicating procedures often suffice.

## Policies and Premises

Out of a broad general philosophy come specific premises that shape and direct policies. These premises apply to profits, customers, employees, quality, expense control, and other areas of operating concern, and they form the foundation on which policy and action are built. The following statement of Varian Associates is a case in point.

This statement of objectives is conceived as a mechanism for the examination and appraisal of working policies. The objectives are based on the following five major points:

a. The Company must be operated as a profitable enterprise, and must serve the needs of its customers, shareholders, and employees. It is our responsibility to think of profits in terms of complex responsibilities involving the shareholders (dividends, stock appreciation), the employees (salaries, benefits, working conditions), and the customers (quality product, fair price, good service).

b. The character of the Company is determined by its decision to operate in highly specialized fields, and to carry a large burden of pioneering in new fields of applied science.

c. The rarest commodities in the world are human intelligence and ingenuity. These must not be wasted, neglected, or allowed to stagnate.

d. The best scientific and engineering talent must be employed and placed in an environment which will facilitate the proper utilization of knowledge, intellect, and skill.

e. The operations of the Company are to be led by a management group which must have the respect of the organization for its business ability, integrity, fairness, and human approach to everyday problems. (8)

Although these premises are not appropriate for all companies, they do indicate the type of thinking that must go into foundation building. Sound premises once accepted become the points of reference for establishing operating procedures and policies.

## Philosophy and Human Resources

The following "cornerstones of human management" are the result of experience in conducting numerous management seminars and leadership programs over a period of years:

1. Human and company achievement is a management leadership responsibility.
2. People want to perform well.
3. People are complete individuals, and the influencing of their lives and destinies should be regarded as a sacred trust.
4. Human behavior is predictable.
5. Motivation and response are related to personal goals and self-realization.

6. The tools and skills of leadership can be identified and improved.
7. Leadership effectiveness is based on attitude, technique, and application.
8. Informative, persuasive leadership achieves best results.
9. Human effort must serve the mutual goal-interests of the individual, the leader, the company, and society.
10. An achieved result is management's moment of truth.

Major decisions in the human area are related to compensation, benefits and working conditions, profits, and long-range investment in the company's future. Charles Hughes, in his book *Goal Setting*, asks the question, "Is conflict inevitable between people interest and company interest?" (9) There need not be a *major* conflict. The employee should have many of the same interests as the company—growth of the enterprise, improved job opportunity, and improved benefits from the company. Management should make every effort to minimize potential conflict through effective communication and the quick resolution of disputes.

Policies should not pit the company against the individual, but should link efforts, creativity, and goals. Neither should they set job standards in opposition to human considerations. High job standards which are reasonable encourage the individual to reach higher, earn more, and thus become more valuable to himself and the company.

Clarence Francis, as part of his basic philosophy concerning people, emphasizes that the very essence of enlightened management is a recognition that the greatest assets in business are its human assets, and their improvement is a matter of material advantage as well as moral obligation. It is clear, therefore, that employees must be treated as honorable individuals, justly rewarded, encouraged in their work, fully informed, properly assigned, and that their lives and work must be given meaning and dignity on and off the job.

The key to quality production, growth, and customer relations is the employee. If the company is willing to work at recruiting and developing the right people and then creating the right environment for effective job performance, the rest of the corporate pieces will for the most part fall into place.

It is the company's basic philosophy as practiced in the human area that establishes the motivational level of the employee group. Countless well-thought-out policies simply don't work in practice because people don't understand them or don't implement them properly. It is assumed that management's values and logic will be shared by the people who implement policies and that management will take great care to formulate guides that will motivate as well as prove acceptable to the employee group. Success in this endeavor can eliminate most of the tensions and subsequent problems that are almost certain to arise if management fails to provide an adequate philosophy in the human area.

## Philosophy and Work

The general purpose of any company is useful work and service—it is this that creates jobs and profits. Company philosophy should give work an honorable status. It is the quality of a person's work that makes him really important to a firm and is the valid status symbol. The German sociologist Max Weber commented at the turn of the century that "capitalism required a religious philosophy that justified a person's position in terms of his own accomplishments and gave divine sanction to social striving. No better example of the manner in which religion justified the social order can be found in the annals of history and anthropology." (10) During the early stages of the Industrial Revolution, religious culture actually supported and placed the stamp of moral rightness on merited success. It became honorable to work and excel in work.

Focus must always be on the work activity that determines the productive achievement of the company. Status, recognition, compensation, and promotions should relate to work contribution. Company philosophy, translated into policies, should keep the spotlight on work as central to the job and the company's need for people.

## Philosophy and Profit

What do the people in the company think about profit? What have they been told about profit, its purpose, its place in management philosophy? Lack of communication in this area can be one of the most serious reasons for mistrust and hostility. Since profit is a stated purpose of the business, investments and work activity are directed to it.

The American business system has been subjected to more criticism and has had to take more lumps for its profits than for all its other "excesses" combined. Reformers, government officials, educators, and others have often leveled their severest criticism of business at the profit system or what they believe to be "excess profits." As stated previously, the company, its system of operation, and what it proposes to be must be acceptable to the employee, the government, the customer, and public groups. A significant factor influencing acceptance is what these groups believe to be the profit goal and philosophy of the company.

Vannevar Bush, when he was chairman of the board, Merck & Co., Inc., said this concerning profit:

> It is the prime duty of management to make a profit. Unless it does, it will not long be present to do anything else. But for a successful company this is not enough. It is not enough, for one reason, because in a democratic society and in the long run a corporation will not be allowed to exert its great economic power without harassment, unless the public believes that it is operating for the public benefit. (11)

The purpose, the essential need for, and the benefits from profits have seldom been adequately communicated to the general public or the employee group. However, better understanding and a reasonable acceptance of profit have been achieved through public ownership of stock as stockholders come to understand the relationship of profit to return on money invested. This group now includes large institutional investors such as colleges, foundations, religious groups, and investment clubs.

The whole area and concept of profit deserves the closest attention and an explanation of how it relates to basic company philosophy. The company should state clearly, for all to know, how it regards profit—its use and its benefits. Employees, customers, and owners should all be made aware of the stake they have in the present and future profitability of the enterprise.

## Philosophy and Growth

The corporation lives and operates in an environment of change, but what is its attitude and reaction to change and the opportunity for growth? Future survival and profitability hinge largely on the manner in which this question is answered.

Consider a few basic facts: The McGraw-Hill Economics Department has predicted that the economy will grow at a more rapid rate over the next 20 years than it has in any period during the past 50. The U.S. Chamber of Commerce predicts significant changes in the population and workforce with regard to age, skills, geographical location, income levels, corporate-related requirements, and purchasing habits. These changes will drastically influence operational procedures and the production of goods and services. (12)

Company philosophy should express an attitude toward change and growth that indicates a willingness to adjust to change and expand when necessary to promote the best interests of the enterprise. People should expect that the company will be progressive, that it will innovate, that it will become more efficient, and that it will work aggressively to fulfill enlarged purposes. The company's philosophy should communicate the belief that change, rather than connoting unsettled agitation, signifies dynamic and beneficial growth as a continuing way of life.

## Philosophy and Society

In 1966 President Lyndon B. Johnson, in a special message to management, stated, "Business leaders and government leaders bear great responsibilities for the economic progress of 190 million fellow Americans. As their trustees, we are altogether responsible for the wise direction of the most advanced, most productive, most rewarding economic system the world has ever known." (13)

Speaking in a similar vein before the National Industrial Conference Board, J. Wilson Newman, board chairman of Dun & Bradstreet, Inc., said:

> Management is going to be faced increasingly with the need to explain not only its operational processes to its customers, but also its basic social and economic philosophy to the public at large—there is a need to make its operational philosophies known to and understood by the general public, investors and non-investors. (14)

Just as every individual has a basic need to serve others, so the corporation has a need to serve the whole of society. Such service should not be limited to byproducts of the company's primary activity but should involve the contribution of talent, leadership, and financial support to individual projects and programs designed specifically to benefit society. The search for human self-expression, fulfillment, and enrichment in work as well as in personal life is one of the unique features of modern corporate existence. The company that fails to support and encourage such satisfactions is doomed—at worst to extinction, at best to fossilization. It is in this area that a company can demonstrate its deepest human qualities through its willingness to serve society, both inside and outside the walls of corporate life.

Company philosophy can and should spell out the company's attitude and actual practices in this significant social area. The individual committed to leaving the world a little better has a right to expect the same commitment from the place where he spends his working life. The discharge of its obligations to society enhances pride in the public image and the private practices of the company.

### Philosophy and the Ultimate "Boss"

Who *is* the boss? "There's only one boss," according to an editorial in the Atchinson *Globe,* "and whether a person shines shoes for a living or heads the largest corporation in the world, the boss remains the customer. . . . Some of the largest companies that had a flourishing business a few years ago are no longer in existence. They couldn't—or didn't—satisfy the customer. They forgot who the boss really is." (15)

The following serves as the customer relations creed for a major retail organization:

> Our Belief
> A sincere and gracious welcome for every customer.
> Merchandise of best value, widest assortment, leading fashions and outstanding service.
> Guaranteed satisfaction with every purchase.
> Customer services which are competitive and courteously extended.
> An attractive, friendly and orderly store.
> Professionally qualified personnel to serve customers.
> Integrity of operation and enlightened community citizenship.
> A commitment to each customer which assures satisfaction and benefit from every visit. (16)

Since no company can be self-sustaining, it must look outside for purpose, for income, and for business. The valid object of its search is the customer. Advertising, the projection of a company image, the mission of salesmen, and all general functions of the corporation are dependent on customers willing to pay for the fruits of corporate activity. It is the customer, alone, who is willing to supply the revenue essential to corporate existence.

The first responsibility of customer philosophy is to recognize this cus-

tomer primacy; the second is to translate this recognition into policies on customer relations. These policies should reflect the regard the company has for
the customer and outline precisely the role each individual is expected to play
in customer relations. This role is of such vital importance that it is generally
included as part of the position description of every individual who deals with
customers. Primary concern for the customer should also be instilled as a way
of life in the control of quality and service.

## Philosophy and the Government

Government continues to exert a constantly increasing influence on the
affairs of society and business, and there is no evidence that this influence will
lessen. Management will therefore have to reconcile itself to the fact that
government, directly or indirectly, is going to have to be reckoned with in corporate decision making.

This will require a change of attitude on the part of many old-timers. As
one veteran stated, "I am glad that my career is coming to an end instead of
just beginning. I am not certain that I could reconcile myself to getting the
permission of the government for everything, or having inspectors with me
every day."

Regardless of personal opinion or feeling, however, a prudent philosophy
provides for effective and harmonious relations with the government. All
units of the Belk Department Stores have been advised as follows:

> We didn't make the laws and we might not be in favor of all of them.
> However, it is the official law of the land. We are a law-abiding com-
> pany; and it shall be our policy to follow both the letter and the spirit of
> the law to the best of our knowledge and understanding. We believe
> that failure to comply with the law will be far worse than compliance. If,
> as individuals, you disapprove of the law, work for its repeal or revision.
> But in the meantime, let's follow it to the best of our ability.

The statement of the Northern Illinois Gas Company regarding government relations summarizes what appears to be the current thinking:

- The Company will encourage the selection of regulators and other
  government officials who are able, intelligent, conscientious, experienced and cognizant of the rights of investors as well as
  consumers.

- Endeavor through proper channels to keep its regulators and other government officials well-informed of the Company's position and problems.
- Deal with these officials frankly, openly and in good faith.
- Accept reasonable and farsighted regulation.
- Make its position known when its interests may be adversely affected. (17)

## Philosophy and Public Relations

Companies view public relations as image making, recognizing that their public reputation has a direct bearing on their success in attracting personnel, capital, customers, and public support and cooperation.

Although a philosophy with regard to public relations may deal first with internal self-interest, it must also describe the company's function as part of the community, the entire industry, and the total business system. In promoting its own profit and business interests, the company should seek to advance the best interests of the other groups on which it is dependent. Although policy statements in this connection may seek to counter misconceptions and negative beliefs, they can also be beneficial by accentuating the positive. Companies, as a whole, have been negligent in selling themselves as honorable human institutions that have no need to apologize for their existence. Corporate public relations has a very real challenge to project company philosophy as a positive motivator of employee and public attitudes.

## Philosophy and Expenses

Corporate policies and guidelines regarding expense control and cost reduction are emphasized when they are stated as part of corporate policy. Thus management notifies everyone in the company that this area will receive its attention, review, and action. Cost control philosophies become effective when they are translated into individual goals and areas of concern.

In the introduction to its official policy, the Marquardt Corporation states its thinking on corporate cost control as follows:

The Corporation believes that the elimination and avoidance of unnecessary costs in the conduct of its operations are essential if the Corporation is to achieve satisfactory growth, remain competitive, and realize a satisfactory profit. The Corporation further believes that significant cost reductions must come about primarily through the efforts of its management personnel as part of their basic responsibility. It is the Corporation's objective to assure that its management personnel motivate constant cost attentiveness throughout their respective organizations and take prompt and appropriate action on cost reduction ideas which are generated. (18)

## Philosophy and Research and Development

Executive Bulletin No. 7 of the Vitro Corporation of America states clearly not only that research and development are reflected in the philosophy of the company, but that procedures exist to insure that progress is made in carrying out policy. The bulletin reads in part:

Vitro recognizes that its business is carried out in a rapidly changing technical economy. For this reason the company must maintain appropriate, active, effective, and aggressive research and development programs in each area of its business. The costs of such programs are a necessary cost of doing business of the division. Because of the diversity of the company's business activities, the responsibility for financing, direction, and execution of research and development will be at divisional or subsidiary level. . . .

In addition, divisions are to submit to the Corporate Office, quarterly, a progress report on research and development programs. This report should include for each project a brief summary of status, accomplishments during the last quarter, objectives for the ensuing quarter, and current appraisal of the technical or market justification for the project. . . . (19)

## Philosophy and Job Evaluation

Another significant concern of company philosophy is the manner in which people are judged. In the individual's mind searching questions arise as to how he will be judged by the company and the effect of this judgment on his compensation, promotions, and security. Although many subjective criteria such as personality and attitude are available, none meets the standard of fairness afforded by judgment based on actual job performance. Perhaps no other plank is more important in the company's platform of employee relations than judging people by what they do. This judgment of performance relates to initial employment, progress in the company, and retention or discharge.

In addition, every comprehensive company philosophy must embrace a sound salary policy. In its Executive Policy Manual the Weyerhaeuser Company states its salary policy as follows:

- It shall be the company's objective to pay salaries which are at least equal to salaries paid by other companies in the respective communities in which we operate and within the industries in which our company competes.
- It is an objective of our salary administration program to pay salaries which will enable us to secure and retain superior employees who will deliver above-average performance.
- It is an objective of our salary administration program to insure that salary increases are used to secure improved performance.
- The levels of salaries shall vary according to the relative importance of the responsibility of the positions as measured by proper job evaluation.
- The levels of salaries of individuals on similar positions shall vary based on their performance.
- Periodic surveys of the prevailing salary rates of similar personnel in other companies shall be made to insure that our rates are set and maintained at the proper level. (20)

The purpose of such policy statements is to communicate publicly, for the information of concerned employees, corporate policies in this important employee relations area.

## Philosophy and Company Excellence

"Zero defects" programs seek to institute, on a companywide basis, the pursuit of excellence as a daily practice. In what areas can a company really make a mark, excel competitively? Answers to this question vary and may include quality, product, research, service, courtesy, location, economy, or a variety of others depending on the ability of the company's human and material resources to produce a particular kind of excellence.

The proper attitude regarding the pursuit of quality can be decisive in building and maintaining favorable work habits and public confidence in the company's products and activities. The guiding principle is to get it right the first time—a belief that there is no justifiable reason for errors, faulty work, or unsatisfactory customer relations. If the pursuit of excellence becomes part of a philosophy that is translated into the daily activity of every executive in both his personal and his managerial duties, zero defects can become a constant standard of job performance. Executives should be continually aware that zero defects can apply in all areas of management, supervision, human relations, customer relations and service, as well as in the production and statistical areas.

## A Philosophy for the Development of Management

One company puts its development philosophy on record with the following statement of policy:

> It is the policy of this company to establish and vigorously pursue a program of executive development, recognizing that this truly starts with the selection and training of supervisory personnel at all levels. The corporation will encourage the establishment of appropriate plans in its various divisions, which will insure that divisional supervisory structures are maintained and are growing with increasing competence. It recognizes that such plans importantly will include on-the-job training and coaching, as well as more formal methods. It is intended that these divisional plans, which are the responsibility of the divisions, shall be ancillary to an Advance Development Program whereby the Corporate Officers will assure that through further selection and training, long-range executive needs of the company and its divisions will be fulfilled.

> The Advance Development Program shall include but not be limited to rotational job assignments, outside courses, self-development assignments, etc., as the needs of the individual indicate. . . . (21)

A total-concept philosophy and program of management development certainly begins with manpower planning and continues with selection, training, counseling, coaching, compensation, and promotion. A statement of policy in this area assures the applicant, and would-be executive, that the program will apply to him if he becomes a member of the executive team. It establishes the operating procedures affecting individuals already with the company and indicates what individual opportunities exist for development and growth. A corollary should be, as explained in the company development policy, a continuing commitment to self-development.

## Management Philosophy and Facts

What criteria company philosophy holds to be valid for management in general is of decisive importance. How management sees itself, its function, its authority, its responsibility, and its clarion call to action will determine all other areas of company activity. For it is management that formulates, modifies, communicates, and enforces the company's basic philosophy and policy throughout the organization.

A management that relies too much on "personalities" to get things done is too often oriented toward subjective criteria and is limited in its potential to the quality of the personalities involved. On the other hand, a management dedicated to a professional approach is fact-oriented and seeks to manage by professionally established standards which are both guided and sustained by performance and results. Such a management is free to change, to adjust, to grow, to innovate, and to improve in accordance with fact-oriented criteria.

The key to fact-oriented management is not a professed philosophy but rather the actual use of facts for developing strategic plans and making decisions. Harlow Curtice, while at the helm of General Motors, went far to explain the success of that corporation when he said: "It is related to our approach to problems. . . . This involves, first, assembling all the facts, second, analysis of where the facts appear to point, and third, courage to follow the trail indicated even if it leads into unfamiliar and unexplored territory." (22) And, in his book about General Motors, Alfred P. Sloan says: ". . . One of the corporation's great strengths is that it was designed to be an objective organization, as distinguished from the type that gets lost in the subjectivity of personalities." (23)

## Management Philosophy and Priorities

Once the facts have been established, the question of priority arises. The incidence of performance deficiencies traceable to inadequate discipline in the area of priority practices is amazing. Awareness of the importance of this fundamental principle was responsible for the adoption of the tenet "First Things First" for one company's management development program. This statement, in bold letters, has been placed in the front of the conference room, and considerable time is spent during the course of the program explaining its importance and meaning.

It is fundamental that individuals and companies find the resources and time to concentrate on those things that they consider to be relatively more important than others. Policy statements that communicate this necessity and clarify the position of the company with regard to priorities should improve individual job performance as well as overall results.

## Management Philosophy and a Sense of Urgency

Related to the establishment of priorities is a proper sense of urgency. An executive of a Midwestern copper producer was lamenting the fact that ". . . too few executives react with any sense of urgency. They seem to feel that competitors are not research-minded—not really hard at work. They snail along without the urgency of 'right nowness.' "

Company philosophy regarding management must realistically recognize and respond to a sense of competitive urgency—to get on with the job, to seize and exploit opportunities, to make decisions (even difficult ones), and to focus on improvements that will increase the company's share of the market. The company's future is likely to be shaped to a significant extent by the sense of urgency which results in response and action in every phase of its operations.

## Management Philosophy and Policy Formulation

The formulation of policies to translate philosophy into practice is usually the responsibility of top management—the board of directors, its chairman, or the president. Although policy formulation is as important as planning, its statement often becomes lost in those of other areas of the corporate structure. Too frequently, it is not considered as deserving of separation as a distinctive subject or component of company structure. Failure to identify these fundamentals increases the difficulty of programming the remainder of the activities of the company.

Executives charged with formulating policies will be well advised to consider the following:

> Today, companies are operating in an environment quite different from the ones of 20 years ago. As the number of government regulations has increased, corporations have had to hire more lawyers to keep themselves posted on current regulatory and legal developments, and they have had to keep a closer watch on their relationship with competitors and suppliers. They have learned to walk a narrower path in maintaining product standards, in pricing the products they sell to their customers and even themselves, in advertising those products, in acquiring companies, in providing employee benefits, even in maintaining their records of accounting. (24)

Since the whole operational procedure is steadily becoming more exacting and sophisticated, the pressure for precise, practicable procedures becomes all the more necessary. During the early corporate years, generalized guides, which existed only in the minds of a few old-timers, regarding "the way we do things around here" might have been sufficient. But no one can count on achieving success in today's frantically competitive and government-regulated world on the same old rule-of-thumb basis. The fundamentals and disciplines of the corporate game have changed, and so has the necessity for philosophies and policy guides that must provide for a maximum of resources channeled in the most productive directions and a minimum of serious errors of either commission or omission.

Policy formulation affords management an opportunity to identify its purpose and the manner in which individuals are expected to become involved in the implementation of them. Guides for policy formulation can be found both inside and outside the company. These might include:

1. Values existing and generally accepted in society and other business operations.
2. Governmental regulations and interests that must be taken into consideration.
3. Guides used by the industry and other companies.
4. Values and beliefs of the chief executive.
5. Values and interests of employees and management.
6. History of the company and previous experience with policies.
7. Climate existing within the company and the type of management available to carry out the policy.
8. All information that will contribute to the composition and the final form of policies.

Although the size of the company and the number and geographical distribution of its units will influence the degree of formality to be used in setting forth the philosophy, the need is always present for stating it clearly and putting it into writing. Since this will become the mold into which the cement will be poured, it should be carefully prepared. Once concrete patterns and habits are set, they are very difficult to change.

Executives have been heard to say, "We don't worry about such formal policy statements around here. This sort of thing will develop on its own. Water will seek its own level, and we'll soon have a policy that meets our needs." They are right in the first instance—policies will develop without deliberate planning—but they are probably wrong in the second, since policy so arrived at is not likely to be one that ideally meets the total needs of the company. This trial and error approach can take too long and cost too much in lost efficiency, lost customers, and lost profit before an acceptable point is reached, if ever. Top management has a clear responsibility to recognize the importance of basic policy guides and to take steps to insure that a philosophy will be formulated that does meet the needs of the company.

Often a special group or an individual will be assigned the responsibility for formulating these basic policy guides. This group will, in all probability, seek advice, guidance, and information from all potential sources. It will then develop a rough draft of proposed policy, which should be thoroughly analyzed, evaluated, criticized, and synthesized. Next, individuals, either inside or outside the company, who are in a position to offer constructive ideas should have an opportunity to suggest revisions. Then a final statement incorporating the best thinking available should be adopted. Last comes the most important step of all—that of disseminating it to all who will be concerned with its implementation and affected by its content.

## Maintaining Policy Validity

A philosophy, like every other management principle or procedure, can never be considered completed for all time. It may represent the most appropriate thinking for the moment, but environment, technology, and competitive challenges change, and it must change accordingly. In order to remain valid, to continue to represent the best instrument for the guidance of the company, policy must be capable of adapting!

The chief executive officer will generally assume or delegate the responsibility for constant re-evaluation. Some questions that might serve as appraisal guides include: Is the philosophy as expressed in writing and practice still valid? Are all the policy statements still necessary? Where and to what extent should they be changed? How long has it been since they have been revised and updated?

It should be remembered that policies serve no useful function beyond the point of effective administration by management. In fact, policies improperly administered can be misleading and exert a negative influence.

## Using Policies to Stabilize Operations and Maximize Excellence

Properly formulated and administered, policies provide both constraint and thrust. They help to prevent errors and make possible the avoidance of detours and roadblocks that could cause a department or even the entire company to stray too far from its primary purpose. They provide a framework that discourages too radical or too sudden changes. They act as a guardrail of constraint discouraging decisions, directions, and activity that would be detrimental to production, profit, and policy goals.

However, policies are not primarily negative. They also serve to give thrust to positive functions of initiative, action, and movement toward goals. Such statements identify what the company will do, when it will be done, the manner in which it will be done, and how well it will be done. They do not advocate a "thou shalt not" approach, but rather encourage a going forth to accomplish, to improve, and to achieve.

Policies can stabilize company operations and create a climate in which the employee will feel comfortable and confident. They also establish a base of integrity in which the general public and customers can trust. Most importantly, they serve to maximize excellence and provide impetus and direction for the achievement of specific goals.

## Company Philosophy and the Individual

In the final analysis, management is not philosophies but individuals. The crux of company philosophy is its contribution to the purposes and practices of management. If the individual executive views the philosophy as purely biblical and not applicable to today's business, then either the philosophy is poorly stated or the executive has an erroneous understanding of it. A philosophy is relevant to the degree that it fulfills the following requirements:

1. *How acceptable is it?* The statement, intent, and purposes of the whole policy framework must sound reasonable and acceptable.

2. *How well is its meaning understood?* "The customer is boss." "All employees shall be treated fairly." The executive's practice in regard to such statements as these can be no better than his understanding.

3. *How effectively is it communicated?* A major fault of company philosophy is not its content or its intent, but its limited dissemination. Although it might be advisable to keep certain policies regarding products and operating procedures from reaching competitors, it hardly seems valid to keep them from employees charged with translating them into action. Although few companies deliberately withhold such information, they do so for all practical purposes when they fail to communicate policies to the affected people.

4. *How effectively is it promoted?* Nothing is sold until the customer buys. There is no benefit to the company or the individual until a philosophy or policy is acted upon. Before this occurs, it is usually necessary to communicate and persuade—policies have to be explained and sold.

5. *To what extent does it contribute to beneficial results?* This is a philosophy's moment of truth. Its practical application must favorably influence employee morale and job performance, customer relations, stockholder relations, public relations, or other activities of the company.

The individual must be able to relate personally and in his job performance to the fundamental beliefs of the company. He should see those beliefs as providing a more favorable working environment in which to spend a large portion of his life.

Management by design assumes and builds on the premise that corporate philosophy can be created to serve the purposes of the enterprise and that this philosophy can be altered, adapted, improved, and constantly updated to serve changing needs. When a viable philosophy is translated into action, the company becomes its living projection. Shape a philosophy, communicate it, sell it, enforce adherence to it—and you have shaped a corporate life responsive to the effective discharge of individual responsibility.

## NOTES

[1] Frederick R. Kappel, "A Business Is an Idea," from a talk given before Graduate School of Business Administration, University of Michigan, Ann Arbor, March 18, 1966.
[2] As cited by Charles G. Mortimer in M. Valliant Higginson, *Management Policies I:*

*Their Development as Corporate Guides*, Research Study 76, American Management Association, New York, 1966, p. 16.

3 *Ibid.*, p. 9.

4 *Idem.*

5 M. Valliant Higginson, *Management Policies II: Sourcebook of Statements*, Research Study 78, American Management Association, New York, 1966, p. 47.

6 Higginson, *Management Policies I, op. cit.*, p. 10.

7 As quoted in Marvin Bower, *The Will to Manage*, McGraw-Hill Book Co., Inc., New York, 1966, p. 23.

8 Higginson, *Management Policies II, op. cit.*, p. 53.

9 Charles L. Hughes, *Goal Setting: Key to Individual and Organizational Effectiveness*, American Management Association, New York, 1965, p. 13.

10 As quoted in Walter Goldschmidt, *Exploring the Ways of Mankind*, Holt, Rinehart and Winston, New York, 1961, p. 479.

11 Vannevar Bush, "Business Management—A Profession," an address delivered at the tenth semiannual meeting and midyear conference of the Manufacturing Chemists' Association, Inc., New York, November 22, 1960.

12 "Economics of Change No. 3," Washington Report, Economic Research Department, Chamber of Commerce of the United States, Washington, D.C.

13 Lyndon B. Johnson, "Message to Management," *Management Review*, June 1966.

14 J. Wilson Newman, "Management's Five Big Changes in the Next Decade," *Stores*, July–August 1966.

15 As reprinted by *The Daily News*, Collier County, Virginia, March 1, 1966.

16 "Statement of Company Beliefs," Belk Department Stores, Charlotte, North Carolina, 1967.

17 Higginson, *Management Policies II, op. cit.*, p. 50.

18 *Ibid.*, p. 69.

19 *Ibid.*, p. 104.

20 *Ibid.*, p. 106.

21 *Ibid.*, p. 88.

22 Statement by Harlow Curtice before U.S. Senate Subcommittee, 1955.

23 Alfred P. Sloan, Jr., *My Years with General Motors*, Doubleday & Co., Inc., New York, 1964.

24 Higginson, *Management Policies I, op. cit.*, p. 34.

# 3

# The Individual in Management:
# Maximizing Personal Effectiveness

John Kenneth Galbraith, in his book *The New Industrial State*, comments on the passing from the American scene of the superstar of business, the individual who was in essence management, board of directors, and decision maker for all major activities. He writes that "in our contemporary corporation setup, it is more and more the management team which provides business leadership, not the individual, that the corporate power 'belongs to a dull and not easily comprehended collectivity.' " (1)

It is true that the old-style entrepreneur, with his unconventional daring and personal courage, has largely passed from the scene, and it is doubtful if corporation presidents will ever emerge again with the charisma or appeal to the imagination of such men as Henry Ford and John D. Rockefeller. This sort of individual, with his daring, his personal sacrifice, and his devotion to hard work, was right for his time—he made a major contribution to the total system of free enterprise. But how effective would his personal leadership and methods be today? How would he deal with government regulations, taxes, unions, computers, and vast worldwide corporate networks? What effect does his departure from the scene have on the relative importance of the individual in today's corporate structure?

If management is the most important element today in the affairs of an enterprise, the most important element in management is man. Management is by individuals. Individuals make decisions, solve problems, incubate ideas, and direct the affairs of the company. Committees and groups cannot manage—they merely provide the framework within which the individual can function.

It is both dangerous and false to assume that the value and the vital influence of the individual are downgraded by systems, bigness, or machines. Actually, all of these increase the company's dependence on the individual executive. The professional approach to management, rather than minimizing the decisiveness of the individual, is totally dependent on the individual for its effectiveness. It emphasizes individual position descriptions, individual performance standards, individual accountability, and individual compensation based on individual performance. The unique feature of successful professional management is that it eliminates the "hiding places" for the individual; he must accept both responsibility and accountability. If he is the chief executive officer, he must accept responsibility for total results; if he is a member of the executive team, a portion of the company is delegated to him for which he is individually responsible.

## The New Demands

If the founding entrepreneur were here today and refused to adjust to the changing scene, he would be as outdated as the cumbersome dinosaur. In fact, many such entrepreneurs have refused to adjust to change and have thereby pulled their vast temples down around themselves. Others have been rescued in the nick of time by leaders more in tune with the beat of modern drummers. The new executive role demands a different approach, different skills, and vastly different attitudes toward specialists and outside influences. Decision making has become more complex; it involves the accumulation of far more information and has far greater effects. Rather than requiring an executive of less stature and competency, modern management demands the highest caliber of intelligence, skill, and judgment.

It is the sheer magnitude and complexity of the modern corporation that have given rise to team rather than one-man management. But, in most instances, each individual member of the team has a greater range of duties and responsibilities than did the "one-man show" types of previous years.

John Berry, writing in *Dun's Review*, comments that this team approach to management creates more room at the top. "The burden of corporate direction is so great that no one man regardless of his intelligence and passion for detail can direct the myriad activities of the modern corporation." (2) Today, no one can be an expert on every phase of business, including all the diverse areas of financing, research and development, production, sales promotion, and marketing. This has given rise to such novel concepts as Ford Motor's three-man chief executive office, National Biscuit Company's four-man executive department, and Itek Corporation's five-man president's office.

### Venture Management: Return of the Entrepreneur?

Although it is self-evident that the day of the swashbuckling captain of industry is gone, companies both large and small have recognized and addressed themselves to the threat that the "organization executive" might become lost in the swirling surf of systems, computers, charts, statistics, speed, and pressure. They know that the inherent strength of management and its catalytic function lie not in the maze of systems, but in the creativity, effort, and activity of the individual.

Dr. Kenneth Lawyer, professor of marketing and merchandising at Western Reserve University, has studied extensively, through interviews and surveys, the value of the individual in the success criteria of business. He concludes that "all business, large or small, to progress and succeed, needs the right man behind it more than it needs sophistication of operating methods and techniques. . . . These same go-ahead qualities will be found in the men who head mammoth corporate structures as well as the man who is basically a one-man operation." (3)

One of the most interesting schemes for harnessing these qualities in a way that will spark individual initiative and imagination has been developed by E. I. du Pont de Nemours and Company. Known as venture management, Du Pont's system emphasizes the importance of the individual:

> The system . . . combines the best features of both old and modern corporations. Venture management is a technique for stopping the buck,

in the sense of defining responsibility. It is also a method for spotting the buck in the first place, in the sense of seizing opportunity.

The system centers on a single individual—a venture manager—who has complete responsibility and authority for all aspects of new product development. He draws people from research, marketing, and manufacturing to help bring the new products to life.

Key to the approach is the venture manager's accountability for success or failure. If his venture needs more lab research, he is expected to get it done. If the market needs to be more clearly defined, he is expected to define it and then develop it. If there are production problems, the burden is his. (4)

The advantage of this approach is that it produces better results for the company and gives the executive something that he can identify as his "own." He is handed the ball, and the venture becomes his to win or lose. In the process, he has the opportunity to recruit the team, organize the strategy, and manage the game. He will be held accountable for results, or the lack of them, but success will go far toward satisfying his hunger for achievement.

The concept of a department store differs most radically from that of a general store in its accountability by departments. Each department has objectives and operating criteria such as sales, markup, operating cost, and profit. The executive, regardless of the size of his department or the number of departments managed, is judged and rewarded on the basis of what his departments produce. He has the opportunity either to succeed or to fail. He knows his objectives and his results. The individual, not the system, is the decisive factor. The system is basically the same throughout the store; variations in departmental results reflect primarily the varying quality of individual leadership.

The top executive of a large national corporation with headquarters in New York once commented: "Wherever we have threatened trouble or unsatisfactory operating results, we try to transfer into the unit a manager with a history of success. Almost invariably, the trouble clears up and results improve. If we have the right individual manager, we know that we can stop worrying—the unit will be operating properly in short order."

## The Individual Executive Versus the System

"Boys, not systems, win football games," said one of the most famous football coaches, Fielding Yost of Michigan, many years ago. Referring to this statement, Harold Mayfield, writing in *Supervisory Management*, adds, "How like business. Men, not systems, get the job done. A poor instrument in good hands will often succeed, while a good instrument in poor hands will often fail. We take this for granted with mechanical tools but sometimes forget that it applies to systems as well." (5)

It is significant that the collective system of communism as practiced in the Soviet Union has come to accept the importance of the individual in an enterprise. In 1966, *Business Week* reported: "As the Kremlin shifts its industrial sights from output to quality and incentive, the manager stands to become a key man—not just a cog in the master plan." (6) Premier Kosygin conceded publicly that there was great need for improvement in training standards; in the education of managers capable of production; and in the development of individuals familiar with economics, management methods, and principles of scientific organization of labor. The Soviets view American management systems with such respect that the U.S.-trained Russian author, Valery Tereshchenko, published a text in Russian on how American techniques could be applied in the Soviet Union—a book which sold out on the first day of publication. The new emphasis throughout the Soviet system is on the qualifications and importance of the individual manager and his use of professional management techniques.

Many who have only a fuzzy understanding of the purposes and functions of business systems view them as placing too many limitations on the individual. This is not the case—it is the system that in reality makes decentralization both possible and effective. In the absence of objectives and controls, more decisions would have to be made centrally and responsibility for collective results would no longer lie with the individual managers.

## The System and Self-Determination

While systematized management may sound restrictive to the uninitiated, in practice it frees the executive for a greater degree of self-determination. Capable executives prefer to work under systems—they like being responsible for a piece of the action and having the opportunity to get the job done. They welcome programmed management as a means of establishing guidelines which they are free to follow on their own without having to check with headquarters. Focusing on results rather than on methods or procedures, they recognize that the purpose of the enterprise is not the sanctification of the system but the attainment of the goal. Systems enable the executive to innovate, facilitate change, and move forward with confidence. He understands his role in the company and respects the roles of others. Systems provide the ground rules for the operation, maintain organized order, clear lines of communication, facilitate common understanding, and enhance the position of the individual executive.

The big challenge to management today is not one of individual versus system, it is the creation of an adequate framework of systems in which individual executives can perform effectively, each interacting with and reinforcing the other. Rather than conflicting, both system and individual are strengthened when each serves to support and enlarge the other's contribution. The individual executive should view management systems as means of identifying and clarifying what needs to be accomplished and as guides to outstanding achievement; a stairway to the fulfillment of his own goals along with the advancement of the company's purposes.

## Profile of an Effective Executive

Perhaps the most sensible way to arrive at an effective-executive "profile" is to take a look at some of the characteristics of executives who are recognized as top performers and to note what they believe to be the bench marks of successful management.

Executive recruiters, chief executives, consultants, and educators—all seem to have developed their own profiles of the effective executive. Each profile is based on personal experience, working relationships with others, and what the particular individual has distilled from his experience as the essence of success or failure. In reviewing these evaluations, it becomes obvious that certain characteristics have unanimous support—all agree that they should be part of the executive's make-up if he expects to manage effectively.

Fred Lazarus, Jr., board chairman of Federated Department Stores, Inc., cites "liking for competition, capacity to organize one's own time, capacity to organize work for others, energy and initiative, sensitivity to others, skill in communicating, and common sense." (7) Samuel Feinberg, a Fairchild Publications writer with more than 20 years of experience working with leading executives throughout the country, would include "drive, skill, imagination, curiosity, action, personality, persuasion, and brains." (8) Jay L. Otis, industrial psychologist and director of Western Reserve's Psychological Research

Services, offers the following list based on depth interviews, questionnaires, and psychological tests: "a gambler, decisiveness, versatility, a finisher, self-confidence, and a benevolent despot." (9)

James Menzies Black suggests in *Assignment: Management* that the qualities of executiveship are "judgment, stamina, organizational and administrative abilities, planning ability, and communications skill." (10) And Peter F. Drucker, in *The Effective Executive*, states:

> The effective executive focuses on contribution. He looks up from his work and outward toward goals. He asks, "What can I contribute that will significantly affect the performance and the results of the institution I serve?" His stress is on responsibility. The focus on contribution is the key to effectiveness; in man's own work—its content, its level, its standards, and its impacts; in relations with others—his superiors, his associates, his subordinates—in his use of the tools of the executive, such as meetings or reports. . . . The focus on contribution turns the executive's attention away from his own specialty, his own narrow skills, his own department, and toward the performance of the whole. . . . As a result, what he does and how he does it will be different. (11)

## Vital Personal Ingredients

Many years' experience in the mainstream of management, including a large variety of companies and types of managers, indicates that the following personal ingredients are vital in enabling a manager to function on a planned, systematic, and profitable basis:

*Mental capacity.* An executive is a quarterback, and football coaches repeatedly emphasize that one of the most essential requirements of a quarterback is that he be able to think. The executive who has limited intellectual capacity or makes minimal or faulty use of his mental potential will come up short in today's competition. Managing is a thinking man's game.

The executive must be able to think ahead, visualize, project, simulate, program, structure, select, reject, and engage in an almost limitless number of activities that must be initiated and carried forward principally at the mental level. It is through mental simulation that he designs his plan for management and determines what will make a profitable contribution and what will be negative or detrimental. Through his powers of reasoning he must determine the practicality of his proposals before actually committing company resources.

The executive's mental faculty is his most important management tool, because through its use he either limits or increases the use of all other tools. His mind becomes an open door, a funnel, a sponge for absorbing historical successes and current information that may make a contribution to his company.

A strong sense of reality should dissuade the executive from rationalizing unsatisfactory results, heaping too much credit on the superiority of a competitor, or attempting to escape from the objective facts of business life. Excuses are easy to come by—the ball may take a bad bounce and the buck may be passed—but what really counts is profitable results. The appropriate application of one's mental processes in management leads not to reasons for failure but to positive contributions to success.

To a greater extent than ever before, mental activity will be decisive in shaping management job performance. The most complex computers and the most elaborate systems will not diminish the importance of the mental contribution. Rather, hardware and speed of change challenge the mental capacity of the manager even more.

*Ability to communicate.* From the manager communications flow in all directions, to all points of the company compass, and they return to him from these same directions and points. Managing is perhaps the least-isolated activity in organized society; its effectiveness is almost totally dependent upon interaction and upon the flow of information connecting it with all other activities. The very process of managing consists of coaching, informing, influencing, feedback, motivating, evaluating, and changing—all of which owe their success to effective communication.

The individual in management must recognize that his contribution to the enterprise hinges on his ability to communicate his plans, ideas, and purposes to others. This need for sound communication covers self-expression in all its forms—oral and written—as well as personal relationships, personal example, and the respect and confidence of others. The individual, whether president or middle manager, relates to the dynamics of managing only as he is able to communicate and receive information regarding the purposes and activities of the enterprise.

*Constructive (not destructive) habits.* The eminent psychologist William James declared:

Habit is the flywheel of society, its most precious conserving agent. The great thing, then, is to make our nervous system our ally instead of our enemy. We must make automatic and habitual, as early as possible, as many useful actions as we can, and guard against growing in ways that are disadvantageous as we guard against the plague. The more of the details of our daily life we can hand over to the effortless custody of automatism, the more our higher powers of mind will be set free for their proper work. (12)

Although James was talking about life in general, his advice applies specifically to management. The influence of habit on job performance is amazing, particularly as it relates to the executive. It has been estimated that over 60 percent of daily managerial activities are not deliberate—that is, the result of conscious thought—but flow automatically from the preconditioned base of habit. The individual carries most of his habits from personal to business life, from job to job, and from one level of management to another. His habits regarding the use of time, attention to detail, relationships with people, use of the telephone, routine duties, problem solving, decision making, and an almost limitless variety of activities are consistent and predictable. He is so addicted to habit that knowledge of these patterns provides one of the principal means of predicting future behavior.

The executive who recognizes the impact of habit on his job performance and management effectiveness will follow the advice of William James in initiating, cultivating, and reinforcing those habits that are most constructive in attaining his own and his company's goals. Negative habits, which become destructive, can be as influential as the positive, constructive ones. Every effort should be made to phase out these negative habits. The individual who is referred to as "his own worst enemy" is probably the victim of his negative habits.

A constructive habit pattern is the best insurance that activity will be appropriate and goals will be achieved in a consistent manner. Habits should be regarded and cultivated as faithful servants of every executive. They can be deliberately initiated and reinforced to the point where they become automatic, requiring no further expenditure of time and energy to assure their continuation.

*Problem-solving and decision-making ability.* Problem solving and decision making are linked here because it is the problem or opportunity that presents the need for decision making. The importance of this ability is almost directly related to the level of the management position—managers in the lower positions are required to make fewer decisions of lesser magnitude; those in the higher positions, more decisions of a significantly greater magnitude.

It is the demand for problem solving and decision making that provides the most striking contrast between the description of a managerial job and that of the machine tender who engages in repetitive activity whose patterns are predetermined by the patterns of machine operation. Criteria for satis-factory job performance at this lower level are not influenced so much by in-dividual problem-solving ability as by speed and manual dexterity. Executive job performance, at the opposite end of the scale, is judged to a significant extent by the quantity and quality of decision-making activity.

A primary function of management is solving problems as they arise and, even more importantly, providing the type of leadership that minimizes the number and severity of problems by appropriate anticipatory action. Since systems cannot make decisions, and since subordinates rely on decisions for guidance, the executive has in this area one of his best opportunities to dem-onstrate his superior skills.

*Adaptability to change.* A resident of Maine was asked, on his hundredth birthday, to comment on the changes he had witnessed. He replied, "Yep, I've seen a lot of changes during my life, and I've been agin' every one of 'em." Unfortunately, this typifies the attitude of too many would-be execu-tives. Change and its increasing rapidity present one of the greatest challenges that both individuals and corporations must confront in the modern world.

For literally thousands of years, the amount of change from generation to generation was barely discernible. Methods of transportation and communi-cation changed very little from Old Testament times to the period of Colo-nial America. Today, more changes of greater significance are occurring over-night than occurred previously during hundreds of years. Many companies are dependent on products and markets that did not exist five years ago.

Edward J. Green, commenting on management by objectives, has said, "There are only three things we know for sure about the future: It will not be like the past; it will not be like we think it is going to be; and the rate of change will be faster tomorrow than it was yesterday." (13) The competitive free enterprise system sounds the death knell for the inefficient, the unchang-ing, and the laggard. It rewards with success, profit, and growth those who are able to offer superior products and services—produced and sold economically and with due regard to changing needs and tastes.

A crucial question facing the individual executive is what his attitude toward change will be. He can resist it like the king who tried to hold back the tide and failed; or he can lead it—discovering new trends, initiating improvements, and setting the pace. The president of General Electric has said that the executive of the future will be judged largely by his skill in managing change. This does not mean that he should ignore or abandon the traditional successes and the past strengths of the company. Rather, he should integrate these pluses into future planning and build on them. The past can serve as an instructive guide, but it should not be unduly restrictive.

*Receptivity to new ideas.* The future-oriented executive will excel both as an individual and as a corporate leader when he proves his receptivity to constructive new ideas by initiating and implementing them. The key to success in this area is a realistic approach to "ideamanship." The following comment cites the importance of facts in developing new ideas:

> Ideas are based on facts—facts accumulated through years of experience, work, and study. Since facts are available to all of us, so are ideas. Edison was a prolific inventor; yet the wonders he developed were not the result of a sudden flash of insight. He built upon fact. He assembled and reassembled information available to all scientists of his time. He studied, analyzed, tested. Every step of the way he questioned: What does it mean? Finally the information crystallized in a new form: an idea was born—after years of hard work. (14)

Ideation involves almost no secrets but requires premeditated diligence and adherence to certain patterns of procedure—both of which involve mental work. No other executive activity offers as much unlimited opportunity as does the development of ideas for constructive change. Almost daily, people—from research and development specialists to average executives and even beginning employees—present ideas that offer potential for propelling the company ahead. It may be a longer cigarette, a new twist to an old problem, a rearrangement of parts, something made larger or smaller, a tiger in the tank, a colorfully painted airliner, or a new slogan. Whatever the suggestion, it is the continuing responsibility of the executive to nurture it—and to come up with beneficial ideas of his own. This should not be viewed as a marginal activity, but should be required by the position description.

*Readiness to accept and discharge responsibility.* One of the most contradictory notions in management is that promotions and increased compensation will somehow come to the executive who declines to accept additional responsibility. He may say, "I already have more work and problems than I can handle. They don't give me enough people, and the ones I do get aren't any good." It has been said that the one characteristic possessed by all top executives is the willingness—yes, even the eagerness—to accept additional responsibility. Acceptance is only one side of the coin, however; the other is effective and profitable discharge of the increased responsibility.

The baseball pitcher must pitch—there is no way that he can avoid throwing to the batter, even on a three-and-two count. In a T-formation the ball goes to the quarterback, who can't refuse it, but must use all his physical powers and every available stratagem to move it toward the goal line. Likewise, the manager cannot do his job without assuming, to the hilt, every ounce of responsibility conferred on him. If he is strong, he will seek and assume more and more responsibility and be willing to be held accountable for still greater results. If he is weak, he will avoid stepping up to bat, pass the buck whenever possible, and becloud the issue with excuses. In dodging responsibility and seeking superficial shields, this weak manager deludes only himself—both subordinates and superiors are aware of his failure to assume and discharge responsibility in a manner characteristic of strong, purposeful leadership.

*The courage to manage.* Many executives fail because they lack sufficient courage to manage. In their sheer neglect of duty or in their search for popularity, they forget the need to be "boss."

Not every individual has the chemical make-up that supplies the kind of courage and daring required of management. It may be that certain individuals have not reached the point of experience and development where it would be either possible or desirable for them to assume command in business. Success is dependent on the courage to make the decisions that must be made; the courage to accept responsibility, even for influencing factors which are beyond executive control; and the courage and strength of character to adhere to principle in the face of severe criticism.

*Attractive personality traits.* Almost every individual is influenced in his human relationships by his general impression of, respect for, and rapport with the other fellow. Personality thus emerges as a significant influence on executive effectiveness.

Important executive personality traits include personal appearance, voice, courtesy, concern for the rights and the privacy of others, willingness to assist others, a genuine interest in people, listening skill, and willingness to be a member of the team instead of a "lone ranger." The good executive inspires trust and a feeling of being comfortable in his presence. He exhibits fairness in giving credit where due, a sense of humor that erases irritation, a disposition to forgive and forget, and a continuing effort to build self-respect and a sense of achievement in the people he is dealing with.

Executive personality, in fact, so influences subordinates and associates that it often overshadows all other factors in managerial performance. And the most constructive executive personality is not the happy-go-lucky, joking, backslapping, always smiling, compliment-one-person-a-day type; he is the one who can produce results in the manner indicated—that is, by winning people's confidence so that they respond with their best efforts.

## Time: A Limited Resource

The company may borrow additional money, build new plants, hire new people, create new products, and develop new markets; but there is one resource that is altogether fixed, and that is time. Time is available in the same amounts and at the same rate for every company and for every executive—it is the attitude toward this time and how it is utilized that shapes the resulting differences.

This concept of limited time has forced companies to think of time as a form of wealth, a resource which the organization must utilize just as efficiently as it manufactures products for sale or devises a new sales-promotion gimmick. Modern business has developed and is still developing a fantastic number of tools designed to achieve better utilization of time. These include the whole arsenal of electronic data processing and computer aids, which create nothing but, instead, rearrange information for quicker answers; company airplanes, which enable executives to oversee operations at more locations in person; communication aids in Buck Rogers style; and a virtually unlimited array of other time-saving services.

Time is the most expensive purchase the company makes—dollars for human time constitute the largest expense item in most operating statements. Management can have no more important responsibility than the efficient management and utilization of this time.

If the company regards time as wealth and as a limited resource, so should the individual executive. He should accept it as providing the only opportunity he has or needs to achieve his goals; but he should always remember that it is a measured, limited, perishable resource. At the time bank he automatically withdraws the same quantity as does every other individual, but the way in which he invests this time can vary considerably.

The effective individual in management has an almost holy respect for time. He plans and programs his days even more carefully than his dollars. He regards time from a total, long-range career point of view as well as from the standpoint of immediate achievement. He guards and uses it jealously, making certain that it is not squandered. This sort of personal time management is indispensable to the individual in both his company role and his personal affairs.

## Managing by Example

The most effective factor in the training of any subordinate is the example of his boss. Development and job performance are influenced far more by what the superior does than by what he says should be done. Ashland Oil's Rex Blazer has commented, "I think the spirit of the team often reflects the spirit of the leader. When Sandy Koufax was pitching, the whole team was fired up."

How many executives are willing to manage and motivate by example? Do they understand that what they are able to get others to achieve is significantly influenced by their own attitudes, behavior, and example? What the boss, by his own actions, demonstrates to be important or unimportant will soon become universal practice throughout the company. He may wish that it were otherwise, that he could avoid management by example—but he can't. If he sets the pace in work habits, attention to detail, compliance with company policy, results orientation, company loyalty, and positive attitudes, it is predictable that most of those subject to his influence will be guided by his example. Rather than limiting the valuable influence of management by example, an executive's personal philosophy meets the challenge best if it includes a willingness to say, "Go thou and do likewise."

## An Attitude Toward People

Critics of business often view the executive's role as one of manipulating people. The individual is important only as he benefits the company, they charge. Such an attitude on the part of any executive would be completely shortsighted.

Successful modern business will tolerate only one long-range attitude toward people, whether employees or customers. That is an attitude which respects the dignity of the individual, recognizes that in a free marketplace both employees and customers may go elsewhere, and acknowledges that the benefits sought by the company must be merited.

The executive approaches his responsibility of getting results through people with the knowledge that all parties concerned—employees, customers, and stockholders—must jointly benefit from the employees' activity. The executive's chief responsibility to his subordinates is to give satisfying meaning to their work and provide a climate that encourages them to develop potentialities that will help to achieve the company's objectives. An appropriate attitude toward employees, therefore, does not encourage manipulation, coercion, or taking unscrupulous advantage; it requires the creation of a corporate environment and system of operation that will maximize the desire of the individual to contribute and benefit in proportion to his contribution. When the subordinate senses this attitude in his superiors, a cooperative atmosphere is encouraged; each employee then becomes a member of the team—not a cog in the wheels of production or a number on a computer card.

It is doubtful if any other area of management competence will be as influential in achieving results as the relationships the executive is able to establish and maintain with other people—those above, beside, and below him in the corporate structure. He is almost helpless—isolated on an island in the midst of the corporate ocean—unless he can interact effectively with other people. And the most decisive factors in promoting successful interaction are his own attitude, his belief in the dignity and value of the individual, and his willingness to take the initiative in creating an environment conducive to maximizing individual potential.

### Commitment to a Viable Personal and Business Philosophy

Every executive should examine what he believes in. Does his personal philosophy agree with that of the company? Will deviations create conflicts that will be detrimental to his health and to his success? Ideally, he should be able to accept the company's philosophy as his own personal business philosophy. Where the two coincide, the executive can give his wholehearted devotion and all his energy to the task of achieving goals that are beneficial to both. This is not to assume that the company philosophy is necessarily perfect or ideal—or that his own is either, for that matter. However, the benefits of compatible philosophies are obvious.

A personal philosophy regarding business does not have to ignore its faults—it is not meant to be a type of blind submission. But it can duly acknowledge the benefits that business and industry have bestowed on the nation—the high standard of living, personal fulfillment for countless millions, and a continuing contribution to the ideals of humanity and freedom throughout the world. The president of a leading chemical company has said this regarding the ends and means of business: "Every mature individual seeks personal fulfillment in useful work. The business manager fulfills his need for useful work in fulfilling the needs of his company—needs that in turn satisfy other human needs on a broad scale." (15)

Any executive can logically believe that the profitable company is one in which individuals will realize greater personal achievement. He should therefore believe that it is his responsibility to operate so as to make a profit and, through this profit, pay higher salaries, provide increased employee benefits, create more jobs, provide promotional opportunities through growth, and, at the same time, provide individual self-satisfaction. As the appropriately organized and efficiently operated company grows and flourishes, suppliers, employees, and customers will all be the beneficiaries.

It would be negligence not to admit that executive profiles come in all sizes, shapes, and ages. Almost everyone can think of numerous exceptions to the stereotype. If many of today's top executives had been subjected to personality tests, they might not have been employed, much less promoted to their present positions of responsibility. This proves the most significant fact regarding the individual in management—that his key asset is not his appearance or walk but his degree of success in producing profitable results.

## The Executive Looks in the Mirror

What do you really think about yourself? The most difficult person to appraise is oneself. Yet all individual accomplishment depends on self-management. The higher the individual rises in management, the truer this becomes. An executive's assessment of himself should include:

- An honest appraisal of his performance and potential.
- A knowledge of the sacrifice he is willing to make for successful achievement.
- A willingness to put first things first—a system of priority in the use of time, talents, and total resources.
- A factual and systematic approach to management as against an emotional, subjective approach.
- A willingness to seek, accept gracefully, and respond constructively to feedback and criticism.
- A firm commitment to high ideals and principles; a willingness to resist corrosive influences, either in business or personal life.

- The courage to be resolute without being stubborn.
- A belief that promotions, status, compensation, recognition, and self-fulfillment are in direct proportion to the value of his contribution to the purposes of the enterprise.
- A recognition that development and progress are the responsibility of the individual—not the company.
- A constant awareness that the company demands and rewards, not the meeting of minimum standards, but uncommon achievement by the uncommon executive who is willing to devote uncommon amounts of time and energy to meet every opportunity.

The executive's personal philosophy either energizes or short-circuits his total relationship with his human and physical environment. He should develop a philosophy that best meets the needs of the company and his own personal goals. He should write it down, appraise it, and utilize it.

## Analyzing Company Needs

A realistic approach to executive effectiveness is to analyze what the company needs. What does the company expect of its executives? If the coach wants to play a fast, mobile game, then the player who goes out for the team had better be or become a fast, mobile player.

Every training and development program, whether on a group or individual basis, should have as its starting point the knowledge and skills needed by the company. The program, if it is to be successful, must meet the needs of the particular company. In the same way, the individual executive who seeks to evaluate and develop his own performance and potential must do so with these same needs in mind.

## Appraising Executive Job Performance

Take an objective look at your executive job performance. Where is it failing to meet standards—or where is it failing to meet the expectations of your superior or your own high personal standards? Ask yourself the following questions:

- How many men have you developed and promoted?
- How much responsibility have you confidently delegated to others?
- How many problems arise within your jurisdiction, and how quickly and effectively are they solved?
- How often are you in the embarrassing position of having to justify a failure to meet goals?
- How much improvement in results has your area of responsibility shown over an extended period of time?
- How many new and practicable ideas and improvements have you contributed?
- How much better off is the company because of your leadership?

### Planning a Program for Self-Development

Those executive leaders who are most out of step with modern practices are the same ones who are least responsive to developmental programs. The alert, well-trained, top performers are first in line for programs that offer potential for still further improvement. In contrast, those being bypassed for promotions, and those whose units are consistently trailing, have responded least to develop opportunities; yet they may never quite detect this correlation.

There is no such thing as a completely self-made man, at least not in the highly competitive and complex world of modern business. Every executive must acquire knowledge, techniques, and guides from others. Researchers, business leaders, and educators are finding "better ways" almost daily. The executive can never assume that he has arrived, that he is educated, or that he has all the technical or managerial skills he will ever need.

He must accept the fact that managing is a dynamic process and requires constant improvement in job performance. Competitors won't let him stand still or do things the same way from year to year. He can improve his company's standing only by improving his own executive job performance. This doesn't mean just thinking about it; it means doing something constructive about it that will benefit the company.

Lack of motivation and initiative continually emerges as the reason for failure in self-development. Executives are not willing to pay the price required to attain their personal goals. Somehow, they retain the false belief that their own case is different, that there is a short cut, that, after all, success doesn't really demand thousands of hours of practice and dedication. Perhaps this is the reason there are so few true superperformers in either athletics or management. The Arnold Palmers of golf spend hours before each match practicing to correct deficiencies in their game. Top executives attend management programs designed specifically to improve their leadership skills.

Most individuals never get around to self-change in the absence of a specific program of action. It may help them to write such a program down, including the "what," "when," and "how." A calendar or timetable should be established. When self-development consists of general statements of good intentions, it usually remains just that. Actually, there are very few mysteries regarding managerial effectiveness—the ingredients can be identified, and the truly motivated executive can develop himself if he is willing to engage in appropriate programs.

## Executive Mountain Climbing

Why do people climb mountains? Simply because they are there. Why does an executive seek to climb the management mountain to the lofty top? The answer might be twofold; the company needs his leadership, and he needs the kind of compensation and sense of personal achievement that exist only at the top. The mountain climber accepts, as fact, that the higher the mountain the more attention he must give to the tools, skills, and disciplines of mountain climbing.

The first step toward the mountain's summit is the will or commitment to climb. Good intentions, daydreaming, idle conversation, "just thinking"— these will never move the individual or the company one step closer to success. International management consultant Marvin Bower states:

> The key to corporate success is a leader with a strong will to manage, who inspires and requires able people to work purposefully and effectively through simple and rational managing processes that are integrated into a management program or system tailored to the nature and environment of the business. (16)

A strong will to manage commits the executive to those management processes that have proved most effective. They in turn will make possible the full commitment of his total personal potential to the activity of managing. We have now entered the era of the uncommon man. Today's executive must be better educated. He must be acquainted with management systems, public relations, markets, production, sales promotion, human relations, and a variety of specialized fields with their related skills. He must be more profit-minded, owing to the rapidly rising costs of doing business. He must adhere to government regulations in dozens of related areas. He must operate within the framework of professional management. And he must resolve the problems arising from the dynamics of change and still be challenged enough by change to charge ahead with bold determination.

Everest was for centuries the greatest challenge to the would-be mountain climber. Only those with uncommon determination, uncommon talent, uncommon persistence, uncommon discipline, and uncommon mobility of resources can expect to enjoy the view from the top. The same holds true for would-be climbers of the management Everest. The future, more than the past, demands uncommon performance on the part of uncommon executives.

Both the burden for results and the opportunity for excellence rest on the shoulders of the individual. When the individual perceives the significance of his true role in management, individual performance will produce group effectiveness, and companies will be more efficiently and profitably operated.

## NOTES

[1] John Kenneth Galbraith, *The New Industrial State*, Houghton Mifflin Company, New York, 1967.

[2] John Berry, "More Room at the Top," *Dun's Review*, March 1967.

[3] Charles M. Davis, "Solving the Riddle of Business Success," *The Rotarian*, March 1966, p. 19.

[4] *The Manager's Letter*, American Management Association, March 20, 1967.

[5] Harold Mayfield, "Good Systems Need Good People," *Supervisory Management*, June 1967.

[6] "Russia Upgrades Its Managers," *Business Week*, April 16, 1966, p. 76.

[7] Fred Lazarus, Jr., quoted in Richard Rosenthal, "High Man on the Totem Pole: How Does He Tick?" *Stores*, May 1967, p. 38.

[8] Samuel Feinberg, *How Do You Manage?* Fairchild Publications, Inc., New York, 1965, p. 27.

[9] Davis, *op. cit.*

[10] James Menzies Black, *Assignment: Management—A Guide to Executive Command*, Prentice-Hall, Inc., Englewood Cliffs, N.J., 1961, p. 8.

[11] Peter F. Drucker, *The Effective Executive*, Harper & Row, Publishers, Inc., New York, 1966.

[12] William James, "Making Habits Work for You," *Reader's Digest*, May 1967, p. 81.

[13] Edward J. Green, "Management by Objectives," *Stores*, May 1967, p. 55.

[14] George J. Kienzle and Edward H. Dare, *Climbing the Executive Ladder*, McGraw-Hill Book Co., Inc., New York, 1950, p. 176.

[15] M. Valliant Higginson, *Management Policies I: Their Development as Corporate Guides*, Research Study 76, American Management Association, New York, 1966, p. 3.

[16] Marvin Bower, *The Will to Manage*, McGraw-Hill Book Co., Inc., New York, 1966, p. vi.

*Part II*

*The Skills of*

*Professional Management*

# 4

# Managing by Objectives
# for Improved Results

T HE total Allied activity during World War II had a *definite goal* and a *master plan of action.* It is not difficult to picture the confusion, waste, and resultant catastrophe that would have ensued without them.

This gigantic effort involved millions of people and activities. Every single activity or mission involved a definite, clearly identified target. On an aircraft carrier, for example, each group and each individual pilot understood exactly what the target was and what part each was to play in hitting it. Each plane carried enough fuel for a round trip to the target and sufficient ammunition to destroy it. Each mission was planned as thoroughly as was humanly possible, with the uncertainties of weather, the possibility of antiaircraft fire, and the probable number of enemy fighter planes carefully forecast. It would have been unthinkable for a plane to take off at will, fly in any direction that appealed to the pilot, and attack mere targets of opportunity. What would have been the chances of victory under these circumstances?

## Management's Basic Choice

Every business enterprise, regardless of size or type, is faced with basically the same choice of establishing goals and then planning to meet those goals—or of suffering the consequences of operating with no target and no plans.

Consider all that an organization must do before opening a department store at a new site. The first step is to determine the location, size, and type of store to be built. This is done by estimating the number of customers in the area to be served, their average annual income, the type of community, the extent of local competition, the proximity to other markets, and the investment required. Once the potential volume and type of store have been determined, the other parts of the picture begin to fall into place. Architectural drawings are made and approved, the building is constructed, fixtures are installed, merchandise is stocked, people are employed, and the store announces its opening to the public by advertising in the newspapers, sponsoring TV commercials, and so on.

Note that it was first necessary to forecast, on the basis of available information, the approximate volume and type of store needed. Only then was it possible to engage in the follow-up planning. And the building of a new industrial plant involves essentially the same principles. The determination of needs and targets must precede planning and action if the best results are to be achieved.

## The Management-by-Objectives Concept

What is management's responsibility for goal setting and the establishment of company objectives? What should management know about the goal-setting techniques and processes? This chapter is written, not for the professional planner, but for the manager who recognizes that goal setting is a vital part of his responsibility and that he is charged with seeing that this activity makes a maximum contribution to the overall success of the company. It supplies information and techniques that a company executive can use to manage the goal-setting phase of his job effectively.

What is meant by the term "management by objectives"? Peter Drucker has stated:

> Objectives are needed in every area where performance and results directly and vitally affect the survival of the business. Objectives enable us to do five things: to organize and explain the whole range of business phenomena in a small number of general statements; to test these statements in actual experience; to predict behavior; to appraise the soundness of decisions when they are still being made; and to enable practicing businessmen to analyze their own experience and, as a result, to improve their performance. (1)

There can be no real basis for planning or other day-to-day activity without the establishment and identification of the objectives toward which the activity is to be directed. Goals may be stated in terms of quotas, percentages, dollar sales, return on investment, cost reduction, increases, standards, targets, deadlines, purposes, volume—in fact, an endless variety. All, however, should identify an established target toward which the company wishes to move by marshaling the necessary resources to reach it.

Regardless of the terms or tags used, goals must be understandable, and they must facilitate the actual measurement of achievement. In other words, they must be reducible to specific figures or standards that are meaningful to the employees whose progress and results are to be evaluated.

## A Responsibility of Top Management

The establishment of overall company objectives must be the responsibility of top management because, as Charles L. Hughes puts it, "major business objectives can be set only by people who are in a position to understand the broad, long-range implications of forecast trends and various strategies which can be expected to meet the company's requirements. Obviously, top management is the only group of individual employees who have the necessary information, perspective, and experience." (2) Not only is management the only group in the company in a position to set objectives, but it has a definite responsibility to the stockholders, the total employee group, and the public to determine the direction in which the company as a whole is to move.

Moreover, top management's responsibility goes beyond the specifics of numbers and time in that it determines not only the style and tone of goal setting but the attitude of other members of the company toward the whole process. Equally important is management's recognition that compensation must be tied in with achievement as it relates to performance against goals.

Management, in short, must not only determine the size and shape of objectives but must then follow through to make certain that responsibility for results is specifically established, throughout every segment of the company's activity, for every individual concerned.

## For Every Size of Business

Establishing targets to shoot for is not a procedure restricted solely to giant corporations. It is just as vital to smaller businesses. No matter whether the targets involve billions or hundreds of dollars, it is the fact of their establishment that matters. The president of a nationwide organization may share his goal-setting responsibility with hundreds of other executives in various locations, whereas in a small business this responsibility might fall on one man alone. In either case, each overall goal becomes a point of reference for the future activity of the entire company.

One divisional manager who was responsible for a multimillion-dollar operation predicted the production requirements of his area well in advance, and experience proved that he never missed his forecast by more than one or two percentage points. Armed with this figure, he made similar forecasts for each department of the division. Purchases were made to meet these predicted production figures; and when it came time to review the division's personnel requirements, it was a simple matter of determining how many people would be needed to produce the targeted volume. The number of people actually hired always matched the estimated needs, and the cost of operation usually was on target. The managers of other divisions, however, seemed unable to establish such goals. They often had too much or too little material, too many or too few people, and the cost of operation was equally erratic. It was no surprise when the successful division planner was promoted to a position with similar responsibility for the entire company.

The same necessity for goal setting applies, in fact, to almost every type of business and to every division and department within that business. Targets must be established before appropriate plans and activities can be initiated.

## Special Considerations

You as president or key company executive should have as a starting point for corporate activity a clear statement of the purpose of the company; that is, its basic philosophy. This is a prerequisite to realistic goal setting and profitable utilization of company resources and effective management, and it is also the surest guarantee that the company will be a vital and dynamic organization capable of meeting its obligations. The same thing applies, on a smaller scale, if you are lower in the organizational hierarchy; you need to know the company's overall purpose and goals in order to establish objectives for yourself and your group. Where no stated company goals exist in writing, you must interpret them as best you can.

Pause and think for just a few minutes about goal setting in relation to your own area of responsibility. The overall company goals become realistic only when you and the other executives have set goals, each of which must make a pro rata contribution to the total results.

As you contemplate your goal-setting responsibility, the following considerations should be kept in mind:

1. Objectives may be general or specific; they may concern the whole organization or just one phase of the company's operations.
2. Objectives involve the public interest as well as the interest of the banker, owner, employee, or manager. Goal setting should take all these interests into account.
3. Goals should be in harmony with each other. Production goals that are out of line with sales goals can be disastrous. In the same way the goals of each company unit should avoid all possible conflict with the goals of other units and with the personal goals of individuals. Both the company and the individual have several roles to play, and each will have its objectives. The setting of goals should make every reasonable effort to insure maximum human effort.

An important consideration is how high a goal should be set. The real question is what the company wants to do. Is it satisfied with maintaining its present position, or is it seeking to grow? If the goal represents growth that is higher than the average for the industry, then management is carving out a bigger-than-average job for itself. It will need better-than-average people to achieve better-than-average results. The better-than-average contribution should result in better-than-average compensation to the people involved and in a better-than-average return to the stockholder.

It is generally agreed that a goal should be high enough to be challenging and to require the company to flex its muscles. It should not be so high, however, that it cannot be reached. In other words, although the goal must be attainable, it is virtually valueless as a motivational force unless it involves improvement or increases over prior goals and results. Also, if compensation is to be tied to achievement, then increases in the one must be linked to increases in the other.

Every business requires a balance of activities and a balance of goals. Establishing objectives is not a mechanical job but one that requires selection, judgment, decision, and adjustment. Financial goals must be coordinated with R&D, production, and sales goals; and, in like manner, the goals of all four must be balanced and coordinated with the goals of the entire company. In addition, company goals must become individual goals, and individuals must be encouraged to realize that contribution to the achievement of company goals will lead to achievement of their own personal, individual goals.

A valid test of effective goal setting is whether achievement of the goal contributes to retained profits, which can be used for further improvement of the productive potential of the company. A further test is whether the various departments and positions are vested with authority and resources to achieve the goals set. It is certainly unrealistic to expect an executive to achieve a given goal when his position description does not include the appropriate duties. Nor is it reasonable to expect results from a department that is not equipped from the standpoint of personnel or physical resources to produce them. The goal-setting process must identify where these inconsistencies exist, and follow-up action must be taken to correct them.

## Bases for Goal Setting

The specific techniques of goal setting will vary greatly according to the size, type, and organizational structure of the company. The exact nature of the stated goals will also be influenced by overall company tradition, history, operating patterns, resources, products or services, and certainly its present and future market potential. The function of management is to evaluate each of these influences properly and then establish a goal based on the total picture.

In general, the following questions should normally be taken into consideration in determining final overall goals.

- What is the potential in the area served for the type of product or service offered by the company?
- In what direction is the market moving, and what is the company's competitive position in the market?
- What and how much can be produced with present resources?
- If present facilities cannot produce sufficiently to meet anticipated goals, how much do they need to be expanded?
- What new products must be created through research and development?
- What new services and markets need to be developed?
- How much additional business must be generated through advertising?
- How much additional financing will be needed to reach the goal if it is set?
- What is the status of the company's human resources with regard to the goal?

Fifty-six company presidents who were surveyed some years ago (3) indicated that they used the following data in establishing company goals: consumer buying power, own industry trends, customer's outlook, population statistics, gross national product, new construction starts, Federal Reserve Board index of industrial production, prices, employment statistics, inventory levels, regional business trends, federal budgets and government spending, and manufacturers' new orders. They also reported the use of trade publications, periodicals, personal contacts, association reports, and forecasts developed by their own staffs. The information gathered from such sources is now being processed and evaluated by EDP in most larger companies, and, as a result, the amount of data that can be utilized and the objective reliability of judgments based on it have greatly increased.

In setting company objectives, all the available data should be given due consideration. The right assessment of each should result in an ambitious but attainable goal, which is most often expressed in terms of dollar volume or percent of profit. It is usually the annual report or operating statement that eventually indicates the company's achievement in relation to goals originally set. One must remember, however, that although volume may be the final form in which a goal is stated, that goal probably represents a composite of hundreds of other goals that must be set and met if the overall objective is to be reached.

## The Right Focus

First-line and middle managers are inclined to see goals only in relation to their own departments or areas of responsibility. Indeed, it is difficult to see how they can do otherwise if they are not familiar with the company's research and development, its advertising program, its management development plan, its financial condition, and the profit percentage expected by the principal owners. The problem is that when asked to participate in the goal-setting process, they may purposely set an objective low in order not to make the mark too difficult to reach.

In any event, goal setting brings to a head the question of how fast the company really wants to grow. In too many companies, goal setting simply means looking at last year's growth rate, and perhaps that for the year before, and then setting a comparable goal for the year ahead. This type of procedure completely ignores the possibility that the previous goals may have been wrong, that the company may be capable of faster growth, and that its potential may have been underrated. It ignores the ups and downs of the economy and the market. And it may also ignore the fact that the "iron is hot"; that the market for the company's products is experiencing a rapid upswing, and management's sights must be raised to take advantage of this increased demand even though it may mean substantial expansion in every area of the company.

Goal setting must not focus too much on the past. It must take the present into consideration, and above all it must concentrate on the future. Goals should not be held down to previous low levels but should represent the maximum that the company's total resources can produce.

## Follow-up on Goal Setting

The ultimate purpose and success of goal setting lie not in the mere setting process but in follow-up and implementation. Nothing of benefit is accomplished by setting a goal and then not communicating it to those who will be responsible for making it a reality. After it has been stated and agreed to, its attainment will depend largely on goal-oriented people and goal-oriented action. The following guides should offer direction as you move from goal setting to goal attainment.

- Goals should be clearly expressed, understandable, and reduced to writing.
- Goals, together with the supporting data, should be adequately communicated to everyone who will have a hand in working toward them. Essentially this means everyone in the company.
- All managers and employees should understand how they and their areas of responsibility are expected to fit into the overall picture.
- Individuals should be able to see how their personal goals can be reached through their contribution to the company goals.
- Motivation must be provided to insure the effort required to attain the goal.
- Management attention must be given to timing, logistics, flexibility, adequate checkpoints, and the adjustment of intermediate goals in relation to the ultimate objective.
- Overall goals should be broken down into subgoals and sub-subgoals until they are meaningful to all levels of personnel.
- Allowance must be made for modification of goals if circumstances change after the target has been set.
- Plans must be set in motion. These must be redefined and modified until company and personal goals reach an effective balance.

It should be kept in mind that a goal is not set for the purpose of enslaving anyone or straining every company resource to that one end. Rather, it is established for the purpose of forecasting realistically what the company can accomplish. It should insure that the company will reach its maximum potential, maintain and improve its competitive position, and serve the best interests of all parties.

## Goal Setting at Subordinate Levels

As a key executive who is responsible for a segment of the company's overall activity, you should make certain that the following guidelines are adhered to in your area:

- All supervisors should set goals for the current year and, where appropriate, three- and five-year goals.
- Departmental goals should be coordinated with company goals and should clearly identify the contribution that the department will be expected to make for the period of time involved.
- Goals should include subgoals, checkpoints, and concrete plans for the achievement of all objectives.
- Goals should encompass the traditional accomplishments of the department and provide for maximum growth and improvement over previous levels.

Goals should be set by discussion and mutual agreement. Superior and subordinate achieve better agreement and understanding when goals are arrived at jointly. The boss must take the lead; he must have fairly precise ideas of ultimate targets and must realize that, while goals must be established within certain limits, acceptance and cooperation can be greatly increased if goal setting is a joint venture. As Charles L. Hughes has stated, "When employees have an opportunity to set standards for themselves, they set higher and more difficult achievement goals. . . . Where standards are imposed, the level of motivation in most cases is lower." (4)

Progress toward goals should be checked at regular intervals, and adjustment should be made where needed. At the end of the time period set for achievement, the results should then be reviewed and compared to the original objectives. Compensation should be in proportion to the contribution made. Goal setting involves precision, but—more importantly—it involves people and therefore calls for a large measure of realism. A balance must be struck between rigid standards and appropriate human considerations.

Every supervisor who is responsible for a segment of the work or a piece of the total goal must accept responsibility for his own results. But he must also be concerned that the organization achieve the total goal; and his management of his own segment should insure that, insofar as he is able, that goal will be met. To put it another way, his responsibility is not limited to his own performance and that of his group; instead, he must accept a share of the responsibility for the entire company's results.

## Goal, Not Task, Orientation

During the goal-setting procedure and as a follow-up to it, management must create and maintain a goal-oriented organization. Every employee who will be involved in results achievement should be encouraged to focus his attention and efforts on the established goals. Task-oriented effort tends to be limited to the moment only, becomes routine, is unexciting; it does not produce the dynamic approach needed in setting and achieving goals. In contrast, goal-oriented effort—with vision—makes daily tasks more exciting, more meaningful, and leads to greater improvement.

Goal setting is an activity which the manager should welcome—it gives him an opportunity to prove his executive ability and judgment while rendering a distinct service to the company and everyone associated with it. When he is convinced that a goal is properly set, he can then proceed with total conviction to the planning and the marshaling of resources as his next steps in management.

One writer has summed up the significance of the goal-setting function in the following words:

> The most critical task of a chief executive is the creative matching of the unique capabilities and potentials of his organization with the infinite variety of present and future opportunities which the world makes available to every organization. When the chief executive concentrates his energy on developing strategies by which these opportunities are translated into the broadest, most imaginative demands on the organization, then and only then will its energies and resources be directed to the biggest challenges. And only then will it rise to its full potential for achievement and for progress. It is a rewarding and exhilarating experience not only for the chief executive but also for each and every member of the organization. (5)

### NOTES

1 Peter F. Drucker, *The Practice of Management,* Harper & Brothers, Publishers, Inc., New York, 1954, p. 65.
2 Charles L. Hughes, *Goal Setting: Key to Individual and Organizational Effectiveness,* American Management Association, New York, 1965, p. 27.
3 *Company Organization for Economic Forecasting,* Research Study 28, American Management Association, New York, 1957.
4 Hughes, *op. cit.,* 27.
5 Robert H. Schaffer, *Managing by Total Objectives,* Management Bulletin 52, American Management Association, New York, 1963, p. 11.

# 5

# Planning:

# Blueprinting the Action

Goal setting often proves to be easier than planning for the implementation of the activities and the acquisition of the resources necessary to reach the goal. Allied leaders had little difficulty in selecting Normandy Beach as the invasion target, but the planning that had to follow was fantastic. It was easy to select the moon as the logical target for space exploration, but planning to reach that target and return safely is the most incredible example of the use of planning techniques in the history of mankind.

Although setting the goal is an essential first step, nothing is accomplished until plans are made that cause things to begin to happen. It is in this area that the true marks of executive ability and judgment begin to appear. And this area generally represents one of the most neglected and inadequately executed managerial functions. If managers only understood the importance of planning and the tremendous contribution it can make to goal achievement, they would approach it with a dedication that would soon result in a tremendously effective program. Business leaders who are concerned about their own success and that of their companies can certainly do no less.

## The Role of Planning

According to Ernest C. Miller, "Managerial planning attempts to achieve a consistent, coordinated structure of operations focused on desired ends. Without plans, action must become merely random activity, producing nothing but chaos." (1) It involves such concepts as predetermining the course of the business, deciding in advance, coordinating, making things happen in the desired manner, eliminating surprises, and anticipating company needs systematically.

Too many executives fail to recognize the need for planning when the company is prosperous and seemingly in excellent condition. They do not realize that it is easy to manage a business when the general level of the economy is rising or when it is on a high plateau. It is possible for businesses to operate for long periods largely on momentum. Often they continue for two and three generations to benefit from the impetus of former leadership.

Wise executives recognize that planning is necessary to maintain this momentum and to increase it still further. They build solid management structures and make plans to insure the soundness of operations at times when the economy may not be booming. They recognize that many businesses survive, not because of good management, but in spite of bad management. But—most importantly—wise management prepares, through adequate planning, for a well-managed and well-operated company regardless of momentum, present economic level, or other environmental circumstances.

Planning takes the results or goals desired and blueprints what is necessary to achieve them. It identifies a range of possibilities, prepares for them, and eliminates most of the surprises.

## Increased Need for Order

The one-man shoe shop and the "mom and pop" grocery store require planning, but on a limited basis. In businesses of this type, one individual can know everything that is going on and plan from day to day without an elaborate formalized program.

It is the fantastic growth experienced by many companies that has made systematic planning essential. Consider the course of three large corporations between 1946 and 1963. Dow Chemical increased its volume by 850 percent; IBM, by 1,620 percent; and National Aeronautical, by 1,170 percent. And many smaller companies have recorded similar growth rates—which would have been impossible without planning for research and development, engineering, production, sales, personnel, and financing. Growth of this type must be planned, coordinated, and kept in balance, as is evidenced by the fact that, during this same period, many other companies that failed to plan adequately went out of business or were taken over by larger ones. Growth itself, especially rapid growth, makes planning a mandatory management function.

Consider the present size, geographical reach, and complexity of your own business as compared with its early years. Many of today's large multi-unit stores were started by peddlers operating out of wagons. Many of today's giant industrial corporations began in a basement or garage. But today's industrial colossus often includes, within one corporate structure, tons of raw materials from every conceivable source, almost every type of manufacturing operation, hundreds of product lines, manufacturing and sales organizations throughout the world, tens of thousands of people in hundreds of different types of positions, and annual sales in the billions.

Although the billion-dollar company may not be typical, there are hundreds of organizations with sales volumes approaching the hundred-million mark. Moreover, few major companies remain local in nature. Communications, transportation, and advertising bring a plant in Cleveland close to one in Los Angeles or one in Japan close to one in Toledo. In other words, the external environment in which a business must operate is changing drastically; and unless all the influencing factors are taken into account, the achievement of the goals will be impossible. Victories in battle, games in athletics, and successes in the corporate world are not won without the type of planning that effectively utilizes total resources.

## Top Management's Responsibility

Planning is a function of top management. Like goal setting, it may be shared with others who develop specific plans for their own areas of responsibility; but the obligation for tying these plans together and making certain that the total program is geared to reach overall objectives remains part of the top executive's job.

The master plan is the top executive's blueprint for keeping the activities of the company on course and for monitoring progress along the way. He must thoroughly understand it, believe in it, and communicate it effectively to his subordinates. He must be able to evaluate divisional and departmental plans and determine whether they are adequate to meet assigned subgoals and contribute properly to the achievement of overall goals. That is why the first and most vital ingredient in sound planning is the support of top management. If top management sees no need for planning, then it will not receive the support of others in the company and will be doomed to failure.

Responsible executives should regard this function as a welcome opportunity to provide for the success, growth, and all-round improvement of the company. Planning, perhaps more than any other activity, can help to avoid the worry, the ulcers, the heart attacks, and even the unemployment that so often are associated with high management positions. The assurance that the entire organization is oriented toward attaining the goals that have been established for it should give everyone confidence that those goals will be reached.

## Specific Advantages of Planning

It would be impossible to list all the advantages of planning. Here are just a few of the most significant ones.

1. Individual effectiveness is greatly increased because each person, regardless of position in the company, has a clear picture of what he is expected to accomplish and is afforded a real sense of personal satisfaction.

2. There is maximum utilization of company resources because planning identifies all such resources and turns them to the best advantage.

3. Standards are set for each segment of the company and for every individual in it. Thus planning makes improvement and growth happen.

4. The purposeful activity necessary to improvement and growth is defined and initiated.

5. People like to know where they are going. The forecasting element inherent in planning provides a large wall map; it enables people to spot their position and plot their course. It gives them a sense of direction and security.

6. There is a common frame of reference, a rallying point for the energies of everyone in the company, regardless of level or location.

7. Perspective and objectivity are gained through the carefully stated view of company purpose and activities that planning provides.

8. The kind of management that ricochets from one crisis to another is prevented.

9. There is less chance of misunderstanding, once objectives, planned activities, and expected contributions have been formulated and written down.

10. Individual potential is enlarged and developed. Robert E. Lewis, while president of the Sylvania Company, emphasized the role of planning in developing people when he said, "The man who can't plan can't manage. . . . The very act of planning develops a person's horizons and abilities. To accomplish this end, planning should be pushed down the organizational ladder as far as possible. A man who has participated in a plan feels a responsibility that could not otherwise be accomplished." (2)

Planning replaces directionless wanderings with firm direction and orientation toward specific goals. The compass and rudder on a ship are of little value without a plan for the voyage. The plan makes the directional mechanism meaningful.

## Planning and Requisites

At least in the large organization, it is customary to delegate the planning function to an individual or group. Normally it is the duty of this individual or group to assemble all the necessary data, guide the divisional or departmental personnel who participate in planning, and coordinate their plans into a master plan for the company. This master plan is then presented to the chief executive or the executive group, who, before approving it, will evaluate, change, and otherwise alter it until it suits the objectives, policies, and resources of the company.

The final plan will be no better than the executives and staff specialists who formulate it. Adequate planning requires vision, analytical ability, an understanding of economics, a recognition of the difference between realism and false hope, the knack of being both rigid and flexible, a feel for balancing long-range needs against the pressures of the moment, a thorough understanding of the company's operations as well as of the industry to which it belongs. It also demands personal drive, persistence, the willingness to take a stand, a high degree of negotiating skill, and the sort of leadership that will swing key executives and others in behind the plan.

Plans can be formulated for (1) doing current business, (2) continuing in business in the same manner next year, and (3) developing and improving business for the future—say, five years hence. Too often planning is viewed as something far in the distance that involves only ambitious programs for growth. It can and should involve such programs, but not to the neglect of current and near-term needs. Thus there are various types of plans.

*Strategic plans* provide for maintaining the health of the business. They utilize resources and specify activities so as to insure that the business will continue uninterruptedly. *Operational plans,* which are more detailed, are designed to put overall or strategic plans into actual operation. In many instances, staff personnel are responsible for overall and strategic plans; but putting them into practice involves operational planning and implementation by operating people. *Corporate plans* are those prepared centrally for guiding the general activities of the entire company. Other types of plans are prepared for divisions and departments or are related to products, functions, geography, or time sechedules.

Planning is not difficult or complex; in fact, it should eliminate many existing difficulties and complexities. However, all kinds of planning involve systematic preparation and specific steps. The following requirements are basic:

1. A *favorable environment.* As indicated, this includes the active support of top management and of others at all organizational levels. This support, to be meaningful, must be translated into active participation and should make available the information and resources necessary for planning.

2. A *clear understanding of management objectives.* Planning, as we have seen, is not intended to be an end in itself; it is a means of setting into motion, as economically and as efficiently as possible, the resources necessary to reach previously established ob-

jectives. All planning should be related to these objectives and oriented toward their achievement. The architect cannot draw plans for the house until he knows what its size, shape, and dimensions are to be.

3. *Knowledge of the organization.* Planning must obviously recognize the history, nature, strengths, and weaknesses of the business, and, to some extent, the internal environment or climate. It must reflect the company as it exists today. Although it will consider expansion, acquisition, and change, it must be formulated on a current base.

4. *Knowledge of the company's external relationships.* The strengths and weaknesses of the company, its competitive position in the industry, and its volume and profit potential are all related to external factors. Planning must take these external factors into account even though the company has limited or no control over them.

5. *Reliable forecasts.* There is little likelihood that the company, the industry, or the general economy will stand still. But in which direction will they move, and how much? Planning is based largely on forecasts which take into consideration trends, the general level of the economy, the international situation, government activities, and all elements of the environment that will affect company operations.

6. *Apparatus for collecting, evaluating, systematizing, integrating, and recording in orderly form all pertinent information.* Planning logically begins with the gathering of many facts from various sources and locations; but these will form a meaningful pattern justifying company action only after they have been ordered, shaped, and worked into the framework established by the company's objectives.

*Preliminary Steps*

The following are some of the preliminary steps that must be taken before planning can begin:

1. *Identification of key problems.* These should include existing problems and also any problems that may arise if contemplated changes are made.
2. *Top management orientation.* If formalized planning is a comparatively new activity, there is a strong possibility that key executives will need briefing on planning techniques and specific responsibilities.
3. *Establishment of a planning organization.* Whether planning is entrusted to an individual, a committee, or a group, responsibility for initiating the necessary activity and seeing it through must be assigned. This includes gathering the information, involving the people, and formulating plans for final review and approval.
4. *Review and evaluation of planning experience.* It is wise to initiate a complete review of any previous planning activity. How was it conducted? What changes and adjustments had to be made? What was the final result? What benefits and guides can be derived from this experience? If possible, planning in other companies—especially companies of the same type—should be checked, along with published guides and recommendations by experts in the planning field.

David S. Atkinson, director of business planning for Standard Pressed Steel Company, has suggested these key questions for planning orientation:

1. Where are we right now?
2. Where are we going as we are?
3. Where do we want to go—what is our goal?
4. What is likely to get us there?
5. When will we get results?
6. Who is going to do it?
7. What will be the resource requirements?
8. Can we reach the goal? (3)

## The Planning Process

After all the ingredients have been gathered, the puzzle must be fitted together. The planner must have a concept of the finished structure; he must be aware of the resources available with which to build; and he must develop a blueprint which takes both into consideration. Just as building specifications should not provide for a building that is unsuitable for the lot on which it is to be built, a plan should not be unsuitable for the organization that is to use it. It should not cost more than the organization can afford, and it should not involve time schedules that cannot be met.

The size and complexity of the company will influence the elaborateness and, in many instances, the size of the plan. It often takes 30 to 50 pages to write down, with sufficient completeness, a set of plans that will cover research and development, engineering, manufacturing, marketing and sales, personnel, and finance. For this reason it may be desirable to summarize such plans in digest form. This usually requires only a few pages of totals and percentages showing what and how much must be done. In the case of sales, it may contain the number of dollars needed for advertising to produce the extra sales as planned. Or, for manufacturing, it may state the number of additional people and machines needed for added production. It is this digest which gets the closest scrutiny by top management.

The master plan, covering the entire company, must of course be divided into dozens or even hundreds of subordinate plans for the various areas. The master plan envisions the final accomplishment, but the separate pieces become the responsibility of executives and supervisors throughout all organizational levels. If the work of planning has been done well, each individual will understand the overall goals and the contribution he is expected to make to achieving them.

The dynamics of planning demand a delicate touch. What it amounts to is selecting, fitting together, adjusting, coordinating, and putting into logical and communicable form the many elements that will constitute a profile of the company's future activities.

## General Advice

Planning involves costs. But the ultimate test of the value of planning is the increased profit it makes possible.

Planning ought not to be an exercise in theoretical gymnastics, but should produce a program that is vital and useful—one that can actually be used by the company. It should not deal in dreams or abstracts; rather, it should be as realistic as possible. And it must be practical. Here are a couple of suggestions for strategic planning:

1. *Plan checkpoints along the way.* When an airliner leaves the ground for a distant city, its flight plan includes a specific altitude, a specific speed, and checkpoints along the way. All planning should in fact have built-in checkpoints. If the initial plan was right, then proper checking should insure appropriate progress.

2. *Include optional plans.* An alternate airport is always selected for the airliner, and sufficient fuel is aboard to enable it to reach this alternate landing field. So, too, business planning should include alternatives. Inevitably, it makes assumptions regarding factors over which the company has little or no control; and, when unpredictable factors change the picture radically, the planners should be able to point to built-in alternates that can replace the existing direction or course of action. This again emphasizes the importance of checking progress against plans and making adjustments along the way.

If the goal of the big-league baseball manager is winning the pennant, he will make plans at the beginning of the season to assure the achievement of this objective. But what if his team falls behind? Some of his players may not perform in accordance with his expectations, or opposing teams may prove stronger than anticipated. In this case he will have to revise his plans. To a similar extent, the business manager makes and approves his initial plans to reach established objectives, but he must be prepared with emergency standby measures.

## Action and Follow-up

There are often two types of people in every company—planners and doers. Professional planners often have limited or no responsibility for putting their plans into action. It is the doers who usually must take the plans and put them into practice.

The top executive must be both planner and doer—having, as we have said, the responsibility for initiating, evaluating, reshaping, and approving the plan and then initiating the action to put the plan into practice. He must have a complete understanding of every phase of the plan: what it is intended to accomplish and how it proposes to accomplish it. He must know what resources are needed and when they will be needed. And he must follow through by mobilizing the leadership, the personnel, and the financial and physical resources to implement the plan.

But before the plan becomes useful, the planners and doers must team up. To the doer the plan is only the beginning, a starting point, a call to action.

Does planning pay? Is it worth the cost? The Stanford Research Institute, after studying the question of why companies grow, drew the following conclusion: "In the cases of both high-growth and low-growth companies, those that now support planning programs have shown a superior growth rate in recent years." Well-managed, profitable companies have grown that way because they planned it that way. Their growth did not result from accident or instinct.

### The Individual Executive and Planning

Participation in planning forces the executive to study company activities and judge how they relate specifically to the work of his department. Planning makes every job more exciting and challenging because the individual becomes part of a comprehensive whole. He gains greater satisfaction because he is in a position to contribute imaginatively to the achievement of company goals.

Whether you are the chief executive, one of his associates, or a lesser member of the management team, you have a real stake in planning. The following suggestions should help you discharge your planning responsibility:

1. Encourage, support, and contribute to the company's planning activity.
2. Make certain that adequate plans are made for your area of responsibility.
3. Work with all your subordinates to develop adequate plans, both short- and long-range, for each unit.
4. Wherever possible, work out plans jointly with others in order to increase understanding and acceptance.
5. Develop the necessary strategies to carry out the plans.
6. Communicate all plans and strategies, in detail, to everyone who will be concerned with their implementation.
7. Coordinate plans with present activities so that what is being done now can mesh smoothly into the new pattern.

8. Constantly review performance to determine what has been accomplished thus far and what needs to be changed in order to stay on schedule.
9. Be constantly aware that planning involves a "rolling forward." Performance today may be the result of plans made five years ago and adjusted dozens of times along the way. By the same token, preoccupation with today's activities should not divert attention from the need to plan ahead continuously. Think of planning as a spotlight covering a time segment from the present to five years into the future. Each day, as the light moves forward, so must planning.
10. Use contribution in terms of goal achievement as a basis for individual compensation and promotion.

Remember that planning serves in a realistic way the best interests of the company and of the executive who has the responsibility for results. The effective manager, unwilling to gamble with his future and that of the company, will instead establish ambitious yet feasible goals, make plans to achieve them, and keep those plans vital, up to date, and target-oriented.

Planning involves a logical consideration of all factors that influence the company's well-being, either positively or negatively. It also involves intangible psychological factors. The winning poker player does not always draw the best cards, and the most profitable company is not always the one with the greatest number of brainy young men.

Successful planning, then, demands the best executive judgment available; the ability to select the right alternative; the courage to aim high; the willingness to take a stand even though it may be unpopular; sufficient persuasiveness to communicate and sell a plan or strategy to others, the initiative to set it in motion, and the tenacity and flexibility to make certain that—no matter what happens along the way—the momentum will last until the ultimate goal is reached.

### NOTES

[1] Ernest C. Miller, *Objectives and Standards: An Approach to Planning and Control,* Research Study 74, American Management Association, New York, 1966, pp. 33–35.
[2] As quoted in James Menzies Black, *Assignment: Management—A Guide to Executive Command,* Prentice-Hall, Inc., Englewood Cliffs, N.J., 1961, p. 162.
[3] David S. Atkinson, "Planning—Long and Short Range," a speech delivered at an AMA top management briefing session, Fort Lauderdale, Florida, January 8, 1966.

# 6

# Organizing for Maximum
# Goal Achievement

Mᴀɴᴀɢᴇᴍᴇɴᴛ by deliberate design requires, in addition to goal setting and planning, programming the company's total resources.

The organizing, controlling, and directing functions of management should not be viewed as having sharp beginnings and sudden terminal points. Rather, these are continuous processes. Also, they serve the essential purpose of clarifying, reinforcing, coordinating, and accelerating company activities. They lock each function into proper perspective, thus assuring maximum achievement.

The football coach's objective is to win the game, and to that end he develops a game plan. But he must still organize, control, and direct throughout the game. He can tell what progress is being made by looking at the scoreboard and observing the remaining time on the clock. He has until the final whistle to reach his goal; but, if he is a wise coach, he doesn't wait until the final quarter to realign his resources in accordance with the results up to the moment.

In a very real sense, the business executive functions as a coach for the company or unit for which he is responsible and must deploy his resources in the same sort of way. That is, he must organize to achieve the results he wants.

## A Systematic Pattern

It is, in short, organization that converts 11 football-playing individuals into a coordinated team. It is the resulting systematic arrangement that enables the team to work together more effectively than its individual members could function alone. The average company obviously employs more than 11 people. And the larger the company becomes and the greater the number of individuals involved, the more essential it is to design a sound organizational structure—that is, to fit the various individuals into a pattern that will enable each to make his maximum contribution to the common purpose.

Organization, like planning, is not a goal or end in itself. It serves only as a vehicle for reaching the goal. The company is not formed for the purpose of setting up an organization; rather, the organization emerges as a process for accomplishing the company's purpose. The type and nature of the organization that emerges, therefore, should be such as will best meet the company's needs. Not only should it enable each phase of the work to move forward with maximum speed and efficiency; it should also facilitate the identification, in precise and realistic terms, of the work to be performed and should thus result in cooperative achievement.

Organization is deciding what needs to be done and who is going to do it. Organizing is moving into the real dynamics of management command. It is a continuing, day-to-day, creative function. It implies the initiation of processes and the assignment of responsibilities; but it is a flow process, affecting and being affected by every part of the company. It implies the total coordination of effort, with every unit and every individual—from the highest to the lowest level—integrated and contributing to the greatest possible extent.

## Means to Efficiency

The question is often asked, "Why organize?" It would be just as logical to ask, "Why be efficient?" or, "Why improve and progress?" The real reason for organizing is that it has proved to be the most logical and efficient way to achieve results. Management is more effective when the company's resources are organized to the point where they represent maximum orientation towards stated goals.

When we talk about a systematic pattern of organization, we are of course anticipating the coordination of activity that must occur. This obviously includes both planning and organizing, and both are the responsibility of the chief executive. It is a responsibility that cannot be delegated, although it can be shared—and many can and must aid in its fulfillment. In the final analysis, however, the chief executive must see that the company has the benefit of top-quality organization to implement first-class planning. It is he who must create and maintain the framework for the organizational structure and for communicating the purpose back of it to managers and supervisors at all levels. And the value of an organizational structure lies not in its appearance on paper but in its effectiveness in providing for the essentials of corporate life. These include the conferring of authority, the assignment of accountability, and the definition and integration of all company activities. Thus a proper framework hinges on a thorough knowledge of the essentials of good organization on the part of every individual concerned with its creation and implementation—a knowledge which should be integrated into the organizing process.

This organizing process should enable the individual to identify his place in the company and to see it as a coordinated, interdependent unit. In the process of helping to develop organizational structure or pattern, and in locating the "boxes" on it, he should come to appreciate both the importance and the techniques of good organization. He should learn also that the same principles that benefit the company as a whole apply with equal validity and advantage to his own department.

Thus it is through the organizing process that the individual executive discovers and accepts the importance of working harmoniously with other managers and departments. He is able to see both the necessity and the logic of cooperative relationships.


## The Basis for Organization


Experts who have studied organizational patterns and techniques in business and industry generally agree that present-day usage owes much to the sophisticated organizational structures developed earlier in religious and military groups. Robert Sampson, in *Managing the Managers*, states that from the management engineering standpoint, organization involves "such things as a short span of control, authority commensurate with responsibility, grouping of related activities, functional specialization, distinction between line and staff, elimination of duplication and overlapping, and unity of command." (1)

Certainly organization implies making basic decisions about the resources and procedures to be applied to company activity. Included are such steps as these:

- Identifying all decisions that are inherent in the objectives and plans of the enterprise.
- Identifying the activities which are necessary if the plans are to be implemented and the objectives achieved.
- Deciding who will do what.
- Arranging the work in manageable units or departments.
- Assigning portions of the work to various individuals and departments.
- Delegating authority and accountability commensurate with the expected results.
- Developing a coordinated "game plan."

When all this has been done and communicated, each individual in each department should understand his responsibilities, the contribution he is expected to make to the total effort, and how he is expected to make it. It is essential that this sort of organizational thinking precede action; otherwise, the random activity which results will seldom be grounded in a dedicated orientation to the company's primary targets, both long- and short-range.

## Guides for Management

The emerging organization structure, as it is put together and set in motion, should be checked constantly by reference to the following questions.

1. *Is the proposed organizational structure the most effective and efficient possible?* Take a long, hard, and critical look at it. Does it have awkwardnesses and "gray" areas? Test it from every conceivable angle. Does it make

the most effective use of the resources available? Does it ignore realities that could make it inoperative? In the final analysis, will this pattern of activity produce the best short- and long-range results?

2. *How effective are the proposed work processes?* Does the plan include all the work that must be done? Does it eliminate all nonessential work, unnecessary reports, overlap, and duplication? Are tasks designed and coordinated so as to complement each other with respect to timing, efficiency, and human effort? Are the jobs and work processes simplified to the point where they are easily understandable but still challenging?

3. *What human resources are available?* If you put the proposed organization into practice, will the necessary manpower be available in terms of both numbers and skills? Will management be able to implement the organization chart fully?

4. *What are the working relationships of the entire staff?* Achievement is dependent on carefully coordinated and integrated teamwork. Is this now present, or can it be accomplished? Has it been built into the organization structure? Will plans have to be made for development, training, and remedial programs to improve cooperation before a smoothly functioning organization can be achieved?

5. *Is the organization structure firm yet flexible?* It must provide direction, but at the same time it must enable people to recognize and adjust to new problems as they arise. Organization is intended to strengthen all work processes, not weaken or hamper them by rigidities that interfere more than they contribute. It should have built-in motivators to stimulate and take advantage of people's increasing skills and experience, promoting rather than restricting the maximization of human effort.

6. *Are all levels of supervision essential?* Is there such a complicated hierarchy of "chiefs" that authority and responsibility become difficult to locate and pin down? How much extra does this cost in payroll dollars, lost motion, confusion, and delayed action? To perform adequately, each employee must have appropriate supervision, but too much can be detrimental to results and damaging to individual morale.

7. *Is each administrative unit self-sufficient and functional?* Can each function alone, and does the manager have sufficient authority and resources to get results? Is he able to concentrate on the work itself rather than on reports and liaison with other management people? Is he results-improvement-oriented?

8. *Are policies contributory or restrictive?* Policies and rules should serve to insure and improve achievement—to keep activity from straying off on

tangents and keep people from jeopardizing their job security and their opportunities for advancement. They should provide ample room for initiative and decision making, yet minimize buck passing on the pretext that "it's policy." They should provide consistency from unit to unit, thereby insuring some standardization of climate for individuals; but they should not interfere with managing for results.

9. *Are there too many specialized compartments?* Specialization tends to breed more specialization, and at times specialists may lack perspective on the ultimate purpose of their activity. Specialization is occasionally viewed as an end in itself—not as a service to the organization as a whole. A function like research or finance can be highly technical, but a good organizational structure will integrate its specific contributions to the company's profit and sales goals. During the organizing process, such specialized functions should not be isolated from the mainstream of the company.

It is as he shapes the organizational patterns to get the job done that the chief executive must stop being an organization theorist and become a practitioner of the art of management. It is indeed a fortunate executive and a richly endowed company when both the strategist and the field general are to be found in the same individual. Short of that, both must of course be represented on the same management team.

## Choice of Organizational Pattern

The type of organization that is right for General Motors may not be right for other companies. The type that will best fit your needs in all probability will not be a perfect match for any other. But the organizational patterns used by other companies can and ought to serve as useful guides, provided they are used sparingly and creatively and—most important—tailored to suit the specific needs of each company.

The organization that will prove most effective in each case is likely to be influenced by the type of ownership, the nature of the business, and perhaps, to some extent, the historical operating patterns of the company. It should be emphasized, however, that there is a real danger in allowing the company to be fenced in by tradition if it expects to grow or, in many instances, even to survive. Insisting that "this is the way the founder operated and we had better stick to the formula" can prove fatal.

The following tags are often used to identify types of organizations: line and staff, functional and product-type, divisional, multiple-channel, and single-channel. Regardless of type, the purpose is to organize functions, people, and activities in such a way that operations will move forward with maximum dispatch. Those units and individuals that are geographically removed, functionally remote, or product-isolated from the central office or the traditional purposes of the company are dependent on a formal plan of organization to know how they fit into the picture.

The larger, more complex companies, which sprawl all over the country and, in many instances, extend throughout the world, are particularly dependent on organizational structure to make them functional and to coordinate the various component parts. Smaller companies may have less need for formal organization. This does not mean that size, number of units, or location alone determines the type of organization that will be appropriate or the degree of formality that will prevail. However, it often happens that in small firms, where a few individuals can personally be in touch with all important activities, the informal pattern of personal contacts and relationships makes a formal structure less essential.

Much has in fact been written about formal versus informal organization. *Formal* organization is generally understood to involve clearly defined lines of authority and formal systems of reporting and accountability. *Informal* organization is based on personal relationships, person-to-person communication, common sense, and proprietary stewardship. Since the two tend to exist simultaneously, the ideal plan is to let the informal organization of a group implement the formal organization. In this manner the formal structure becomes more human and understandable. People do the things that need to be done whether the person normally assigned the responsibility is available or not. Needless to say, an informal organizational pattern must not be allowed to usurp anyone's place in the formal structure, to bypass the structured reporting relationship, or to water down anyone's accountability for results.

In making the final judgment about what type of organization to set up, how much to put on paper, and what degree of informality to tolerate, the needs of the enterprise—as always—should be the decisive guide. The chief executive should never become enchanted with a type of organization that is not necessary or even desirable for his company. To repeat: The focus should be on the results desired, and the organizational structure should be specifically designed to obtain those results in the most direct, simple, and effective way.

Executives should be cautioned against becoming overorganized from either a personal or a company standpoint. When this happens, the false illusion is often created that because a good formal organization exists, it necessarily follows that the company is being operated in the best possible manner. In other words, the process of organizing has become an end in itself rather than a useful tool.

The type of plan finally adopted should be one in which everyone feels comfortable, one in which everyone will have confidence. It should satisfy the individual involved and insure that everyone will work cooperatively within its framework. An organization that is "letter perfect" but restrictive, awkward, and largely unaccepted is bound to be a failure.

## Company Need or People Available?

Organizing must be based on some premise or projection. The two most obvious foundations or backdrops are company needs and the people or human resources presently available.

There are many strong and obvious reasons for using company needs as the basis for organizing in preference to people available. Total programming should be predicated on maximum utilization of all resources for goal achievement, and this can occur only when attention is focused on overall company need. An organizational structure designed to meet the need is more reliable than one which has been compromised to fit the so-called qualifications of the people available.

Once the ideal structure has been devised, every effort should be made to employ, develop, transfer, or otherwise adjust individuals to suit the needs of the enterprise. This may require making some adjustments in position descriptions—if possible, only on a temporary basis. Such descriptions should, however, be completely rewritten to fit the incumbents. J. Keith Louden, on the other hand, recommends

> letting the "gap" in experience or ability remain in order to serve as a built-in personal development program for the man in question. Whoever has the "gap" elements or duties assigned to his area should recognize that they are of a temporary nature and that it is his responsibility to train the incumbent on the basic job to take over these elements and thus move toward the ideal organization. (2)

The important principle to keep in mind is that an organization based on enterprise need is more permanent than a makeshift structure based on individual ability and subject to rapid change through resignations or transfers. It is much easier to put the ideal organization down on paper and communicate it to everyone concerned than to try to explain a structure based on particular individuals.


## The Activity Analysis

Ask an airplane pilot what is necessary to make a trip, and he may reply simply that you have to take off and fly to your destination. Ask a manager what is necessary for enterprise success, and he may just tell you that the human and physical resources of the company must be directed into appropriate channels. A logical question follows: What *is* appropriate activity? Thus organization requires an analysis of the activity which must occur before company goals can be reached. Such an analysis may include:

1. A list of all the major functions which you consider to be essential: research and development, manufacturing, finance, marketing, personnel, and so forth.
2. A further listing of all the activities normally associated with these functions—as, for example, marketing research and advertising might be associated with marketing.
3. The quantification of all these activities in terms of money to be budgeted, numbers of people required, and so on.
4. Building on this foundation, a detailed step-by-step description of every essential procedure from beginning to end. This should include each position involved, action to be taken, and authority and accountability at each point.
5. A statement of the various levels of authority with descriptions of the positions involved.

After activities to be performed have been identified, they should be grouped into logical units according to location, time, customers, processes, functions, or any other criterion that will result in better management or more efficient operation. Before considering the analysis of activities complete, however, these checks might be applied:

- Have all the essential activities been accounted for?
- Is each major activity treated in sufficient detail for understanding and communication?

- Is each step or sequence identified and described to such an extent that it can be followed?
- Does the analysis include an estimate of the full resources essential to each activity?

## Span of Control

How many people, units, or activities can the executive effectively manage? Sound management principles dictate that there be only a minimum number of levels. There must, however, be a sufficient number to help each manager's span of control within practical limits.

Johnson & Johnson, in a statement on "Fundamentals of Management," recommends that the span of control be determined by the following:

1. Homogeneity or complexity of the work.
2. Ability of the manager involved.
3. Level of supervision and activity.
4. Experience and ability of the subordinates.
5. Type of organization framework in which the activity occurs.
6. Distance to be covered—distribution or separation of the activities to be managed. (3)

Decisions in this area must consider both the advantages of enlarging a manager's span of control and of such limiting factors as the distance over which effective communication can be maintained, the expense entailed in various layers of supervision, and the effect on morale of under- versus over-supervision.

We have stated that an organization structure should be devised with the needs of the company as a guide rather than the capacity of the individuals concerned. From a practical, short-range standpoint, however, consideration must be given to the specific abilities of those individuals and the contributions that each executive can be expected to make. The batting order of every major league club is based on the recognized strengths and weaknesses of individual players; each manager knows that he will win more ball games with power hitters who keep their batting averages over the 400 mark, but when such talent is limited, he plans his strategy to utilize the bunting and base running of the average players. In much the same way, the manager in business and industry must know the precise strengths and weaknesses of each of his subordinates and be guided accordingly in his thinking on span of control.

"The dimensions of this span always possess considerable flexibility," says William N. Mitchell, ". . . depending upon subordinates' intelligence and resourcefulness, the capacity of the executive himself to understand and coordinate dissimilar operations, and the general complexity and diversity of the work to be coordinated." (4) The danger here, of course, lies in extending the span of control beyond the point of optimum administrative efficiency. Thus James C. Worthy, of Sears, Roebuck and Co., argues for a "flat" minimum number of management layers. He believes that "relatively wide supervision facilitates communications within the management team—prevents over-supervision, achieves higher morale, and enables the closer relationship to provide improved coaching for subordinates." (5)

Certainly, the degree of responsibility that the executive has for the direct development of his subordinates will influence the span of control that he can effectively manage. Also, subordinates who are in relatively structured jobs, where most operating procedures are clearly defined, will require less control than subordinates in relatively unstructured jobs. Comparatively specific and objective standards for a position tend to minimize the degree of supervision required, whereas frequent changes in job structure, in methods and procedures, and in job tenure tend to increase it and, therefore, limit the supervisor's span of control.

### Delegation of Responsibility

Organizing human resources and activity involves delegating responsibility. This means determining how much responsibility is to be delegated and to whom. At the moment when the chief executive realizes that he cannot make all the decisions and personally supervise all the work, he must begin to think about delegation—with the full awareness that in delegating he cannot abdicate accountability for the results for which he is responsible.

We are concerned here with operational authority rather than with legal or technical authority. According to William H. Newman, "delegation of such authority involves three aspects: assignment of duties, granting of permissions, and creation of obligations or responsibilities." (6) Actually, delegation is the means by which the manager puts the organization plan into effect.

The advantages, disadvantages, limitations, and techniques of delegation will be discussed in a later chapter. Let us point out at this point that the individual executive must delegate appropriate authority to the people under his supervision so that they will make their expected contribution to the programmed plans.

## Organization Chart and Position Description

The organization chart is a picture, on paper, of the levels of management, the reporting relationships, and the vertical lines of authority. It shows where all the activities and all the people fit in. As each executive finds his place on the chart, he recognizes whom he reports to, who reports to him, and what other executives are on the same level.

If the chart is properly drawn, it is obviously a useful device—but, like the organization itself, it is no more than a means to an end. When it is ignored, as organization charts often are, it is not worth the paper it is printed on.

Much the same thing holds true for the written statement of duties, or position description, which usually contains four basic parts:

1. The objective or purpose of the job; the work activity involved.
2. The responsibility and authority assigned to the position.
3. The boundaries of the position.
4. The working relationships with other people and other activities.

The benefits of such a statement are obvious. When an individual is assigned to a position, he needs a sharp and comprehensive understanding of what that position entails. The position description should clarify what is required of him so long as he occupies that position.

## Organization and Committees

A practical, much-used device within management is the committee. Its chief virtue is that it owes its existence to and is accountable to top management—and therefore has top management support. It is a grouping of individuals brought together for the pursuit of a common goal, for communication, for coordination, or for the solution of a specific problem.

The chief executive often sets up a management committee, an executive committee, a policy committee, a committee of major department heads, or a committee consisting of active officers, whatever its title may be, to assist with the managing process. This generally assures that everyone has the opportunity to participate in the overall management of the company and, at the same time, is kept informed of what other operating executives are doing and thinking. J. Keith Louden sums up the rationale for such a committee as follows:

1. It must have a reason for being, and that reason must not be a substitute for sound executive action. A committee should not be a decision-making body.
2. Its aim is to provide a more comprehensive view of a given problem than can be gained from or by a single member.
3. Its use is advisory—a means of intercommunication and coordination—particularly in matters concerning policy and performance against plans.
4. Its purpose is to generate a result that contributes more to company revenues than can otherwise be generated. (7)

Committees are by no means restricted to top management; they can be utilized at all levels, and they can be either permanent (with permanent or rotating membership) or temporary (that is, appointed for a specific one-time purpose). Appropriately used, they can convert human limitations, individual lack of understanding, and disjointed activity into significantly strengthened team action.

Indeed, the chief executive faces a tremendous challenge in the discharge of his responsibility—the effective utilization of company resources to meet company needs. Every department, every individual, and every activity must be informed, motivated, and equipped to make a maximum contribution to identified goals.

NOTES

1 Robert C. Sampson, *Managing the Managers*, McGraw-Hill Book Co., Inc., New York, 1965, p. 145.
2 J. Keith Louden, "Organizing," an address before an AMA top management briefing session, July 13, 1964.

[3] As reproduced in Elizabeth Marting, AMA *Encyclopedia of Supervisory Training,* American Management Association, New York, 1961, p. 13.

[4] William Norman Mitchell, *The Business Executive in a Changing World,* American Management Association, New York, 1965, p. 97.

[5] As quoted in Thomas A. Mahoney, *Building the Executive Team,* Prentice-Hall, Inc., Englewood Cliffs, N.J., 1961, p. 43.

[6] William H. Newman, *Administrative Action,* Prentice-Hall, Inc., Englewood Cliffs, N.J., 1951, p. 176.

[7] Louden, *op. cit.*

## 7

# Controlling
# Conformity to Plan

Goal setting, planning, and organizing are all preparatory processes which anticipate subsequent activity. At this point in the management sequence nothing has happened, nothing has been produced, nothing sold, no money earned. A vital key to the successful implementation of all these advance preparations is the systematic and purposeful control of the activity generated. Call it what you will—administration, direction, coordination, or anything else—control is the mechanism designed and used by management to insure that the operations conform to plan and fulfill expectations.

The subject of this chapter is the creation and maintenance of continuous control processes which, adequately constructed and administered, will provide management with an automatic pilot specifically programmed to show the company's current status in relation to plans at all times—and provide for corrective measures when deviations from plan occur.

*Basic Assumptions*

The impetus to design and use control devices comes from a recognition on the part of management that—

- Advance planning without constant follow-through is inadequate to insure desired results.
- Once resources have been expended and time has elapsed, it is too late to take corrective action.
- Controls make it possible for each group and each employee to make a programmed contribution to the collective effort and for that contribution to be kept on target and coordinated with the other activities throughout the period in question. Each supervisor and unit needs adequate procedures for the constant checking of progress in relation to plan and goal. Management itself must have adequate methods for coordinating and gauging all activities in relation to the total plan.

Control points and procedures, then, are an essential feature of management by design. The benefits to the company are self-evident. In addition, they are an ideal source of stimulation for the individual executive. They promote self-supervising as a result of self-appraisal, and they provide opportunity for self-improvement.

*Requirements for Control*

An adequate control program is dependent on the presence, proper systemization, and effective administration of certain fundamental management ingredients. It is designed simply to measure progress and adherence to plan and schedules, and it should never be expected to replace or compensate for inadequacies in any of the other management processes. The primary function of control is not creation, not initiation, not decision making, but the monitoring of other activities. It is the slide rule, the tape measure management uses for evaluation.

The basic requirements of a comprehensive control program can be stated in the following steps set forth by J. M. Juran:

1. Selection of control points.
2. Definition of units of measure.
3. A systematic means of measuring and summarizing actual performance.
4. Selection of standards of performance.
5. Interpretation of the difference between actual performance and standard.
6. Decision on what action to take.
7. Action to comply with the decision. (1)

D. H. Jaquith, speaking before AMA groups, has added to this list:

1. Clear-cut objectives as a starting point.
2. Sensory devices for the measuring process.
3. Timing of comparison of actual performance versus plan.
4. Effectiveness of decision making and commitment for action. (2)

The control process is most often referred to as a circular flow—planning, organization, delegation, feedback through comparison, and corrective action. As one such cycle is completed, the next is under way.

*Planning for Control*

These key facts should provide a guide for planning effective control procedures:

- Sensitive control devices become more essential as the pace of change is accelerated.
- Control is concerned with people's job contribution—and this can be determined only where standards of performance have been established.
- Each manager and supervisor should know at all times where he and his group stand in relation to expected results.
- Every individual must know precisely the extent of his responsibility, the scope of his authority, the standard of performance he is expected to maintain, the assistance available to him, and—ideally—the rewards he can expect for a job well done ("What's in it for me?").

- Control assures the retention of accountability, but it does not imply centralized decision making.
- Effective control requires that everyone be oriented to objectives, procedures, individual contributions, required feedback, and corrective action.
- The proper approach to control is one of preventive maintenance in preference to constant breakdowns and continual "fire fighting."
- No control package is workable without a continuing flow of two-way communication.

### What, How, and When to Control

Planning for control requires several basic decisions on the part of management. These involve the fundamental questions of what, how, and when.

Decisions regarding *what* to control must be based on a recognition of what is critical, what indicates trouble, and what must be measured against the projected plan or schedule. Decisions on *how* concern the methods for effective control. Control systems should not be overly complex, costly, or time consuming. Above all, they must be practical, they must indicate the current status of activities quickly, with minimum demands on the time of the manager. Ideally, they should be programmed so as to generate self-correction almost automatically. The thermostat on the wall with its built-in system for correcting the room's temperature didn't just happen—it was planned to meet an anticipated need.

Decisions as to *when* concern the points in time at which progress is to be measured and corrective action taken. In determining these critical control points, it should be clearly recognized that "water over the dam"—that is, expended time and resources—cannot be controlled; the corrective focus must be on the future. (The thermostat provides for correction of the temperature whenever programmed tolerance limits are reached.) Therefore, while there may be weekly or monthly checks, for example, control should ideally provide for immediate correction of any beyond-tolerance deviations.

### Essential Ingredients

Management by design, like engineering or building construction, demands adherence to fundamentals that determine the shape, composition, function, and reliability of the finished product. If any specification or principle of construction is ignored, or if any ingredient is deliberately omitted, a knowledgeable builder realizes it is at the risk of subsequent flaws in the structure. In the same way, a knowledgeable manager realizes that to ignore or misuse any management principle, or leave out any essential ingredient, will endanger the value of his entire system. He knows, moreover, that this is just as true in this important area of control as in any other phase of management.

To insure the success of the control system, then, the following ingredients must be present.

1. *An adequate understanding of objectives.* Before concentrating on procedures and correction, every effort should be made to communicate the purpose of control so that everyone has a clear concept of what is wanted and what he is expected to contribute.

2. *Participation in construction.* The control system should be a joint effort. It should not be a top management package forced down the throats of subordinates. If this is attempted, the program will be suspect and probably ignored. Jointly constructed, it will involve everyone and is more likely to insure that appropriate activities are being checked.

3. *Clearly stated performance standards.* How far can production or sales stray off target before performance is judged unsatisfactory and corrective action is demanded? Not only should satisfactory performance be defined precisely, but—even more important—it should be made clear that this standard constitutes minimum acceptability.

4. *Adequate supervision.* Emphasis should be placed on the exception principle. Activities that are running smoothly, according to plan, require a minimum of attention, but deviations demand immediate and thorough scrutiny on the part of the accountable executive.

5. *Adequate inspection.* Executives must accept responsibility for sufficient personal, on-the-scene inspection to determine accurately whether expectations are being met.

6. *Provision for self-correction.* Ideally, a maximum of self-checking should be built into the system. Too often, there is a considerable time lapse before the responsible manager becomes aware of a deviation and can initiate the required adjustment. However, the on-the-spot supervisor can act immediately to make a correction if he is aware of the deviation, if he understands what correction to make, and if he knows that it is his responsibility to do so.

*Construction of the Program*

To tailor-make the control program to meet the needs of a particular company activity, the manager must select those points at which the status of the work will give him the best indication of what is going on and how clearly it conforms to plan.

No manager can be on the scene, personally, every time a vital operation is taking place. Neither is it practical, from a cost standpoint, to require excessive reporting of information. This only creates mountains of figures whose reading will consume a vast amount of his time. The alternative, and the practical course, is the selection of strategic control points of a sufficiently sensitive nature.

Most companies have learned by experience what must be checked—and when—in order to keep on target. The typical company operating plan spans the fiscal year and is ordinarily subdivided into six-month, quarterly, and monthly segments. This means that at least monthly the cost of raw materials, amount of production, size of payroll, volume of sales, cash flow, and other indicators are noted and compared with established expectations and standards.

The key to the wise use of such indicators is the selection of checkpoints that will give a complete profile or cross-section of the company's between-check operations as a whole or of one particular function or activity. The intervals should be as long as possible without undue risk of damaging deviations from plan. The practices of similar companies, plus managerial judgment in adapting these to the situation at hand, will usually provide sufficient guides.

The adage "Everyone's responsibility is no one's responsibility" applies in this connection. A large overall control program must eventually be divided into units that can become the responsibility of one individual. The workman is responsible only for his personal production, and his production record provides the basis for gauging his contribution to achieved results. The supervisor must control the output of the group as a whole—and so on up the ladder to the chief executive officer, who must concern himself with controls for the entire company. The important thing is that responsibility for control match assigned job duties and accountability.

For example, International Telephone and Telegraph's European operations are tied together by

. . . ITT Europe's "business plan." This consists of an elaborately detailed map of targets and timetables spanning two years and projected ahead to the fifth. It is rewritten every year and reviewed every month; in some critical areas—consumer products lines, employment, and inventories—it is reviewed weekly. . . . The plan pushes goals and controls down through the organization—even to the shop foreman. While most European executives tend to think about earnings on a corporate or continental scale, ITT managers worry about the profit of each individual product line. (3)

In other words, the principle of matching control and accountability to individual responsibility is applied to the man in charge of European operations in the same basic manner as it is to the shop foreman. Layers of controls corresponding to layers of management, integrated vertically through geographical managers, provide a means whereby the chief executive is supplied with the information he needs on the entire organization.

## Types of Control

There are almost as many types and methods of control as there are varieties or types of businesses, but certain basic patterns can be identified. Since most goals and plans are stated in statistical language, so must the appropriate control procedures.

*Operating expense* is perhaps one of the best guides to whether the company is making a profit. This is usually budgeted as a dollar amount and a percentage of production or sales. Control budgets are generally established for every operating unit and category. The control program indicates at what points results to date will be checked and the level at which expense should stand at each of these points. Typically, the trend—if portrayed chronologically—ought not to show a straight line. The very nature of many operations involves seasonal peaks and valleys; so the executive who reviews operating expense statistics must know whether, for example, the doubling of a cost figure from one month to the next is normal and appropriate to the operating plan.

Quality control measures performance in terms of *waste, rejects, returns, customer complaints,* and the like—all of which have cost implications. It was Henry Ford who first stated that if cars were made properly in the beginning, it would not be necessary to start each one to determine whether it worked properly; and the customer, whether purchasing a jet airliner or a pop-up toaster, wants it to work right every time. Industry has labored for years to narrow its tolerances to acceptable limits. Now, with the improvement of machinery and the increase in company training programs, "zero defects" has become the battle cry. And why not? Why not do it right the first time— whether you are making a pair of shoes, selling a dress, answering a business telephone, or conducting a program? Quality control should be an integral part of every operation.

A major airline applies quality control with good effect to its reservations personnel. A supervisor monitors a fixed percentage of all incoming calls which each clerk receives. The manner in which each is handled is evaluated against a predetermined standard that includes such factors as how much time elapses before the call is answered, whether sufficient information is obtained from the caller, how the information is given, and whether the operator asks to make the reservation (general factors such as courtesy are considered as well). Any operator falling below the quality standard in any category is counseled, and anyone whose total score is below standard must undergo additional training.

Controls can and ought to be established over every activity in the organization. Major oil companies operate efficiently and profitably throughout the world by applying controls to everything from quality and safety at giant refineries to the courtesy and the cleanliness of the restrooms at local service stations.

To repeat: The best executive judgment is demanded in selecting appropriate controls and control points. Although considerable variation can be expected from company to company and from operation to operation, the following guides are important:

- Controls should be sufficient for detecting important deviations in time to take corrective action.
- They should be practical and economical to operate.
- It should be possible to integrate each control into a comprehensive system that consolidates and summarizes large blocks of activities.
- Controls should be balanced so as to promote the company's best long- and short-range interests.

### Reporting and Action

Controls can be no better than the measuring instruments or the reliability of the reporting channels. The executive who reviews performance and makes decisions regarding corrective action must have confidence that the information he receives does, in fact, compare performance accurately against plan. Any inaccuracy or distortion, whether intentional or accidental, will be magnified by his decisions.

The executive's concern for reliability should involve him personally in the establishment of all controls and stimulate him to verify the system's validity through personal observations. Although, in the last analysis, he is responsible for the performance of his people, he cannot check it directly except in the smallest organization.

The most effective and most practical method for assuring a reasonable degree of control from above without stifling individual initiative requires that only exceptions from standard procedure be authorized at a higher level of management. For example:

- All budgeted expenditures may be handled in the routine way except those that exceed $1,000. These must be authorized on an individual basis by the general manager.
- The employment of persons whose salaries exceed $200 a week must have prior approval.
- Pay changes beyond salary ranges must be approved.
- The credit manager may use his own judgment in approving credit in amounts up to $5,000.
- The purchase of supplies from new sources must first have the approval of the purchasing officer.
- Relocation of floor-mounted machines must be cleared with the plant manager.
- The advertising budget may not be exceeded except by prior authorization.
- All approved training may proceed on schedule, but new programs must be approved.

These types of controls are different from those that measure conformity to plan; they draw basic lines of operation and authority. They establish boundaries which indicate that the individual is free to exercise authority up to a point, but within the prescribed patterns and budgets. Control is achieved by requiring that authorization be obtained before exceeding this point.

The forms used to report exceptions or request approval for deviations from standards should be models of simplicity. They should contain no nonessential chaff and should provide for prompt action.

*Taking Corrective Action*

The J. L. Hudson Company, in Detroit, conducted a zero defects program throughout its $300-million-plus operation. Its success is evidenced by the thousands of corrections it prompted. The program had several significant features:

1. Instruction regarding correct job performance.
2. Commitment on the part of the employee group, from chief executive to truck driver, to the purpose of the program.
3. Forms for reporting errors, defects, or deviations from accepted job standards—with space for stating how these could best be corrected and prevented in the future.
4. A committee to follow up and make certain that required corrective action took place.

Fundamental to the success of this massive undertaking was the involvement of every employee, the provision for prompt reporting of trouble, and the existence of a system for effecting the required adjustment.

Corrective action is taken, it should be remembered, because controls have indicated that it is necessary if ultimate goals are to be reached. The proper approach, therefore, is to determine *why* production was 5,000 units short, *why* the sales campaign failed to produce targeted sales, *why* expenses were 5 percent over budget. Also, exactly what is needed to bring activity back on target toward the next control point?

Typical correction includes adjustment of physical surroundings or of the internal or external situation, in the event that unexpected obstacles have been encountered. The failure of one division may be the fault of another —over which the first has no control. For example: Salesmen for the Eskimo Air Conditioning Company miss sales quotas for the first quarter by 20 percent. Cause? A shortage of manufactured units owing to a steel strike. It is obviously important to morale in such cases for the executive in charge to acknowledge that the people involved—in this instance, the salesmen—are not to blame for the variance from plan.

The executive has to exercise discerning and often firm judgment in discriminating between excuses and facts. It may even be necessary to modify the original plan. But this is a last resort and should be used sparingly. Habitual excuses and changes weaken the entire structure of commitment to planned results.

## The Human Element

Corrective action should involve all essentials of goal management. Attention should be given to the human element—training, motivation, supervision, appraisal of performance. If it has been determined that all physical facilities are meeting standards, all materials are being received in acceptable quality, and all external influences are unchanged, then the correction may have to come through change in the human element. Retraining, reassignment, alteration of the organizational structure, new quotas, supervisory development programs—any one of numerous devices for influencing job performance may be called into play.

All other factors being satisfactory, it is reasonable to assume that goals have been set too low if control-point checks still reveal deviations. Executives or subordinates, or both, may be functioning below the level of maximum commitment and effort. This highlights the need for focusing on motivation —which, owing to the vital influence it exerts on job performance, deserves the continuing attention of all managers. (4) (See Chapter 15 for more on motivation.)

## "A Stitch in Time"

It is comparatively easy to correct the missile that is only slightly off course; but, when it has been permitted to deviate for too long a time or for too great a distance, correction is a major task. Likewise, the company operation that is kept profitable, that conforms to plan, that is never permitted to wander dangerously off course, will require far less major surgery and in-depth reorganization than the one which lacks adequate controls. Not only are major changes expensive in direct dollar costs, but they are almost inevitably detrimental to morale and operating efficiency. It is far better to insure adherence to plan.

To effect adherence, controls must be of a continuing nature. They must involve constant analysis of the validity of objectives, policies, procedures, position descriptions, performance standards, financial framework, reporting procedures, and incentive systems. Day-to-day operations should be structured in such a manner that deviations correct themselves with little if any management intervention. When this becomes fact, fewer deviations will occur and fewer corrections will be necessary. But for the few deviations, there must be a system that will signal the need for attention. Hence the use of *warning* controls. In mechanical operations, these are the buzzers that sound or the lights that flash when limits are reached or faults have been detected. For example: the warning light on the dashboard of the automobile indicates that the oil pressure is dangerously low or that the radiator temperature is excessively high. Just so, managers need comparable warnings that an activity is not meeting standards.

According to D. H. Jaquith, warning controls of this type are primarily quantitative. They include:

- Timely and adequate data on results.
- Reports on deviation from plan.
- Progress reports on specific programs.
- Critical-item tabulations—orders received, backlog, inventory levels, rejects, accidents, and so on. (5)

Not strictly of a numerical nature but no less essential are performance reviews, progress reports, and personal observation.

## Management's Purpose in Using Controls

To sum up, control keeps performance in line with plan. It should provide force and direction without stifling individual initiative; the focus is on results rather than personality problems. Such a focus makes control more acceptable to the individual; and, since the company is concerned not with molding personalities but with producing profitable results, it is eminently practicable.

Significantly, control also creates a constant awareness of existing problem areas. This awareness is the first step in facing up to problems and doing something about them. A failing of management that is all too common is not knowing that anything is amiss—or not doing anything after being told about it. Many a manager has to have too many "under his nose" deviations called to his attention. Too often, even though he knows what his problems are, he fails to correct them.

Since collective results are dependent on individual performance, the most valid measure of managerial ability is the results produced by subordinates. Management is primarily the creation of an environmental climate in which people are willing to perform to their maximum potential. Controls invariably identify the success or failure of individual executives in this decisive area.

The revealing glare of the control spotlight discloses actual rather than assumed achievement—it eliminates hiding places, buck passing, and diversionary tactics. Either you're on target or you aren't. Whether you're a salesman, a production worker, or an executive, you can be judged by the record.

The spotlight must be on the vital few areas rather than the trivial many. And the executive must be able to see the difference and react accordingly. The way in which he uses his time, the issues on which his attention is focused, and the types of reports he requires are indications of the quality of his selectivity.

Controls provide built-in guides and protection for the individual. They reveal whether he is meeting interim goals, provide an opportunity to make corrections before it is too late, and give him the satisfaction of knowing he is doing a good job. Rather than stifling individual initiative, controls bolster it. The manager is forced to use his ingenuity, to solve his problems creatively, and to strive daily for results based on the maximum utilization of available resources.

### NOTES

[1] J. M. Juran, "Universals in Management Planning and Controlling," *Management Review*, November 1954, p. 755.

[2] D. H. Jaquith, "Control," speech made at an AMA briefing session, October 1965.

[3] "How ITT Tightens Its Spreading Net," *Business Week*, June 24, 1967, p. 58.

[4] Ray A. Killian, *Managers Must Lead!* American Management Association, New York, 1966.

[5] Jaquith, *op. cit.*

# 8

# Identifying the Job:
# The Position Description

THE individual executive's first step toward effective performance on the job is to acquire an adequate understanding of that job: its purpose, its scope, its responsibilities and authorities, and its working relationships. Most unsatisfactory job performance is the result of simply not knowing what is expected of a particular position and what the individual occupying it is supposed to do. This knowledge of the job, or lack of knowledge, appears to be one of the major differences between hit-or-miss management and professional management.

A position description is a summary of the important facts about a particular job. It is an attempt to clarify for all concerned the basic purpose of the position, the duties and responsibilities assigned to it, the extent and limits of its authority, and the relation of the position to others, both inside and outside the company. An organization chart is analogous to a line drawing of the company, showing the location and relation of each position. A position description goes one step further and identifies that portion of the company activity and responsibility assigned to a particular "box" on the chart. The chart identifies the "where" with respect to other jobs, and the position description describes the "what."

The position description enables management to subdivide the total workload into manageable units, assigning to each position reasonable but challenging portions of the work. It identifies for management what can reasonably be expected by way of job performance. It communicates to the individual assigned to the position, whether veteran or novice, precisely what management expects. And it describes the interactions and relationships that should occur in the discharge of the various duties and responsibilities.

### Why Describe the Management Job?

In *Defining the Manager's Job*, it is stated that "today almost every well-managed business maintains some formal descriptions of the content of production jobs. Such descriptions are accepted because they have proved useful in recruitment and selection of new workers, appraisal, wage and salary administration, training, and many other subsidiary activities." (1) A more recent development, but now a firmly established and widely accepted practice, is the writing of position descriptions for managerial jobs. Descriptions reflect an existing set of circumstances. During periods of rapid expansion, the information becomes out of date very rapidly. However, properly written descriptions can be extremely helpful in organizing and planning expansion programs.

Often, when the addition of another position is being contemplated, the following questions prove invaluable: What portion of the present work is not being done? Where is there an overload on present executives? Will the new position involve additional work or portions of the work now being done by others? How much better will the work be done? What additional results can be expected? Has a position description been prepared? Can it be used to justify the need for the new position to management and to the new executive?

When position descriptions are written in a company for the first time, they are likely to reveal many organizational shortcomings: overlap in authority and responsibility, ambiguities in the chain of command, and even duplication of work by whole departments. Obvious benefits can be gained if someone in authority will study the situation and take remedial measures.

However, if the situation is one of stubborn unwillingness to make any changes in the basic organizational structure, position descriptions lose much of their value and the effort of writing them has been wasted.

Position descriptions will probably be of minimum value if they are dashed off in a hurry simply because other companies are preparing them and management wants to keep in step. Or, if they are prepared merely to give the president an overall look at his organization or because one lone individual insists that they are important, they will soon be tucked away and fail to fulfill their potential.

Setting up a position description program usually takes about a year. This includes three months to organize and initiate the program, several months to complete the written descriptions, a couple of months before they are finally approved, and several more months before the "bugs" are eliminated and the program becomes an integrated part of company operations, functioning on an almost automatic basis.

The writing of position descriptions requires a sizable commitment of management time, attention, and expense. It may be necessary to assign someone full time to the project or to bring in a specialist from the outside. Considerable judgment is necessary if descriptions are to be accurate; and, since each becomes a sort of "charter of authority" for the executive occupying the position, the damage from improperly written descriptions can be extensive. If maximum benefit is to be derived, changes in organization and possible reassignments may be advisable. However, changes of this nature should not be initiated unless they have been thoroughly thought out and judged to be in the best interests of both the company and the executives concerned.

The basic decision regarding the initiation of a position description program should be a weighing of benefits against costs in terms of time, money, and possible effects on the company. The ultimate benefit can be a significant step in the direction of orderly professional management; but, like other management tools, position descriptions must be skillfully formulated if the results are to be fully satisfactory.

## Variety of Uses

Before initiating a job description program, it is also wise to determine the various uses that will be made of the resulting descriptions. *Defining the Manager's Job* lists external compensation comparison, internal compensation comparison, performance appraisal, management development, recruiting, hiring and placement, orientation of new executives, promotion, agreement with superior, organization clarification, and organization planning.

But, whatever companies may state as intended or proposed uses for position descriptions, the real test of their value is the *actual* uses to which they are put. In an AMA survey of 108 companies, most reported using position descriptions as follows:

1. To clarify relationships between jobs, avoiding overlaps and gaps in responsibility.
2. To establish a just basis for the organization's internal salary structure.
3. To help executives acquire greater understanding of their present job by analyzing their duties.
4. To revise the basic organization structure and division of responsibility.
5. As a foundation on which to compare jobs inside the organization with others outside it, in order to pay salaries in line with current rates.
6. To evaluate individual executives' job performance.
7. To acquaint new executives with their jobs.
8. As a hiring and placement aid to find the right executive for each post.
9. To develop lines of promotion within the organization.
10. To predict kinds and numbers of executives which will be needed in the future.
11. To determine the organization's training needs.
12. To rearrange work flow and revise procedures. (2)

If position descriptions are put to use in all these ways in the daily operation of the company, they will constitute a significant plus for systematic management and overall effectiveness.

## Initiating the Program

Establishing a position description program, like the whole process of management, involves goal setting, planning, organizing, administration, controls, appraisal, and adjustment. Top management support is probably the most vital requirement for launching the program. High-level endorsement and active involvement emphasize the program's importance in the eyes of all executives. It is therefore advisable for the chief executive to demonstrate this support by making the first announcement concerning the program, holding the first meeting, sending out the first directives, and making it clear that the director of the program is carrying out his wishes and acting for him.

Top management support also is demonstrated when the initial authorization of the program comes from the executive committee or chief executive officer. In addition, top management must understand its essential role in the program. A reluctant nod or even enthusiastic approval is only the first step of the way. Reviewing progress, providing direction, settling areas of disagreement, acting on information gathered, and in general seeing the descriptions through to successful adoption are essential. Nothing else will demonstrate so clearly to all other executives the importance of the program and the need for their support and cooperation.

## Gaining Acceptance for the Program

Even though the company president announces the program and sends out a memo to all executives explaining that the project has his full and enthusiastic support, this does not mean that everything will be coming up roses from this magic moment on. It should be remembered that executives who are asked to reveal the "secrets" of their jobs and to run the risk of change tend to be suspicious of programs or gimmicks that they do not thoroughly understand. They may therefore react by saying, "Convince me." This is precisely what must be done—the entire executive group must be convinced of the value of position descriptions.

So long as a man suspects that the program may unduly restrict his activities or isolate him in a "little box," he is not convinced. It might help to ask him to imagine what would happen if the shortstop on the baseball team were permitted to wander all over the field, play where he wished, and neglect his assigned position. Through this type of dialogue the individual executive can often be made to see and appreciate the benefits to be derived from a position description program.

Extreme care should be taken to transmit complete information to all executives whose positions will be included. This should be done as soon as possible after deciding to proceed with the project in order to forestall possible false rumors. The methods used for communicating this material will depend on the peculiarities of the executives involved and the structure of the company. The majority of position description programs are announced and explained in group meetings; only a few companies appear to depend solely on written communications. It is, of course, possible to combine the group meeting with written communications. Introductory material typically includes the following points and ideas:

1. An explanation of the benefits to be derived by the individual and the company—often with specific examples of problems and inequities the program is expected to cure.
2. Assurance that the project has been evaluated and approved by top management and has its full support.
3. A short history of the project's origin, together with typical instances of the use of position descriptions by companies with which members of the group are familiar.
4. Clarification of the fact that the program involves a description of the job, not of the person holding it or how well he is doing it.
5. Assurance that the program will not cause anyone to lose his job or have his salary reduced.
6. Explanation and specific illustration of the types of involvement expected from individual executives. This should include a review of all the forms to be employed.
7. Solicitation of the support and cooperation of all concerned.
8. An opportunity for everyone to ask questions and to speak freely. Important and as yet unidentified problems may thereby come to light.
9. Assurance that the project will have the continuing support and active participation of top management and that, individually, every executive will be given as much assistance as he needs to complete his essential part of the program.

Because enthusiastic acceptance and support can be crucial, it may be necessary to have more than one meeting. This will give everyone an opportunity to think about the program, study the forms, and ask additional questions. However time consuming, the additional meeting or meetings make up for any delay by providing excellent insurance against possible failure.

## What to Include

Virgil K. Rowland, in *Managerial Performance Standards,* suggests that one of the best ways for determining the "what" of the management job is group discussion and agreement. (3) Basically this method involves a discussion leader and a group of executives engaged in similar or related jobs—for example, a sales manager and his subordinate managers. During the session, the leader asks the others what they do as managers and makes a list of their responses. He continues this procedure until all the essential activities have been listed.

The meeting then moves to the second stage—that of discussion, evaluation, and eventual agreement on major segments of the job to be included in the description. The final stage involves agreement on what specific duties and responsibilities of the position are to be included.

Another approach, and one that often saves time, is to begin with a list of common responsibilities of most managerial positions. The Alan Wood Steel Company suggests the following common responsibilities of all managers:

- Planning work.
- Assigning responsibilities and delegating authority.
- Directing work and guiding people.
- Maintaining and improving quality.
- Improving work methods and reducing costs.
- Keeping others informed.
- Safety, health, and good housekeeping.
- Reports, correspondence, and procedures. (4)

Company surveys and generally accepted procedures suggest that position descriptions divide logically into four areas.

*Basic function or purpose of the position.* This is a brief description or digest of what occurs in connection with the position and the contribution it makes to the company. Take, for example, the job of manufacturing manager at Boeing: "The Manufacturing Manager administers and directs all manufacturing activities. In addition, he assists in the development of Division objectives and advises management regarding manufacturing aspects of product proposals. He establishes Transport Division manufacturing philosophy in accordance with overall company policy." (5)

*Duties and responsibilities of the position.* This is usually the longest and most detailed part of the description. It includes a listing and brief explanation of the principal activities of the position, often in order of importance and commonly grouped under such headings as planning, administration, personnel, organization, controlling, and appraisal of results. A typical statement might read:

> Office Manager: Responsibility for the administration and control of all Home Office and building service functions [a list follows]; . . . formulates and recommends policies and procedures concerning office and building service functions and sees that approved policies and procedures are effectively carried out; works closely with all units of the Company on matters relating to general office and building service . . . ; and is responsible for coordination and administration of specialized functions such as: allocation and reservation of conference rooms on Company property and the assignment of space to personnel in executive garage, and the authorization of schedules for use of Company cars and chauffeur. (6)

In order to insure that the list of duties and responsibilities will not be restrictive and will not prompt some executive to use failure to list some activity as an excuse for its neglect, these two categories might well be appended to the list: (1) "duties and responsibilities normally discharged by executives of this level" and (2) "such other duties and responsibilities as might be temporarily or permanently assigned to this position."

*Limits of authority.** The executive is given a grant of authority to take certain action and to make certain decisions in the performance of his duties. This authority must be spelled out as a part of the position description. A machinery manufacturer uses the following statement to describe the limits of the authority delegated to the vice president for personnel and public relations:

1. To operate within budgetary limits as approved by the President.
2. To implement new policies and programs of major changes in previously established policies only after the approval of the President.
3. To approve budgets and expenses submitted to him by his subordinates.

---

\* Many companies feel that responsibilities and authority are inextricably interdependent. For this reason "duties and responsibilities" and "limits of authority" often are combined into one section of the position description.

4. To approve capital improvements recommended to him by Personnel Relations Director above $2,000 and not exceeding authorizations.
5. Line authority is limited to his immediate subordinates. (7)

When the extent and limits of his authority are not made clear, an executive may either fail to assume the full responsibilities of his job or attempt to exercise authority beyond the intended scope of the position.

*Relationships with others.* This section describes the working relationships of the individual executive with subordinates, superiors, other departments, and people outside the company. Robert D. Melcher, of North American Aviation, Inc., emphasizes that, in the main, position descriptions resolve most work problems but too often fail to resolve the relationship puzzle adequately. The organization chart shows the basic division of the work and indicates who reports to whom, but it does not describe functions in detail or explain how individuals are to relate to these functions—which, in reality, is how the organization works. (8) Mr. Melcher further suggests that the following types of delicate and often nebulous generalities need clarification: "general responsibility," "operating responsibility," "specific responsibility," "must be consulted," "may be consulted," "must be notified," and "must approve."

The following is a typical relationship statement:

1. The Plant Manager is directly responsible to the Technical Vice President.
2. The Chief Chemist, superintendents of the Rayon and Nylon Departments, and heads of auxiliary departments are responsible to the Plant Manager.
3. The Plant Manager will maintain close liaison with the heads of all staff departments in carrying out the Company programs and policies.
4. He will also maintain close relationships with outside organizations, suppliers, and contractors with whom the plant is doing business. (9)

Position descriptions should include all the significant areas of activity, stating these concisely and clearly insofar as is practical. The executive group itself should be involved in the development process; otherwise there is very little opportunity to resolve human differences and improve essential communication.

The "Management Responsibility Guide," developed by Ernst Hijams and Serge A. Bern, attempts to "relate management positions, functions, and responsibility relationships to each other; to draw the executives concerned into active participation in position description programs. This approach has provided a dynamic means of objectively describing the work to be done and clarifying the role each manager plays in it—and it has proved to be a major factor in improving management communications and interpersonal and intergroup relations." (10) Here, certainly, is support of John Dewey's statement that "people believe to the extent that they participate."

### Preparation and Writing

The process of preparing the position description usually requires the following steps:

- Gathering the information necessary to describe the work.
- Writing the first draft.
- Approving the first draft, usually after comparison with first drafts of other positions relating to it.
- Writing the final version and making any changes required by company policy. (11)

The actual writing can be done by the incumbent, the incumbent's superior, or staff specialists. Occasionally, outside specialists are employed. The manner in which the necessary information is gathered varies significantly in accordance with who does the writing. The incumbent probably knows the position best, but he may need considerable assistance in wording his description concisely. Specialists who are not familiar with the positions to be described customarily rely on interviews with both the incumbent and his superior, questionnaires, personal observation, and similar position descriptions already in existence.

The first rough draft is merely the starting point. Time should be scheduled for considerable review, revision, and rewriting before the final draft is submitted for approval. Primarily concerned are the incumbent, his superior, and the director of the position description program.

In contrast, the final version of the description is usually the work of one individual. Writing this final draft is generally not as difficult or as critical as preparing or revising the first draft. The task is usually assigned to one man in order to insure standardization of form and consistency of content.

## Updating the Position Description

A position description is like any other management device in that it is subject to change and must therefore be updated periodically in order to be fully useful. The difficulty of keeping up to date is one of the major problems in using descriptions as day-to-day job guides.

Normally, descriptions are reviewed on one or more of the following bases: at regular time intervals (six months, one year, two years); when the job content changes; when the incumbent changes; when the incumbent asks for a review; or when the incumbent's superior asks for it. A review will certainly be merited when disagreement arises over revision of duties—or, for example, when someone calls attention to inaccuracies in a description or the program head suspects that changes in job content are developing, when a general review of the salary structure is in progress, or when the organizational structure is being changed radically.

It may even be a good idea to ask executives to reread their job descriptions periodically and propose any changes they feel are desirable.

## Use and Distribution

Nothing has been accomplished if money and time are spent in preparing position descriptions, only to have them tucked away in confidential files where no one bothers to consult them. The following sums up their use and distribution in forward-looking companies:

- Any incumbent should have access to his own description.
- Any executive should have access to descriptions of positions under his jurisdiction or within his own particular department.
- Nonmanagerial employees need not have access to managerial descriptions, since they are of little value to production workers and

clerical people. This is not true, however, when the descriptions are written in easily understandable language and in a style which would make them useful as induction aids for new employees.

- If the firm is using the descriptions exclusively or in large part for salary determination and it seems likely that at least some adjustments will cause disagreements, access to the descriptions is sharply restricted unless such access will help the situation rather than aggravate it.

- The percentage of employees having access to description manuals is, roughly, in inverse proportion to the importance of salary administration in the uses which a given company makes of the descriptions. (12)

The writing of position descriptions and the administration of a sound position description program constitute one of the clearest examples of how management provides an orderly and systematic framework for executive performance. A major advantage is the systematizing of activities and job groupings in the process of formulating position descriptions. The clarification that results from this process, as responsibility, authority, and relationships are reduced to writing for continuing reference, gives the company one of its most effective tools for shaping both human and material resources toward maximum goal achievement.

## NOTES

[1] C. L. Bennet, *Defining the Manager's Job: The AMA Manual of Position Descriptions*, Research Study 33, American Management Association, New York, 1958, p. 9.

[2] *Ibid.*, p. 36.

[3] Virgil K. Rowland, *Managerial Performance Standards*, American Management Association, New York, 1960, p. 46.

[4] Bennet, *op. cit.*, p. 421.

[5] *Ibid.*, p. 221.

[6] *Ibid.*, p. 314.

[7] *Ibid.*, p. 330.

[8] Robert D. Melcher, "Roles and Relationships: Clarifying the Manager's Job," *Personnel*, May–June 1967, p. 33.

[9] Bennet, *op. cit.*, p. 233.

[10] Melcher, *op. cit.*, p. 34.

[11] Bennet, *op. cit.*, p. 80.

[12] *Ibid.*, p. 140.

# 9

# Performance Standards:
# Assuring Goal Achievement

Every golf course has an established par for each hole and for the entire course. The golfer knows clearly at all times the standard of excellence toward which each individual shot and, indeed, his whole game should be oriented. From the first drive to the final putt, he is results-minded. He knows not only the total number of strokes that constitutes par for the course but also the maximum number allowed for each hole, so that he is constantly aware how well he is doing. The golfer negates the often-heard criticism of standards—that a man is satisfied once he achieves them, and then slacks off. Instead, the golfer tries for a birdie on every hole. He is competing with himself, as well as with others, and if he is a professional he knows that par will not be good enough to win many tournaments.

Thus the standards involved in the game of golf manage to attract and hold millions of dedicated players who willingly sacrifice time, money, and convenience to participate in the game. In the same way, standards in the business world are capable of attracting and holding executives dedicated to maximum job performance. The motivating factor for both golfer and executive is the ultimate target at which each aims; and the inducement to continue is provided by the intermediate targets that serve to measure performance and progress.

### What Is "Satisfactory"?

A standard of performance is an expression of the conditions which will prevail when a job is being done well. The typical statement begins: "Performance with respect to this responsibility is satisfactory when. . . ."

Performance standards are not new, but historically have been a part of almost every activity, often evolving through experience. The workman and his boss may not discuss standards, but when the boss says, "You're not producing enough," or, "Your work is too sloppy," he is implying that there is a standard which is not being met. Similarly, when the sales manager says to the salesman, "Joe, your volume last week was too low. Reorders are not big enough. You're not opening enough new accounts," Joe concludes that his performance is below acceptable standards. Obviously, what Joe needs to know is what sales volume will be considered satisfactory, how big reorders must be, and how many new accounts should be opened each week. The incumbent in any job is in the impossible position of being unable to perform satisfactorily until performance standards have been established and communicated to him. Only then will superior and subordinate alike know where they stand.

It can be assumed that standards of some type exist for every function or job. In most instances they are the result of trial and error over a period of time. The superior has an idea of what he considers satisfactory job performance, and the subordinate thinks he understands what the boss will accept. The best interests of the company, the superior, and the subordinate will be served when these standards are clearly identified, mutually acceptable, and objective; are reduced to writing for future reference; and have become the focal point for discussion of job performance. Standards shift such discussion from subjective generalities to objective specifics on which both can agree initially and which can later be used for the purpose of evaluation. They provide a systematic and orderly basis for on-the-job interaction and a solid foundation on which to build work expectations. They also facilitate maximum individual achievement and self-realization.

## Standards for Everyone

Standards can be developed for functions as well as individual positions. For example, conditions can be described which will prevail when the engineering department is doing a good job. And standards can be set which will be indicative of conditions under which the sales department can be said to be doing a good job.

Standards can be developed for the entire company too. These identify the scope and purpose of the enterprise as a whole. The function standard then becomes a portion of that total, and the position standard is a portion of the overall function standard. It is of course important that the individual understand the essential dependency of both function and company results on his own contribution. Logically, company standards are established first, then function standards, then individual position standards.

Production and sales standards have been a fact of business life for years. Industrial engineers have computed the output that must be achieved by each machine in order to break even or insure a profitable return on investment and related costs. Each operator is then given a production standard based on the machine or machines for which he is responsible—or, in the case of an assembly line, there may be a collective standard. So, too, the sales manager figures very quickly what each salesman must sell in order for his department to meet its quotas. These standards have been generally accepted because they are objective and relatively easy to establish and use in appraising results.

The establishment of performance standards for executive and managerial positions is a more recent development. Professional management theorists now believe it is possible to set such standards for everyone: chairman of the board, president, vice presidents, department heads. The task may be more difficult than at lower levels, and measurements may be more subjective than is the case in production or sales, but the need for standards is just as valid and the benefits are far greater. Managers, too, need targets to shoot at; the identification of results to be achieved eliminates the temptation to seek hiding places, to avoid challenge and the glare of appraisal.

The acceptance of standards for top management positions is the most persuasive argument for the application of standards to all other positions. It would be difficult for the manager of the auditing department to contend that standards should not be established for his department when they exist for higher-level positions.

## Overcoming Skepticism

Skepticism and even opposition should be expected when the subject of performance standards for managerial positions is first raised. The typical reaction is, "Maybe it's possible to apply standards to other jobs, but mine is far too complicated. There is just no way of reducing it to simple statements or determining statistically when performance is satisfactory." This reaction usually occurs because the incumbent does not think of the position in terms of its component parts, of the individual responsibilities with respect to which results are expected, or of established criteria for performance in each of these significant areas.

An office manager stated flatly: "It would be nonsense to worry about standards for my position. Why, I'm responsible for at least a half-dozen things, and I have to use personal judgment in handling all of them." Considerable progress was made with this man by asking such questions as these: "What variance from budget do you allow yourself in managing the financial affairs of your office?" "What rate of turnover in personnel do you consider excessive?" "What is the maximum length of time an invoice should be in the office before it is paid?" "What are the latest dates by which monthly reports are to be submitted?" Slowly the manager, who had answers for most of these questions, began to understand the meaning of standards. Since he wasn't at all certain how some of his existing yardsticks had been arrived at or how valid they were, the idea of sitting down with his superior for the purpose of jointly examining and establishing standards for all his important areas of responsibility actually appealed to him.

## Types of Standards

Standards may not always be so obvious. Logical first questions in seeking to establish a standards program are: Where do they come from? What relevant information do we have, or where can we obtain appropriate guides? Generally, standards fall into four principal categories.

*Objective or engineered standards.* These are usually established through observation and scientific analysis—a process that is often associated with the stopwatch, time and motion study, and the activities of the industrial engineer. It is an attempt to count the number of pieces, measure the amount of work, determine the volume of sales, or define the results that performance of a particular job can be expected to contribute in a specified time. Standards of this type are usually stated statistically on the basis of elapsed time. The salesman should make 30 sales per week. The typist should complete 150 insurance policies a day. The machine produces at the rate of 50 units per hour; therefore, an operator must be able to receive and inspect 50 units per hour.

*Historical standards.* Historical standards are based on comparisons of performance for one period—month, year, and so on—with performance for a similar period in the past. The automobile dealer considers that he has done a good job when he has sold more new-model cars during their introductory week than he did during the comparable week of the previous year. The safety director considers that he has done a good job when the number of lost-time accidents for a given period is lower than the number for the same period a year earlier. The controller considers that he has done a good job when operating costs are no higher relative to sales than at the same time last year.

Unfortunately, most standards originate in just this manner. Yet this year's performance target is no more valid than last year's actual results, and last year's results probably were considered satisfactory only because they matched or exceeded those of the previous year. The weakness of this system is that it does not incorporate factors which influence the ideal bases for performance standards—that is, reasonable capabilities, return on investment, and desired percentage of increase.

*Comparative standards.* A comparative standard, as the name implies, compares performance with what is generally acceptable in the industry or in competitive companies. Sales are satisfactory when they compare favorably with figures reported as national averages. Payroll cost is satisfactory when it compares favorably with averages published for the industry. Advertising costs are in line when they do not exceed those for similar companies. This type of standard is based on the assumption that, if your company keeps up with its competitors or performs slightly better, it is doing a good job. Again, like historical standards, comparative standards fail to incorporate objective yardsticks.

*Subjective standards.* Subjective standards reflect primarily the demands or expectations of the individual executive in viewing his subordinates' performance—they might be termed the special phases of the work which he considers important. Often, for example, an executive will set his own standards for functioning as a committee chairman, writing reports, and a variety of other duties. In the case of a subjective standard, the executive is saying, "This is something that I feel should be done in a certain way, and I will not consider that you are doing a good job in this respect until you are doing it that way." Thus merely getting the order may be acceptable to one sales manager, but a second sales manager may not consider that a good job is being done until all the paperwork connected with the sale is completed and the merchandise has been delivered in acceptable form.

What generally happens in the case of managerial performance standards is that appropriate use is made of all types—objective, historical, comparative, subjective. However, standards can also be labeled positive, negative, and zero. *Positive* standards reflect what is expected in terms of results. A good job will be done when sales are increased by 5 percent a month. Performance will be considered satisfactory when machines are kept in operation 98 percent of the time. A positive standard is usually established when results can be determined statistically.

A *negative* standard states what should not occur or sets limits that are not to be exceeded. If the standard is not met, performance will be considered unsatisfactory. For example: Quality control is satisfactory when no more than 2 percent of shipped products are found to be defective. Customer relations are satisfactory when no more than three justifiable complaints are received monthly. Returns are satisfactory when they do not exceed 6 percent of sales.

A *zero* standard allows no margin for error. It requires that the job be performed in a prescribed manner every time—without exception. Thus: Safety policies are not carried out satisfactorily unless every accident is reported. Job performance is not satisfactory unless the report is filed before the tenth of every month. The cashier must verify every total on the machine.

Good standards reflect certain basic characteristics. William C. Treuhaft, president of The Tremco Manufacturing Company, suggests that standards may be considered acceptable and functional when they are—

1. Jointly developed by employees and supervisors.
2. Statements of basic results required of an operation.
3. Worded to include references to accurate means of measurement.
4. Worded to prevent misinterpretations.
5. Measurements of quality and/or quantity of work performed.
6. Set up in officially approved form.
7. Attainable by at least one member of the group concerned.
8. Continually revised with use. (1)

It is also desirable that standards be based on factors that are easily determinable and that they be complete and broad enough to cover all major aspects of a position or function. Although many standards may be arrived at on a subjective basis, they become functional and beneficial in relation to the effectiveness with which they are written in objective terms.

## Tools for Preparation

It is neither necessary nor desirable to initiate standards in a vacuum without regard for the past, present, and future of the business. They should fit naturally into the company structure. They can be much more accurately and easily arrived at when all influencing factors are considered and all the available tools are employed.

*The organization chart.* Basically, the organization chart clarifies the relationships of the position under consideration with all other positions that touch it either vertically or horizontally. Since standards often involve statements of conditions for which other departments and other individuals are responsible, it is important that these relationships be clearly understood and taken into account.

*The position description.* This can often be used as a foundation on which to base standards of performance. When properly written, it constitutes the best statement of responsibilities available, and is often used as the actual outline. Should an appropriate position description not be available, it is generally necessary that one be written as a preliminary step to the establishment of performance standards.

*The company planning setup.* Standards should reflect the general long- and short-range plans of the company. If these call for a significant change —such as a 10 percent increase in sales for the coming year—then both production and sales standards will have to reflect this increase if the expected results are to be achieved. In other words, whenever standards are being set for collective functions or individual positions, total goals must be considered. Projected changes in company activity affecting type, quality, quantity, and so on all require changes in performance standards.

*Past experience.* Just as the second golfer to putt profits from the experience of the first man, so should the formulators of performance standards profit from experience. Past complaints and conflicts should be examined and dealt with. Vagueness, confusion, irrelevance, excessive lenience or severity —all should be corrected or eliminated.

When these tools are used effectively, standards can be much more easily related to objective criteria. The job incumbent and his superior can proceed with full knowledge that they are on solid ground and that the final list of standards will be both practical and acceptable.

## The Importance of Wording

The real challenge, however, is to get down on paper—out of the heads of superior and subordinate—what the position demands in terms of performance and results. Indeed, the key to the acceptance and effective use of standards lies in clear, precise wording.

An established standard holds job content to a steady and consistent norm. It keeps performance from varying too greatly even when the job is occupied by different individuals; it tends to insure that a uniform contribution will be made to the achievement of goals; and it encourages the development of each incumbent.

The current incumbent will normally have considerable impact on the standards that are set for his position and will naturally understand and accept them—in fact, such standards cannot be satisfactory without his full understanding and acceptance. However, it must be remembered that these standards may be used as a hiring tool, in which case they must be sufficiently clear so that the employment interviewer can display them and say, "Here is what we expect by way of results."

Standards of performance also become a tool for orienting the new employee. Allowance must of course be made for his newness, and he must be permitted a reasonable length of time before his failure to meet the established standards can be considered unsatisfactory performance. When he does succeed in meeting them, it can be assumed that he has mastered the job.

## Techniques for Describing Standards

Here are the two essential steps in stating standards as accurate measurements of results:

1. Start with a complete story or description of the position. This consists of a listing of all essential functions and areas of re-

sponsibility. When standards have been established for each of these functions and responsibilities, the position will be fully covered.

2. To define each area of responsibility, begin with the words, "Performance will be satisfactory when. . . ." Complete this statement by specifying the conditions that must prevail in order for results to be acceptable.

It is critically important that this task of writing performance standards be handled with absolute objectivity. Completed statements should answer these questions: When? In what manner? How well? ("When" refers, not specifically to time, but more to the conditions that must prevail.) Thus satisfactory performance for a branch bank manager might be expressed as follows:

| | |
|---|---|
| *When?* | A complete accounting of the previous day's operations must be in the main office by 10 o'clock the following morning. |
| *In what manner?* | The report must be accurate, balanced, in conformity with bank procedures, and must reflect established standards in each operating category. |
| *How well?* | The report must show actual amounts, number of transactions, percentages, and so on. Any unusual conditions should be indicated. |

Objectivity and preciseness begin to evaporate when too many general terms or words are used. It is preferable to avoid "many," "reasonable," "adequate," "few," "satisfactory," "most of the time," and similar generalities that depend too heavily on subjective interpretation. There will be little room for misunderstanding if expectations are stated in terms of quantities, dollar values, percentages, ratios, elapsed time, quality levels, and other statistical measures.

The first attempt to reduce standards to writing typically ends in generalities. It takes a lot of objective thinking, reworking, and rewriting to produce a clear, concise statement. Every word must be analyzed in order to minimize the possibilities of misinterpretation. It is at this point that semantics becomes important: Does everyone have the same understanding of the terms and phrases used? If the superior and subordinate can interpret these differently, seeds of trouble are sown—much of which can be avoided by discussion. Find out what the new incumbent thinks a standard means. Does he interpret it in the same way as his boss, who held the same position for many years?

There are basic terms on which there can and should be no difference of opinion. Everyone should understand, for instance, that "reached" means "equal to"; that "not reached" means "under"; and that "exceeded" means "over standard." Other concepts can be made more precise by qualifying them as follows:

| Vague Term | Suggested Qualification |
|---|---|
| "Adequate" | State exactly what is adequate. |
| "Approximately" | Omit—or use an average figure. |
| "Few" | State exact number. |
| "As soon as possible" | Be precise. |
| "Reasonable" | Omit. Whole standard is assumed to be reasonable. |
| "Justifiable" | Qualify or omit. |
| "Desirable" | Omit. A standard of performance is assumed to be desirable, but it must be stated in exact terms. |

To repeat: The desired goal at all times in writing standards is precision of measurement. General and indefinite criteria often serve only to water down and confuse. The writing and refining process should continue until the expected results are clear beyond all possible question.

### Who Should Develop Standards?

The several basic approaches to developing standards vary according to who is made responsible for their development. Often their usefulness hinges on this factor. Possibilities include the job incumbent himself, his superior, incumbent and superior together, a committee or other group, or a staff specialist.

*The superior.* A boss should develop standards for his subordinate only when no one else is available—where, say, the job is new, responsibilities have been drastically changed, or a department has been reorganized. Only the superior can know for the moment what he expects by way of performance; therefore, he is the only one who can realistically set standards. However, in instances where standards are developed by the superior, it is imperative that, as the subordinate gains experience, he have an opportunity to participate in revising and updating them.

*The incumbent.* Why shouldn't the incumbent develop his own standards? Who knows the job better? It is common practice for the first draft to be developed by the man in the position. The disadvantage of this procedure is that such standards usually reflect the man's own performance rather than objective considerations. The principal advantage is that the man has been involved in the process; he is familiar with the results and they are his; they have not been thrust upon him without his participation and approval.

It is not unusual for the incumbent to set standards higher than his present performance would seem to call for—he often sets them unrealistically high. When this occurs, it affords an opportunity for joint discussion with the superior, and the resultant easing off may help the superior to gain the subordinate's respect and confidence. In many instances the subordinate will then continue to seek the advice and guidance of his superior.

*Joint approach by subordinate and superior.* Fred Lazarus, Jr., while chairman of the board of Federated Department Stores, Inc., was asked what services the corporate office had offered its member stores. He replied, "We set standards and goals, with the participation and agreement of the person who was to achieve them, and then helped him do the job." (2) This Mr. Lazarus considered a major reason for Federated's position as one of the nation's largest and most profitable department store groups.

The joint approach does confer the benefits of mutual participation. The procedure may be one of several: Standards are set wholly by joint discussion; a list prepared by the subordinate is subjected to joint discussion; a list prepared by the superior is discussed by superior and subordinate together; or simultaneously but independently drafted lists are later compared and discussed. Regardless of the starting point, the key to the success of this method is the exchange of ideas. It enables the subordinate—the man who knows the job best—to communicate his understanding to his superior; and it enables the superior—who knows what he expects of the position—to clarify these expectations to the man who is depended on for results.

Again, special attention must be given to setting standards for the position and not for the incumbent. However, when standards have been arrived at jointly and accepted by the subordinate, they constitute a challenge that he will more often than not meet successfully.

*Group or committee development.* Although this method of standard writing can take several forms, the typical one is to assemble a group of individuals in similar jobs (either subordinates or superiors) or an appropriate management committee. The group might consist of all plant managers, all regional sales managers, or all shift foremen. If properly managed and followed, this approach has most of the advantages of the three previous methods of preparing standards, and the group often brings to light problems that might otherwise be overlooked or discovered only through subsequent experience.

A modification of this approach was used in the Belk organization to establish performance standards for the "buyer-department head." Many managers were uncertain about the duties and responsibilities assigned to this position; standards of performance or expected results, if they existed at all, were based principally on subjective opinion. The incumbents had totally inadequate targets toward which to orient their efforts. It was difficult for either the superior or the subordinate to know what conditions must prevail before a good job was being done.

A group consisting of superiors, incumbents, and staff people was assembled. Through discussion, selection, elimination, and refinement, agreement was first reached on the areas in which results were expected. The next step was agreement on what kind of results were expected in each. Finally, standards of performance for each of the areas were established. This set of job standards was then made available to all units in booklet form. On the page opposite each performance area was a blank sheet headed "Adaptation for My Position." The superior and the incumbent took the standard developed by the group and jointly modified it or added to it. The resulting set of standards then became the incumbent's own, had the approval and support of the superior, matched the official standards for the position and—most important —was no longer an arbitrary document imposed by headquarters. Installed and operating, the system has successfully served the intended purpose.

*Development by specialized staff.* There is always the temptation to "let the specialists do it." After all, they are supposed to have special training in the techniques of developing performance standards. And there is much to be said for this approach, principally because of the skill of the usual staff group and the fact that standards involve management policies, plans, and goals—all of which should be familiar to the specialists. However, although assistance can be an important adjunct to the development of standards, the responsibility should rest with the line organization. The eventual acceptance and attainment of the standards are too significantly dependent on line personnel not to involve them directly.

When time is short or experience in developing standards is lacking, there is often the temptation to purchase "packaged" standards from outside. Obviously, standards developed for similar positions in comparable companies, or made available through specialists, can serve a useful function as guides to the initial phases of getting the program under way. But, so long as any standard remains someone else's, the job incumbent will be unimpressed and unresponsive.

Again, as with previously mentioned approaches, effective use of standards for purposes of performance improvement is dependent on the incumbent's acceptance and support of those standards as his own—standards that he personally is challenged to meet. This is not likely to be the case unless he has been directly involved in their development.

### Examples of Specific Standards

Typical areas in which standards should be developed for individual managerial positions include research and development, engineering, production, finance, marketing, and personnel. Typical management functions within these areas include planning, organizing, coordinating, controlling, motivating, and the like.

Performance standards for a specific position will probably average between 5 and 15 functions. The more precisely these can be stated, without becoming too detailed, the more useful they will be. Duties, responsibilities, and relationships with others should be covered. All available material, including past experience and current operating policies and procedures, should be used as resources.

The following excerpts are from the standards of the products pipeline division of a major oil company. Each was developed through consultation in which the job incumbent, others holding similar jobs, and the incumbent's immediate superior participated. In each case, also, only one standard of many is listed, and performance is considered satisfactory when the stated condition is being met.

> *Safety:* Frequency of serious injuries is less than 10.0 per million man-hours.
>
> *Personnel Administration:* Hours paid for, not worked (excluding vacations) are less than 15 per 1,000 man-hours.
>
> *Maintenance:* Pipeline maintenance labor cost is less than $150 per year per mile of pipe maintained.

*Operations:* Gaugers required to run 1,000 barrels per day are less than .90.

*Communications:* The supervisor visits each gauging district and each pump station at least once each month.

*General Administration:* All accounting and financial procedures will be followed with less than 2 percent of adjustments and errors.

*Public Relations:* At least two planned visits per year are made to operating offices of other pipeline companies in the area. (3)

A wholesale distribution company has listed the following performance standards:

1. Cost of deliveries does not exceed 20 cents per truck-mile.
2. Inability to fill orders due to "out of stock" does not exceed 2 percent of all items listed in the catalogue.
3. Loss of stock value due to damage, breakage, and shrinkage does not exceed 1 percent of inventory value.
4. Cost of operating the warehouse does not exceed 8 percent of sales volume.
5. No more than 4 percent of all orders received will require longer than 48 hours before they leave the loading dock.
6. Sales volume will increase by at least 6 percent monthly.
7. No more than five justifiable complaints from dealers are received monthly regarding factors controllable by the company.

Note that most of these typical performance standards present quantitative measuring criteria. They are—by way of further emphasis—statements of conditions that will prevail when a good job is being done.

## Use of Approved Form

Considerable benefit can be derived from using a standardized form throughout the company. Individuals moving from one position to another find this uniformity helpful, as do superiors concerned with a variety of positions. Special, temporary, and emergency assignments—"helping the other fellow out"—have a way of confusing incumbents and superiors alike as to the valid, permanent standards of performance for a specific position.

Use of approved standards and approved form insures consistency and guards against changes on the part of either superior or subordinate which are not communicated to or accepted by the other party. It means greater objectivity and clearer language, and therefore minimizes the possibility of incompleteness or misinterpretation. And, as an added benefit, a practical form for performance standards interacts with all other forms in company use, each contributing examples of clear wording and insights into the jobs concerned.

## Agreement and Acceptance

The initiation and installation of a standards-of-performance program may well occasion resistance, misunderstanding, and disagreement. However, almost the same precautions can be taken as in implementing any other new management technique or program. These reminders should prove worthwhile:

1. There is no substitute for complete, accurate, factual information that both the superior and the incumbent can realistically relate to this area of concern.
2. The proved benefits of standards should be cited. This is especially advisable when a subordinate appears to feel that the purpose of performance standards is to "force him to work harder."
3. Sufficient details should be presented concerning the exact nature of standards and the procedures to be followed in establishing and administering them.
4. The experience of other companies may prove persuasive.
5. It should be stated unequivocally that the individuals concerned will be given an opportunity to participate in the development of standards.
6. It should be stated, further, that not only will the establishment of standards be a joint venture, but the program will have built-in provisions for review and updating where experience proves this to be desirable or where changes occur in the work environment.
7. Top management should state and demonstrate its approval and support by developing performance standards for its own positions.

8. Most important, the program should be implemented exactly as it was explained. Each successful step paves the way for additional approval and support.

## Standards as Living, Changing Guides

Positions change. Relationships change. Job requirements change. The agreed-on performance standard should at all times reflect the job as initially conceived, but it should be revised as quickly, as often, and as drastically as necessary to keep pace with changed expectations. The probability of change has been used as an argument against established standards. However, it follows that if a man has the right to know the job initially, he also has a right to know how it may have changed.

The validity of present standards may be reviewed at stated intervals, in connection with each performance appraisal, or at times when too many incumbents fail to meet standards, when standards are too easily exceeded, when the job contribution does not appear to be worth the money being paid for it, or whenever either the subordinate or his superior feels that standards merit review. Any proposed changes call for agreement between the individuals concerned, as in the case of initial establishment. This process should insure understanding and up-to-date standards. And the resulting appraisal climate is likely to be a healthy one.

In summary, according to William C. Treuhaft:

1. When agreement has been reached as to what constitutes satisfactory performance, there is immediate improvement in the work.
2. Relations between the man and his boss have been improved.
3. Setting standards is conducive to the growth of the individual.
4. It is difficult to get adequate performance by decree; however, participation in group discussion often affects future performance.
5. Social pressure in the group causes high standards to be set.
6. Self-appraisal has been made easier. Motivation is strengthened and development of the individual is accelerated.
7. There is opportunity to see how logical the thinking of the group members is, and to spur those whose thinking is not too orderly to greater effort in this area. (4)

These are not one-shot or temporary benefits. They function on a continuous basis to the advantage of the individual and of company goal achievement. Potentially, standards can be rated as one of the most valuable techniques available to professional managers. And, as is true of other management-by-design techniques, the manager himself benefits in proportion to his increased contribution to the company.

Standards of performance, skillfully used, are guides and motivators—not clubs to be wielded against the individual. They should be utilized only to the extent that they facilitate achievement relative to the individual's own goals and those of the enterprise. Like policies and procedures, they must be consistent and firm or they will lose much of their value. At the same time, they should make allowance for circumstances beyond human control. In football, deciding whether the safety man for the defense has interfered illegally with the pass receiver is often referred to as a "judgment call." Similarly, the manager must rely on judgment in balancing rigidity of standards against human considerations. He is accountable for results, but he must also consider the welfare, both short- and long-range, of the individuals working under his direction.

## NOTES

[1] William C. Treuhaft, "Standards of Performance," in General Management Series 183, American Management Association, New York, 1956.
[2] Fred R. Lazarus, Jr., "Expanding with Confidence," *Nation's Business*, July 1966.
[3] Treuhaft, *op. cit.*
[4] *Ibid.*

## 10

# Improving Performance and Potential: The Appraisal and Counseling Program

$M$ODERN corporations are spending billions of dollars to purchase human time, to assure contribution to current goals, and to develop future potential. A logical question is: How are we doing? The managerial device for answering this question is the appraisal and counseling program. Appraisal seeks to evaluate actual contribution and future potential; counseling, to promote improvement in both.

Appraisal and counseling are areas in which many managers feel inadequate. Where possible, they avoid them, believing that both require leadership skills which they do not possess and create problems instead of solving them. Such managers, basically, are reluctant to apply the same objectivity and principles in these areas that they apply aggressively and profitably to most others. They are willing to let executives and supervisors roll along unaware of their failures and shortcomings, not to mention their successes, thus denying them the benefits of developmental leadership. As a result, the greatest possible opportunity for strengthening the weak and making the strong even stronger is denied to all. The essential need to know how one is doing can provide input for job satisfaction and development only when met by the man's superior in such a way as to achieve these desirable goals.

## Guides to Mastery

Those who master the techniques of appraisal and counseling to the extent that the program achieves the desired results have the inside track in successful management. In reality, the generation of an increased contribution to current goals and the development of future potential constitute two of the principal functions of management. The practice of effective leadership in these critical areas holds the key to maximum achievement.

Essential to such effectiveness is an appropriate understanding of the purpose and role of the appraisal and counseling program and the steps involved. The following suggestions may serve as guides to such understanding:

1. *Focus on the future.* The coach reviews the films of last week's game and appraises the performance of every player, but he does so for the sole purpose of influencing future performance. Too often, appraisal and counseling degenerate into arguments about water already over the dam. What beneficial purpose can be served by this? Typically, it is more damaging than conducive to future contribution.

2. *Concentrate on job activity.* Individual personality is not an appropriate subject for appraisal or discussion—except as it relates to present contribution, future potential, and development. The company does not purchase the individual; rather, it makes an investment in his time and talents. This is the only subject that can properly be considered.

3. *Aim to develop, not to discipline.* The appraisal and counseling program is not an occasion to downgrade or chastise an individual for past errors or inadequacies. Rather, it provides an opportunity to improve future results through development. When the emphasis is on development, neither superior nor subordinate is preconditioned by the traditional "merit rating" concept.

4. *Be specific.* The superior should regard appraisal and counseling as a

chance to provide the constructive coaching leadership that benefits both the individual and the enterprise. This requires specifics as to time, method, motivation, and implementation of improvement activities. The superior's primary purpose is the provision of this programmed package, structured specifically to benefit the individual concerned.

5. *Eliminate roadblocks and escalate progress.* Most executives confront roadblocks as they seek to appraise performance and develop for the future. Appraisal and counseling can serve an important function in identifying and minimizing the negative influence of these obstacles. It is management's responsibility to eliminate them and to provide a climate in which people can grow.

6. *Realize the importance of the individual.* Games are won by the team, but the strength of the team is in the talent and performance of its individual members. The superior, or coach, is rightly concerned with department or group results, but it is through appraisal and counseling of individuals that the collective results are improved.

7. *Relate appraisal and development to standards.* Expectations should be based on goals and on standards of performance. Appraisal, then, should be an evaluation of achievement in relation to expected results. There can be no other valid basis for appraisal, which is in reality a continual measuring of actual performance against pre-established goals or bench marks. This should be clearly understood by both the superior and the subordinate at the beginning of the period which the appraisal covers.

## Basis for Leadership and Control

Appraisals are the end product of a process of analysis and judgment. Lawrence A. Appley has stated, "If a basic function of an executive is to establish objectives, to determine how well people are performing in relation to those objectives, and discover methods by which they can bring actual accomplishments nearer to the objectives, performance [appraisal] is the very heart of that function." (1)

Appraisal not only is an essential responsibility of managerial leadership, but in actual practice forms a foundation and guide for that leadership. Day-to-day supervision and coaching are based on an analysis of the individual's performance in relation to objectives and standards. Judgments, training, assignments, individual development plans, and individual counseling are the results. This style of leadership is thus based on objective factors related to job contribution, not on generalized personality traits.

Executives, no less than other people, are sometimes unduly influenced by the unusual, the dramatic, and the exceptional. The system must therefore be geared to guard against the errors of judgment that can result when appraisal is affected by such influences; otherwise, the quiet executive who has managed well and prevented crises may be ignored, while the executive who heroically puts out "fires" is applauded. This is a frailty that managers must constantly attempt to overcome. If it is not compensated for, the steady man will be forced to conclude that his type of preventive management is not desirable. Or, still worse, he may be tempted to let fires start just to prove how clever he can be in extinguishing them. The unwary manager may also be tempted to place "fire fighters" in important positions, thereby losing control of his operation.

No superior can control his organization adequately without accurate and intimate knowledge of his people's performance. To assure this knowledge, he must establish and maintain a system by which he can observe, analyze, and draw conclusions in an orderly manner about actual results, not merely superficial events. (We assume, of course, that he has selected control points and that responsibility for checking the appropriate indicators has been assigned to individual managers.) Appraisal involves a judgment of achievement in relation to goals or targets; counseling proposes to improve the probability of goal achievement. In this manner, appraisal and counseling become the technique and process whereby the superior seeks to review and change performance in order to achieve success.

## Motivating Individual Development

It can be assumed that the subordinate wants to do a good job, perform successfully, and gain the approval of his superior on the basis of equaling or exceeding established standards of performance. Like his superior, he knows that achievement of his personal goals is dependent on the achievement of job and company goals—and on the awareness of his superior that this has been done. Appropriately executed appraisal and counseling programs thus become the best vehicle not only for providing the necessary information but—even more—for motivating self-development and subsequent performance.

Nothing of practical benefit is achieved by merely identifying past performance levels. Increased achievement is the primary purpose; and, since it will provide still more compensation for both the superior and the subordinate, the appraisal and counseling program should supply sufficient motivation to insure that the needed development will take place.

## Gauging Future Potential

The quality of future executive leadership depends on the development of that which is currently available, and appraisal provides a realistic basis on which to gauge individual potential. Actually, it is the most reliable method available for this purpose.

Several experimental projects have sought, in recent years, to develop skills in managerial processes and, at the same time, evaluate the individual's promise insofar as his ability to handle high-level responsibility is concerned. One of the most notable and ambitious efforts in this area is AT&T's assessment center program. This seeks to observe how selected individuals behave under standardized conditions and thus determine their capacity for management. Douglas W. Bray, AT&T's director of personnel research, states the purpose of the program as follows:

> To obtain as comprehensive a picture as can be had of men at the beginning of their careers in management. In order to do this, it is necessary to discover their abilities, aptitudes, goals, social skills, and many other qualities. The most effective way of doing this, it appears to us, is to assemble the subjects, a few at a time, and have them spend several days together going through interviews, tests, group exercises, and individual administrative work under the observation of a special staff. (2)

This program simulates actual activities requiring responses that will be indicative of managerial potential. Its so-called in-basket phase attempts to duplicate the paperwork aspects of the actual job, confronting the individual with typical problems that a manager might face during a day's work. Candidates are rated by three managers on such factors as planning, organization, decision making, and flexibility. The staff evaluates all findings and estimates promotion potential. Results based on test groups have proved the program to be far superior in gauging potential than traditional wait-and-see methods. The tremendous advantage of the system is that it is able to predict an individual's capacity for leadership early in his career.

*Pitfalls and Problems*

The principal pitfall of appraisal and counseling is that it is a human activity, beset with all the built-in human errors that occur when one person seeks to judge, develop, and change the behavior of another. The degree to which judgment can be exercised on a strictly objective basis will determine how many of these human-judgment and personality errors can be eliminated.

The personality and expectations of the superior loom large in the appraisal picture. So do weaknesses in the operating environment: foggy objectives, lack of job clarification, lack of specific development plans for the individual, difficult terminology, and the reputations of both superior and subordinate.

C. R. Grindle, writing in *Nation's Business*, suggests that the following constitute potential trouble spots in appraisal:

- Deciding which traits and performance factors are to be rated.
- Reaching agreement on a definition for each factor.
- Evaluation of traits and factors for the particular position.
- Overcoming the natural prejudices of the superior.
- Concentrating on performance in relation to established standards rather than dealing with judgments of people. (3)

Charles J. Coleman suggests that most such pitfalls can be avoided through successful effort in these areas:

- Superior and subordinate jointly reach agreement on critical elements of the subordinate's job.
- Superior and subordinate jointly decide on ways performance will be measured.
- Superior and subordinate jointly develop short-term targets.
- Main emphasis is placed on superior-subordinate counseling, using objective data wherever possible.
- Appraisal focus is placed on the results achieved by the subordinate rather than his personality characteristics. (4)

Both the superior and the subordinate should be familiar with the shortcomings of appraisal and counseling. Both individual executives and their company will be unwise to promote a program without making every attempt to compensate for difficulties that are inherent in it. Results will be no more satisfactory than the effectiveness of those concerned in avoiding anything that may negate, or prove detrimental to, the purposes of the program.

### Program Formulation

Formulating an approved program, or understanding one already established, demands a knowledge of appraisal types, forms, performance areas to be covered, methods of reaching agreement, and appraisal procedures. The finished appraisal product will blend and shape all these ingredients in proportion to the skill of the individuals involved.

*Types of appraisals.* Appraisals may be divided into two basic types—individual and group. Specific attention here will be devoted to the individual appraisal, whose effectiveness depends on—

- Acceptance of responsibility for the process, in depth, by several managers up the line, not just the immediate superior.
- Appraisal of the conditions under which a man works as they relate to his opportunities for achievement.
- Evaluation of the group within which the man works as to its bearing on his performance results.
- Concentration of the appraisal process at the point of action rather than in a central office.
- The perception of the superior, which should be challenged and increased by the appraisal process.

Appraisal, in other words, seeks to assign appropriate values to certain factors in terms of the degree to which they are within the control of the individual being appraised. For example: The W. T. Grant Company bases the evaluation of a manager's performance—and his compensation—on assigned accountability areas and action that he is able to take. Neither is affected by factors beyond his control.

The appraisal is normally completed by the man's immediate superior, although occasionally several superiors may be involved. The emphasis is on results, but the process also serves as a review of management methods and techniques.

The individual appraisal has the advantage of being economical in time. It is far easier to handle than group appraisals of the type that a few organizations have experimented with, and what is said can remain confidential between boss and subordinate. On the other hand, there is danger of it being unduly influenced by personalities, by recent events, and by personal bias.

*Appraisal forms.* A large variety of forms are available for appraisal, ranging all the way from the "blank sheet of paper" through the formalized fill-in type to the descriptive essay. The essay method of appraisal requires written statements concerning job performance, the individual's weaknesses and strengths, and his future potential. The graphic scale that is sometimes used permits the drawing of a kind of profile based on listed criteria. The check-off sheet calls for rating traits or performance areas by checking the most applicable term or description. For example, planning may be outstanding, adequate, or poor; while a manager may be immediately promotable, promotable at some future time, or satisfactory in his present job but not—so far as can be seen now—promotable. Question-and-answer forms are often used, as is the summary-of-weaknesses sheet that shows the major areas where improvement is needed.

Many forms that are ultimately adopted for company use involve a combination of several of these types. But, regardless of the form used, it should be designed to provide an accurate, in-depth picture of job performance and developmental activities in which the subordinate should engage.

*Areas to be appraised.* The two general areas for appraisal are present performance and potential for future performance. Appraisal in each of these areas involves the selection of appropriate factors and their measurement. Typically considered are job content, objectives, standards of performance, actual results, relationships, methods of performance, and action to be taken.

One company form provides for appraisal of the following:

> *Quality:* standard of excellence of work done on assigned job.
> *Cost:* cost results, efficiency, getting full value from money spent for payroll, supplies, and equipment.
> *Leadership:* impact of his personal leadership on his men, associates, and others with whom he works. Effect of his actions on others in promoting his job objectives.
> *Personal development:* increasing his own skills, ability, and effectiveness through work experience, exchanging information with associates, training, and study.
> *Overall effectiveness:* overall results on a current job. (5)

Under the heading of "Leadership," the following explanation is given:

> This is not an appraisal of the man's popularity. It is a judgment of the results to the company that flow from his business actions and work with others. Do his actions promote harmonious and constructive effort, as opposed to disruption and conflict?
>
> Does he inspire his men? Through his management actions, how well does he cause his men to want to do a good job? Through his business action and manner toward people, his associates, and others, how well does he promote cooperation to further our common objectives?
>
> Is he effective in gaining cooperation? Does he build good relationships? Is he well respected? Is he known as being fair in all of his actions and relations with people? How effective are his actions and manner in getting others to help willingly in promoting his job objectives?
>
> Considering all of these questions and any others you think are pertinent to his particular job, please evaluate his "results of personal leadership in gaining respect and cooperation." (6)

*Reaching agreement.* After making the necessary decisions regarding the "when" and "what" of appraisal, agreement on judgment factors must be reached. What is "adequate" performance? What evidence will be allowed? Do failings in one area offset strengths in others?

The quality of performance that will satisfy minimum requirements is most difficult to determine. Subordinates must measure up to certain levels in order to justify their retention in the job they hold now, and then must exceed certain levels if they are to be in line for increased responsibility.

One procedure, and the one most often recommended, is the consultative approach. It involves the gradual evolvement, through discussion, of acceptable standards, including tolerances and definitions of unacceptable and exceptional performance.

Chronically difficult to judge is the validity of the evidence on which appraisal must be based. Suppose, for the sake of illustration, you have just been told that you are in line for a substantial promotion; meanwhile, you must present evidence that you have a subordinate in your department who can replace you without serious sacrifice of department results. What sort of evidence will prove this? It should be objective, revolve principally around statistical data, and identify the contribution of the assistant. For a production manager, such information as the following should prove pertinent:

- Production has been maintained at a level sufficient to provide a 5 percent inventory over and above current sales and shipments.

- All costs for plant operation have averaged within 3 percent of projected goals and have at all times been within acceptable tolerance levels.
- There is satisfactory morale, as evidenced by less than 8 percent employee turnover, below-average lost-time accidents, standard costs for employee benefits, and no excessive number of justifiable employee complaints.
- Development is above average as shown by training programs and subsequent improvement in performance, the number of individuals promoted to higher-level jobs, and the numerous instances of self-development encouraged and guided by the manager.

Such statistical evidence is truly convincing. The more general and intangible factors in performance should be translated into objective terms —as, in the example just cited, skill in human relations and morale building are measured in terms of turnover, number of accidents, payroll costs, complaints and disagreements, absenteeism, and evidence of employee development. Agreement on "how well" a job should be done becomes relatively easier when the supporting evidence is of this type.

*Appraisal procedure.* William N. Mitchell, in *The Business Executive in a Changing World,* states that "correct evaluation of ideas, events, things, operations, or persons always includes three stages:

1. Gathering, analyzing, and testing pertinent evidence.
2. Searching for valid criteria or standards by which to judge results.
3. Establishing objectivity in formulating judgment." (7)

Once again, the executive making an appraisal should be reminded that familiarity with the factors being appraised and with the actual performance of the individual involved is absolutely essential. Appraisal by remote control, or from a physically removed location, must of necessity be based to some extent on hearsay evidence. Because there is no real substitute for personal observation, personal judgment, and first-hand impressions, the absentee appraisal should be understood to have limited value. Actually, it is only a partial appraisal, since so many significant factors cannot be considered.

The actual recording of the appraisal results is the easiest and quickest phase of the program. The preparation of the material, its evaluation, and the gathering of supporting evidence are more difficult and far more time-consuming.

*The Counseling Interview*

The counseling interview is the most difficult and, at the same time, the most important link in the entire chain of evaluation, development, and improvement. Improved performance involves changes in behavior; this depends largely on the success of the counseling interview, which should follow appraisal and should focus on opportunities for individual development.

*Purpose.* Johnson & Johnson and affiliated companies have developed the following statement of purpose for the counseling interview:

1. *Getting the subordinate to do a better job* through making clear your standards of performance. Remember that you too have peculiar traits and expectancies. Here is a chance for the subordinate to learn your preferences in quality, quantity, and methods of work and to understand your reasons for these standards.
2. *Giving the employee a clear picture of how he is doing* with emphasis upon strengths and weaknesses. Showing how well he meets your standards. We assume that much trouble results in business and industry from subordinates whose self-rating is sharply at variance with their superior's evaluation.
3. *Discussing together plans for improvement* and projects for better utility of the subordinate's strengths.
4. *Building strong, personal relationships* between superior and subordinate in which both are willing to talk frankly about the job, how it is being done, what improvement is possible, and how it can be obtained. Improving human-to-human understanding so that closer, stronger relationships will exist.
5. *Eliminating or reducing anxiety*, tension, and uncertainty which may exist where individuals do not have the advantage of planned counsel. (8)

Keeping these goals in mind and remembering that motivation for constructive change is paramount will guard against unproductive concentration on past performance or on personalities.

*Preparation.* The success of the counseling interview rests largely on advance planning and use of objective data by the superior. This preparation should include such steps as these:

1. Review thoroughly the appraisal results, especially the "how" and

"why" of the rating, in the light of both job requirements and job performance.

2. Evaluate the man: his training, experience, and record; his relationships with others; and any influencing factors.

3. List specific facts or illustrations from his job performance to substantiate your appraisal.

4. Determine exactly what you want to accomplish during the interview and design a plan to achieve it. Attempt to build a greater will to work than the man had when the interview began. Work out specific steps that both of you are willing to take to better his performance. Send him away with as much knowledge of his strengths and weaknesses as he is able to accept.

5. If it will be the first interview of its type for either the subordinate or the superior, anticipate a degree of anxiety, curiosity, or tension. Recognize its presence and plan to minimize it.

6. Decide on the use that will be made of the appraisal record. If the interview is to concentrate on a review of it, special attention should be given to each rating, to the language, and to the supporting information. The subordinate will have to be assured that the rating form is merely a convenient way of recording data and is not to be used against him; rather, it is designed to stimulate further development.

7. Project various approaches for leading up to the ratings and other points that will be stressed. How will these be illustrated and supported?

*Problems.* The superior is naïve if he plunges into the interview without anticipating that certain problems may arise and without being prepared to meet them. For example, the employee might disagree with the evaluation and present evidence to support his case. His reaction may be constructive and unemotional, and he may be in possession of significant information that appears different from that on which the appraisal is based. The superior should willingly accept this information, asking appropriate questions to verify it. He should also be willing to change the appraisal if, after investigation and evaluation of the facts, there appears to be justification for it. He may find it advisable to delay completing the interview and schedule a second session after the new information has been checked and the appraisal revised.

The employee, however, may agree to everything that is said with suspicious readiness. When this occurs, it can be presumed that the man either does not understand the appraisal or is keeping his objections to himself. Deeper questioning should determine which is the case. The challenge here is to make certain that he will commit himself strongly to taking the action necessary to correct his weaknesses and thus increase his future potential.

Then, again, the employee may view the interview as an opportunity to talk about promotion and financial gain. He may be too eager for advancement. The superior should remind him that these rewards come as the result of outstanding performance over an extended period of time and that his chances will depend on a variety of circumstances, some of which cannot be anticipated at the moment.

The man may lose his temper, become emotional, angry, or even abusive. The best response is to remain calm, not argue, but simply hear the man out. It may be advisable to terminate the interview and schedule a second one later.

Sometimes an employee refuses to accept responsibility for unsatisfactory performance. He may contend that he has done everything possible and that any shortcomings are the fault of others. His superior may have to reason with him before he is willing to see his role in the job-performance picture. He certainly doesn't want to be blamed for someone else's unsatisfactory work, and his sense of fairness should prevent him from wanting to shift the blame for his own poor performance.

The employee may have shown no improvement since the last interview and may actually be on the way out. Although this situation reflects an admission of defeat by the superior, the subordinate, or both, the superior has to make the best of it by breaking the news in as kindly a manner as possible. He may also try to make the man face the reasons for his failure.

*Climate.* Acceptance, by the subordinate, of the appraisal concept is often more heavily dependent on climate than on objective factors. The subordinate must believe that the appraisal is fair and that the superior is sincerely interested in his development and future potential. Beyond this, climate may be influenced favorably in a variety of ways:

- Insuring privacy and time for the interview.
- Placing primary emphasis on development and growth.
- Assuming an attitude of firmness based on the knowledge that the employee has been evaluated against measurable, objective criteria. However, the interviewer should not be rigid to the point where the subordinate gets the impression that the appraisal is a closed issue.
- Avoiding the appearance of a cross-examination. The purpose of the interviewer is not to entrap the subordinate or prove that he is

wrong and the superior is right; it is to motivate constructive change in performance and future potential.

■ Letting the subordinate do most of the talking at certain stages of the interview. His feelings, opinions, and objections can come to the surface only if he has a chance to talk. And, by talking, he gains a better understanding of himself that will enable him to work constructively toward change.

*Conduct.* As the interview begins, the superior should have devised a strategy and selected the most important factors for discussion. He should be prepared to ask questions that will lead the subordinate to recognize his need for improvement. Taking the initiative, he should explore ways in which the employee can improve his performance, and he should assist the employee to make plans for improvement and accept the responsibility for carrying out those plans. The superior should conduct himself so as to maintain a good relationship with his subordinate at all times, and he should control the interview so that it achieves its objectives within a reasonable time.

As the superior, you will want to make notes of things you intend to stress. Then, as the interview progresses, you should ask questions and *be willing to listen to the answers*. Every time you are tempted to make a speech, ask a question instead. Above all, don't dwell on your own success—it isn't important, at the moment, when or where you started with the company or how hard you had to work to get where you are today. Concentrate on your subordinate. Make him want to respond to the program in a positive way.

If the subordinate appraises himself more favorably than you have, ask him to tell you why. In appraising mistakes, remember that no one is perfect. How many things did the man do *right?* Try to separate your personal feelings from your judgment of his value to the company. If you are at fault, and part of the man's failure can be laid at your doorstep, admit it. Separate, in point of time and in the subordinate's mind, appraisal and discipline. If the employee is really deficient, explain to him exactly where. Point out that you have faith in him and get him to agree with you on what he must do to improve. Be sure to offer your help. And, if the man is outstanding, let him know it. Make this a part of his record and encourage him to even further development.

Although the exact procedure to be followed during the interview should vary according to the situation and the skills of the interviewer, Bernard J. Cover, of Dunlap and Associates, Inc., suggests the following basic outline:

- Have your preparation completed and everything in a state of readiness.
- Establish a climate of rapport.
- Discuss the purpose of the interview and the appraisal plan.
- Give the subordinate an opportunity to respond.
- Present the overall rating.
- Give the subordinate an opportunity to respond to both the good and bad.
- Cover all of the favorable or strong points.
- Give him an opportunity to respond.
- Present the points which are weak and those which need greatest improvement.
- Give the subordinate an opportunity to disagree or respond.
- Discuss the ways in which the subordinate might improve.
- Give the subordinate an opportunity to ask additional questions or discuss other points which he might have on his mind. (9)

In closing the interview, review the points made. Encourage the subordinate to summarize them, using his own words. Reassure him once more of your interest in him and his progress. Indicate your willingness to take up the discussion again at any time.

### Results and Benefits

Joseph F. Tripician, while director of personnel for the Pennsylvania Railroad Company, listed these benefits of his company's appraisal program:

1. It developed an excellent group of promotable personnel.
2. It brought to light many competent personnel.
3. The percentage of promotable personnel was greatly increased.
4. The reaction of the men appraised was almost unanimously favorable.
5. Appraisers were forced to appraise and improve their own managerial performance, thus deriving a personal benefit from the program.
6. Appraised people were given an opportunity to make suggestions regarding the improvement of the company, and many excellent ones were made.

7. A study of supervisory appraisal reports pinpointed the areas where training could be most profitably concentrated. (10)

Companies continue to derive additional benefits from appraisal and counseling programs. For example, one personnel director suggests that it assists in identifying instances where position descriptions are out of date. In the final analysis, however, the primary benefit for most companies is improvement in achieved results and increased future potential.

## Self-Appraisal and Self-Development

The principles and recommended guides in this chapter have been aimed primarily at appraising and counseling the subordinate, but they apply with equal validity to the superior.

The executive should be encouraged to appraise his own performance in relation to standards and expected results in the area for which he is accountable. He should make use of statistical and other objective criteria to determine his batting average in achieving goals and maintaining effective control over his operation in accordance with established standards. He should appraise his job performance and make plans to further develop his managerial competence, improve his results, and increase his future potential. The higher he goes in management, the less direction he should need in correcting, expanding, and refining his performance.

## Counseling and Coaching: A Summation

David W. Ross has remarked: "Many a boss either shies away altogether from counseling his subordinates or bungles the job, because he doesn't understand the true nature and function of this key executive responsibility." (11) And Lawrence A. Appley has said that "coaching means that when the rookie goes to bat for the first time he has supporting him the concern and experience of the manager and every member of the team. He does not stand alone, unsupported, unaided, uncoached, or without all the assistance coaching can supply."

Vince Lombardi, ex-coach of the Green Bay Packers, feels the main job of a coach is to bring out the best in every player—to make sure that each will play up to the absolute maximum of his potential. This involves basic skills but relates just as importantly to attitudes and self-confidence. The player must believe in himself and the coach. He must know that, when game time arrives, everything humanly possible has been done to enable him to do his part in winning.

Individual and team coaching on the part of the manager involves no less responsibility for developing the fullest potential of the individual. It eliminates the problems that block starring performance. It reinforces self-confidence and encourages the application of every ounce of mental and physical effort the individual is capable of exerting.

The executive should remember the following basic guides as he carries out his counseling-coaching responsibility:

- Job-related managerial counseling is a part of the manager's function. It should be treated not as a psychological exercise, but as a normal part of the manager's opportunity to guide subordinates into more productive channels.
- The essential work of counseling is done by the superior. He must be willing to present the facts, examine them, and draw logical conclusions concerning courses of action.
- Thorough knowledge of the individual's background, work history, relations with others, and all other influencing factors is essential to counseling.
- Subordinates must be allowed sufficient time to think and work through a problem. The continuing challenge to the superior is the patience and time that are part of effective counseling.
- The discussion should focus on the barriers to progress. The superior should avoid identifying these himself where possible—it is preferable for the subordinate to arrive at them through his own logic.
- Follow-up involves attention to future behavior. If no change occurs for the better, the superior may want to initiate subsequent counseling sessions—or, after a number of attempts, seek professional assistance.

"The goal of counseling is the elimination of any problem that interferes with workforce morale, productivity, acceptance of change, or interferes with the harmony of the group." (12)

In summary, an appropriately structured and executed appraisal and counseling program could conceivably hold the key to the current and future productive results of the company. Such a program offers essential benefits to both the objective and subjective goals of the company and the individual.

## NOTES

1 As quoted by Charles W. L. Foreman, in "Appraisal: Appraising the Management Team," from a speech delivered before various AMA sessions.

2 As quoted in Jaala Weingarten, "Companies Take a Close Look at Employee Appraisals," *Dun's Review and Modern Industry*, September 1966.

3 C. R. Grindle, "What's Wrong with Performance Appraisals?" *Nation's Business*, May 1967.

4 Charles J. Coleman, "Avoiding the Pitfalls in Results-Oriented Appraisals," *Personnel*, November–December 1965, p. 26.

5 Foreman, *op. cit.*

6 *Ibid.*

7 William Norman Mitchell, *The Business Executive in a Changing World*, American Management Association, New York, 1965, p. 75.

8 Earl G. Planty and Carlos E. Efferson, "Counseling Executives After Merit Rating or Evaluation: A Project in Executive Development," *Personnel*, March 1957.

9 In Joseph M. Dooher and Vivienne Marquis, editors, *Effective Communication on the Job*, American Management Association, New York, 1956, p. 153.

10 Joseph F. Tripician, "Appraisal in Action," in Robert E. Finley, editor, *The Personnel Man and His Job*, American Management Association, New York, 1962, p. 200.

11 David W. Ross, "How to Be a More Effective Counselor," from a speech delivered before various AMA sessions.

12 Donald A. and Eleanor C. Laird, *The Technique of Personal Analysis*, McGraw-Hill Book Co., Inc., New York, 1945.

*Part III*

*Maximizing*

*Managerial Performance*

# II

# Assuring an Appropriate Resource
# of Management Talent

I$_N$ due course, Mr. Knorr will discover, as did many who came before him, that managers, whether they think with their larynx or their head, are successful in almost exact ratio to the caliber of the talent at their command." This statement was made in 1956 regarding the new president of the Detroit Tigers, Fred Knorr. It could have been made, says Marvin Bower in *The Will to Manage*, of any new corporate executive. "Success in business," Mr. Bower declares, "is in almost exact ratio to the caliber of executive talent at top management's command." (1)

Winning teams do not come into being by accident; they are recruited carefully because of special talent and potential. Each person is placed in the position where he can make the greatest contribution to the team, each is coached and developed, and each must perform consistently. One spectacular play will not win pennants; it takes the superstars who make spectacular play a way of life.

Similarly, successful companies can grow profitably only when they, too, have superior performers in key positions who do most things right most of the time.

## Unique Challenges

The executive personnel administrator must be concerned with the quantity and quality of the management team in much the same manner as the regular personnel administrator concerns himself with employees at lower levels. However, there are some unique challenges facing executive personnel administration:

- The scope of the executive position and its significant influence on company operations.
- The limited supply of high-caliber management talent and the competition for it.
- The high costs in beginning salary, training, and time involved in developing top management talent.
- The critical continuing cost of this individual to the company and the need for his contribution to grow in proportion to his salary.
- The problems involved in assuring top performance in the more general areas of management.
- The close personal relationships that must exist among members of the management team.
- The long-range nature of executive employment.
- The decisive role that executive personnel administration plays in determining the future course of the entire company.

Executive personnel administration is decidedly a top management responsibility. The accountability for its successful implementation cannot be delegated. It has been stated often that the chief executive's primary task is to acquire and develop a management team capable of guiding the company effectively. He can delegate certain duties for the discharge of the executive development program, but it must have his personal attention in order to insure results.

Lack of management leadership is the principal cause of most business failures. It is largely for this reason that companies find it necessary to seek mergers. Unfortunately, mediocre or poor management has caused many companies to be rejected as acquisitions.

The chief executive who becomes convinced of the critical importance of his management team will give executive development more than mere grudging lip service. He will set in motion and fully support a program that will guarantee high-caliber executive personnel administration. And, in so doing, he will most likely be assuring the profitable growth and even the very survival of his company.

## Components of the Program

After the commitment has been made to an executive personnel program, planning, organizing, and implementation logically follow. An effective program can be divided into the following key areas:

1. *Executive manpower planning.* This should be a total-concept program aimed at determining the company's requirements for executive and professional personnel in terms of numbers, types of talent, and time when needed.
2. *Inventory of executive personnel.* This inventory of present personnel should include—for each man—age, performance on current job, and potential for future promotion. It should estimate probable turnover and give the whole manpower picture, present and future.
3. *Recruitment of executive manpower.* It may occasionally be necessary to employ experienced executives from the outside, but this can be minimized and almost eliminated if an adequate supply of potentially qualified trainees is recruited and developed.
4. *Executive development.* This usually includes an appropriate mix of formal projects within the company, outside assistance, individual counseling and coaching, and specific developmental techniques.
5. *Provision for promoting, retaining, and separating.* The system should offer promotional opportunities and other inducements for remaining with the company. However, it should also facilitate the spin-off of the subpar and surplus personnel.
6. *Incentive compensation.* Compensation should be linked to re-

sults in such a way as to reward executives in direct relation to performance and contribution to the company. This provides the balance of opportunity and rewards essential to the star performers and enhances the economic performance of the company accordingly.

## Gauging Executive Manpower Needs

Shortly after the Korean conflict, the president of a leading New York bank was heard to say, "We will have a shortage of vice presidents in ten years." When the surprised listener asked how this could be predicted so far in advance, he was told that the bank could project the number of each year's trainees who would rise to that management level and, therefore, the number the bank must hire to compensate for losses and failures and still have enough vice presidents left. During the Korean conflict the bank had not been able to hire sufficient trainees. However, the executive manpower planning program had projected, on the basis of anticipated growth, statistical experience with management trainees, and the bank's promotional program, exactly the number of trainees needed to fill vice-presidential positions eight years in the future. This is the type of realistic executive manpower planning every major organization should engage in.

The beginning point for all executive manpower planning is a determination of needs. This can be done through an extensive, detailed plan that is geared precisely to all company activities. Or it can, as is too often the case, exist only in the head of the president, who has decided, but told no one, who are the "heirs apparent" to certain positions. He has also probably assured himself that he can hire additional executives from the outside if and when they are needed. Since well-managed companies require better means than this for providing vital management resources, more sophisticated systems are in order.

Although techniques vary with each company and systems should be designed to meet specific needs, most comprehensive plans include the following:

1. A forecast of the number of executives needed in light of the present size and estimated future growth of the company.
2. An analysis of the company's organizational structure and posi-

tion descriptions to determine present validity and probable changes as well as a forecast of how these changes will alter the numbers and types of executives needed.

3. Determination of the numbers of executives that will be required at various levels of competence and at established intervals.

4. An evaluation of anticipated changes that might alter the company's needs for executives: automation, technological advances, new products, phasing out of unprofitable operations, trends in the economy, and so on.

5. Estimates of other factors in the executive employment picture:
   a. Anticipated turnover as reflected in the number of probable retirements as well as voluntary and involuntary resignations.
   b. The speed with which trainees will move up the promotional ladder.
   c. The potential of trainees and how effective the development program will be.
   d. The overall effectiveness of the organization in utilizing executive manpower.

6. Determination of the probable number of beginning-level executives or trainees who will have to be employed in order to supply company needs as projected by these data.

The effective program provides manpower in sufficient supply, but not to the extent that it slows promotions and adversely affects morale. An oversupply is not only expensive but potentially harmful. Real talent is always ambitious and, when overcrowded, seeks more promising opportunities with competitors—and the executives who leave may be the ones most essential to the healthful growth of the company. Although the problem of oversupply will correct itself in the long run, its immediate effect may be to involve management in the expenditure of unnecessary dollars.

## A Perpetual Inventory

Only a few years ago, says Lyle H. Fisher of Minnesota Mining and Manufacturing Company, a glance around the lunchroom was all the inventorying of executives that was necessary in that company. But with rapid growth and decentralization, "name and reputation" gave way to a formal inventory system based upon three general beliefs:

1. A belief in promoting from within: The company's officers have an average of 26 years of service.
2. A belief that a company can only make development opportunities available: Basically, each individual has to develop himself. The rapid growth of the company, of course, affords many such opportunities.
3. A belief in management committees as a source of training. These committees, operating at both corporate and division levels, act as review boards and guiding lights for major activities. Members get liberal opportunities to observe and take part in running a large corporation. (2)

IBM, to cite another instance, has more than 120,000 employees, but a perpetual inventory is maintained. This includes typical personal data, such as age and education; but it also contains evaluations, comments on promotability, and a listing of company and outside courses completed. Because the information is updated monthly, changing qualifications are taken into account; and the manner in which the information is stored enables the company to identify needed skills at all times. Less complicated systems are used by smaller companies, with or without computers, but the purpose is the same—that of maintaining an inventory of available executive and professional skills and being able to retrieve this information with maximum speed when needed.

Of all the assets a company possesses, the most vital is executive leadership. It is only logical, therefore, that managing by design should include a system for maintaining an accurate record of its availability, its changing patterns, and its possible utilization.

One of the largest and most successful U.S. companies matches the inventory system to its organizational chart. To each position on the chart are attached three removable colored cards, each with a name and birth date: that of the present incumbent, his understudy, and another possible candidate. The colors indicate the current evaluation of each man's long-range potential. These mechanics reflect a simple but highly effective system for long-range executive manpower planning. . . . (3)

Such an executive data profile should certainly include such basic information as age, education, experience, performance appraisals, and indications of potential. The information should be sufficient to enable management to make decisions concerning the man's current functioning level and his qualifications for lateral transfer or for promotion. This assures the company not only of the availability of needed manpower but of the efficient utilization of its most valuable resource. The individual, in turn, has the assurance that he will not be inadvertently overlooked.

Month after month articles appear in professional management magazines emphasizing one theme: We're wasting our executive manpower. (4) The implication is that companies which pride themselves on their elaborate and highly complex mechanization in production areas are attempting to function with antiquated horse-and-buggy methods in providing for the effective utilization of their executive manpower. Many companies are limited by traditions or by rigid beliefs on the part of certain key executives which, in effect, block transfers and promotions. Such comments as the following are indicative of faulty manpower utilization and the resulting low morale:

- "Anyone who expects to become part of top management around here will have to start where I started and come up the hard way—there's no short cut."
- "There's no use wasting executives by transferring them across divisional lines."
- "The trouble around here is that every unit manager downgrades his best people in the eyes of top management in order to keep them hidden. He fights to keep them from being promoted out of his division, and then he ends up losing them to a competitor."
- "Executives just don't believe that they're being considered when better positions become available or that they have a realistic opportunity of being considered for the job for which they are best qualified, wherever it may be in the company."
- "Why is it that the best jobs are always filled from the outside? Does the man across the fence always have to look better?"

It is evident that the company suffers most from this sort of thinking and, too often, the competitor benefits.

There must be more than just a philosophy of promotion from within. Actual practice, from top to bottom, must assure that every individual will be given maximum promotional opportunities in accordance with his qualifications and the positions available. The key to the success of the program is a soundly planned, consistently implemented system. It is the responsibility of top management not only to approve this system but to audit it in order to insure that men are not being arbitrarily held back or bypassed in making promotions. To do otherwise is to neglect one of the most important functions of management—that of utilizing every company resource to the maximum benefit of the individual and the organization.


## Recruitment of Executive Manpower

"Where are tomorrow's leaders?" asked Frederick R. Kappel while he was AT&T board chairman. "Are we doing all we can to find and develop the men who have the drive, the character, and the vision to assert the needed kind of leadership? I do not think so. I think that we must do better." (5) The pyramid of management is constantly changing as the stones are rearranged. The quality of the structure tomorrow will be determined by today's success in recruiting and developing leaders.

The search for tomorrow's executives usually focuses on three major areas: management itself, outside sources of experienced men, and trainees with executive potential. Employment of experienced men from outside is often a symptom of poor trainee recruitment and faulty promotional practice and, for this reason, will not be discussed as a component of managing by design.

*The search for qualified management trainees.* Not only is there a critical need for executives to supply the rapidly expanding and almost insatiable demand, but this shortage relates particularly to the better-qualified, more capable executives—performers who can make the first team in the major league of professional management. The most critical limitation on the growth of companies, giant corporations as well as small businesses, is the supply of promotable executives capable of providing the competitive superiority demanded for profitable growth.

Cloud Wampler, while chairman emeritus of Carrier Corporation, stated that his No. 1 job was "to have our younger men ready for the responsibilities that come with leadership." (6) And Dr. Frank Stanton, as president of the Columbia Broadcasting System, declared: "Manpower is our most important need. Not just bodies to fill jobs, but the creative man who won't stay within the stereotyped framework which, unfortunately, much of industry is today." (7)

"Help Wanted—and Very Badly." This caption (8) is symptomatic of the scramble now occurring among recruiters for the limited supply of qualified graduates. The situation is critical because—

- Business and industry are expanding at an astonishing rate.
- There is increased demand for executives in both quantity and quality.
- The armed forces are taking sizable numbers of the available candidates.
- College graduates, increasingly, are going on to graduate and professional schools.
- A pathetically small percentage of graduates is seeking careers in the professional management field.
- Numerous graduates simply fail to meet the high standards set by well-organized, demanding companies.

In short, some of the strongest competition in business is coming—not necessarily from salesmen seeking markets—but from recruiters competing for the limited supply of executive trainees.

Publishing houses, management consultants, professional management organizations, and companies themselves are all giving increased attention to the problem of attracting, hiring, screening, and selecting the right candidates for executive jobs. Guidelines have been drawn up for recruiters, placement officers, employment agencies, and, most importantly, the applicants. The National College Placement Association and its various regional organizations have been in the forefront of this movement. In addition, colleges, employers, and employment agencies are cooperating to develop and abide by certain codes of ethics in the recruitment of executives and of management trainees. This has tended to keep the competitive scramble from getting completely out of hand.

It is certainly true that recruiters have, at times, engaged in practices that are not only costly but hardly in the best interests of a young trainee. The manner in which he is initially wooed (consider, for example, the New York engineering graduate who flew to the West Coast for an interview by one company, interviewed another while there, and collected expenses from both) is often calculated to produce a prima donna complex. The sought-after graduate begins to feel that the company needs him far more than he needs the company—an attitude that is bound to have a negative influence on the effort he is willing to put forth for professional development and growth after being employed.

Where does all this leave the chief executive who wants to adhere to ethical practices and keep costs in line, but who recognizes that he must compete not only for share of market but for share of talent? In his search for operating guides in this area he should—

1. Base activities and decisions on projected company needs. Avoid "stockpiling."
2. Attempt to establish and maintain contacts with colleges where recruiting will be done. This may include grants of money, but most often takes the form of furnishing speakers for classes and campus groups, arranging for company tours, working with professors, and participating in college management programs. Professors in particular exert a considerable influence on both the career and the company eventually chosen by the graduate. (9)
3. Be selective. Recruit in those colleges most likely to furnish candidates who have the wanted skills and will be favorably inclined toward the company.
4. Use recent graduates or other former trainees as members of the recruiting team. Graduates want to meet and talk with operating executives and find out what the company is really like.
5. Don't oversell the company. The pressure put on recruiters to produce bodies has caused serious problems: the employment of unqualified applicants, expensive turnover, and disenchantment with the company on the part of trainees.

Of vital importance is an understanding of the graduate—what he wants, what will influence his initial decision, and what conditions will produce a commitment on his part. This is the key to attracting and retaining his interest—not the ability to "sell" him. The company certainly should not be remodeled to cater to his whims, but management should recognize that it might best serve its own long-range interests by providing the developmental environment most likely to motivate the young executive group.

Attendance at professional recruitment conferences, interviews and discussions with graduates, and research in the field all indicate that graduates want challenging, meaningful, important work. They want to be able to use their minds, and they certainly expect to find challenges and stimulation beyond college levels. They have been led to expect that the company will be well organized, that it will function smoothly and efficiently, that it will be objective in its decision making, and that compensation and promotions will be based on merit. Serious disillusionment occurs when they discover disorder, pettiness, partiality, "sacred cows" that can't be disturbed, and a power structure and pattern of operation behind the chrome-plated facade that are completely different from the picture painted by the campus recruiter.

The graduate wants responsibility as soon as he can handle it—and he expects an early chance to prove himself. Failure to give him this chance is a chief cause of turnover. The fact that he wants to be a participating member of the management team does not mean that he expects to make top management decisions from the start, but it does mean that he wants his ideas, suggestions, and contributions to be taken seriously. He is much more interested in being judged on merit, engaging in challenging activities, and being able to contribute and belong than in being treated with paternalistic "tender loving care."

It must be assumed that the graduate has something to sell, something that the company needs. He does not have to accept employment with your company; therefore, you have to take the initiative in seeking him out and making him want to join your company—even to the point of changing certain aspects of the environment to make it more appealing. Top executives too often assume that the paths they took to success are the only ones; therefore, all trainees must follow the same road map. They fail to recognize the urgent need, in bidding for a limited supply of talent, to structure recruiting and development programs for quicker and greater "return on investment."

A willingness to listen is the campus recruiter's most valuable asset. He *must* listen to get the message from placement officers, from prospects, and especially from recent graduates who have joined the company. It can be assumed that many future trainees will react in much the same way as the present crop. What are their reactions to the company, their place in it, its training programs, its compensation and promotional practices? What do they believe their career opportunities to be with the company? Management has at times failed to ask these questions because it doesn't want to hear the answers. Yet, in reality, this is the type of feedback management needs when seeking ways to improve not only its recruiting performance but also the way the company is managed.

## Selecting the Most Promising Candidates

What are your criteria for deciding whether to employ a trainee or an experienced executive? The right answer can be far more decisive for the future of the company than deciding which machine to buy or the color of the annual report. The aim here is "zero defects," and the selection criteria and the skill with which they are used will determine the batting average. Standards should not be so stereotyped that the company never has the benefit of the "rule breakers." Every company needs a couple of mavericks, unconventionals who are not blinded by tradition and whose receptors never pick up messages to the effect that something cannot be done.

The chief recruiter for the Aluminum Company of America posed these questions before a college placement association meeting: "I wonder how many of today's recruiters can see no deeper than the Brooks Brothers suit, the sharp clear eyes, the firm handshake, and the fraternity personality? I wonder how many of today's sharp recruiters would have hired Steinmetz?" It is sobering to think of the number of good, competent potential employees who may have been bypassed because they didn't seem to have the "right part in their hair."

Although exact criteria will be as varied as the particular needs and preferences of the company, these basic guides should be given consideration in most selection procedures:

- The individuals making selection decisions should be thoroughly familiar with every phase of the company's operations and have detailed knowledge of all job and manpower specifications.
- Interviewers should be thoroughly trained and skilled in the difficult art of interviewing.
- Executives who will participate in group interviews, or otherwise share in the selection process, should be given—and be willing to accept—some guidance.
- Characteristics, mannerisms, appearance, motivation, personality, impression made—all these should be considered together with such factors as scholastic record, extracurricular activities, and experience. Neither too little nor too much weight should be attached to any single factor; rather, each should become a part of the appropriate mix.
- Use should be made of professionally accepted tests and other appraisal tools.

It has been suggested that companies ought to accept the fact that executive selection is a compromise—one searches for the ideal but settles for the practical. In brief, one should—

*Seek accomplishment.* Aim for the individual who has established a record of success in a responsibility that closely approximates the position you wish to fill.

*Evaluate strength and weakness.* Assume an objective, critical, and analytical posture toward the candidate.

*Use multiple evaluations.* Arrange for those company executives who would be expected to interrelate with the new man to interview and evaluate the candidate.

*Choose competitively.* Don't hire the first man who looks good just to take the pressure off by filling the position with a warm body. (10)

With regard to specific personal characteristics, those most advantageous in management trainees were rated by 41 companies as follows: (11)

|  | Times Appearing in Top Five | Percent |
|---|---|---|
| Intelligence | 41 | 100 |
| Maturity | 33 | 80 |
| Interpersonal skills | 33 | 80 |
| Integrity | 28 | 68 |
| Analytical ability | 28 | 68 |
| Communication skills | 27 | 66 |
| Temperament | 9 | 22 |
| Health | 4 | 10 |

Regardless of the slide rule used in evaluating the qualifications of the potential trainee or the experienced executive, the employment decision should be viewed in proper perspective—that is, as a major economic decision. It can influence the affairs of the company as significantly as any other decisions made by management.

## Developing Management Potential

Potential executive talent has little value until it is developed and used for the benefit of the company. Perhaps even more challenging, therefore, than persuading the potential executive to join the company is the maximization of his potential through systematic programs. Management development, by whatever tag it may be identified, has occupied the minds of leading executives and been in the spotlight in seminars and conferences with increased regularity as operating costs have risen and the importance of executive leadership has been more fully recognized.

Executive development can be compared to a journey, with top management assuming responsibility for advancing the individual along the way. By coaching, encouraging, counseling, and appraising, management seeks both to accelerate and to insure the trip. However, development philosophy recognizes that the acquisition of new knowledge and skill is primarily the responsibility of the individual, even though most companies attempt to provide both individual and group guidance.

Management development can be divided into two basic categories: programs for inexperienced trainees and programs for experienced executives. This distinction, of course, is made purely for convenience's sake—development ought to be viewed as a total concept. Each potential executive has a starting point from which he begins developing and advancing; the development process is not terminal in nature but must continue at a level of maximum effectiveness so long as new knowledge and skills are being discovered, changes are occurring within the company and its environment, and the individual desires to advance to levels of greater responsibility.

Perhaps no other business activity has received more attention or been the source of more disillusionment than management development. Too many programs have simply failed to produce effective executives. Maybe too much was expected to begin with—there were too many magic formulas and panaceas. Development programs must be planned, evaluated, and conducted with the realization that—

- They cannot succeed if the wrong people were hired.
- They cannot compensate for faults in the areas of policy, organization, compensation, appraisal, promotion, or management systems.
- Development must have specific goals but should not be viewed as an end in itself. Its function, given the size, shape, and nature of executive performance requirements, is to prepare the individual to meet these standards.
- They cannot succeed if artificially structured without regard for the true nature of the company and its effectiveness in utilizing the individual.

Planning development for newly employed trainees involves both formulating a program and constantly revising it so as to meet the changing needs of the trainee and the company. The planning job deserves the same careful, systematic attention as any other management responsibility. In many instances, a top management committee is assigned this task; and it may, in turn, seek the advice of specialists, the help of educational institutions, and the lessons to be learned from the experience of other companies. Consideration should be given to job requirements, the knowledge and skills that the program will be expected to instill and improve, the way in which the program will be implemented (who will conduct it, when, and where), methods of presentation, visual aids and other materials needed, and a continuing system for measuring effectiveness, appraising results, and changing the subject matter as necessary.

No "canned" program is likely to contain all the component parts considered essential by every company, and this is as it should be, since each should be structured to meet specific needs. Most effective programs contain varying degrees of training in the following:

1. The duties and responsibilities of executive leadership.
2. The ability to understand people and communicate with them; to motivate and deal with subordinates.
3. An overview of the management process, plus training in the management techniques of goal setting, planning, organizing, controlling, and appraising.
4. Specifics regarding the products and activities of the company.

Who should conduct the training? Whoever is the best qualified and will be the most effective. It is unfortunate, but true, that some of the most successful managers turn out to be the poorest trainers, especially when they have to participate in group or formal programs. The "best"-qualified trainers may include line executives, staff specialists, outside educators and consultants, and others who have a contribution to make. Training programs often take the form of company-run institutes, possibly located away from company premises, thus affording a neutral environment and an opportunity for participation by a cross-section of company leadership. It is highly desirable, above all, that line management play an active role in the program. Trainees need to have the opportunity to meet these executives and be exposed to their thinking and methods. Staff specialists and outside educators can present facts and generalities, but they cannot substitute for the line group.

There should be training programs for the trainers in order to improve their effectiveness and increase their self-confidence. No one—executive, staff

member, or outsider—should be used as an instructor or supervisor of a
trainee, regardless of his reputation, unless he is a good trainer. Fred J. Koch,
while director of executive development for F. & R. Lazarus and Company,
stated emphatically: "It is essential that the junior executive get his on-the-
job training from a good teacher. And it should be borne in mind that a successful executive is not always an inspiring teacher; he may be a loner who
expects juniors to learn by proximity." (12) Actually, the effectiveness of the
trainer should influence the trainee all during his early years with the company. This formative experience is likely to have far more impact on his per-
manence with the company, and the contribution he makes to it, than the
formal phases of the development program.

The specific developmental techniques used by various companies would
make an impressively long list. Undoubtedly this list would reflect two
goals: (1) training the individual in short-term specifics and (2) developing
the individual to the point where he can achieve maximum results through
accepted management processes. Balanced programs attempt to combine
both.

*The formal, organized, systematic training program.* This is structured in
advance and planned down to the last detail of timing, participation, and
material to be covered. The program has continuity from year to year, but is
constantly undergoing change and refinement.

*Job rotation.* The way to the top at Du Pont, General Foods, Texaco, and
Federated Stores is through frequent transfers to different jobs, sometimes in
different divisions. The rotated trainee or executive learns not only the basic
facts regarding the various operating areas, but also the skills demanded. For
example, in a staff job he will be trained to think, to analyze, and to be creative. In a line job he will be more concerned with specific results regarding
units produced or dollar sales. Job rotation is an accepted technique for development, but many companies ignore its potential. They cite as reasons the
trainee's lack of experience and the risk to the company of below-standard
performance while he is learning the job. However, consider the long-range
advantage of a competent executive with balanced training as opposed to the
short-range gain of rigid adherence to standards. There will be disappoint-
ments, but the benefits far outweigh the risks and the costs. As John Gardner
says:

> In an organization, a well-designed system of personnel rotation will
> yield high dividends not only in the growth of the individual but in
> organization fluidity. Free movement of personnel throughout the or-
> ganization reduces barriers to internal communications, diminishes hos-

tility between divisions and ensures a free flow of information and ideas. (13)

*Delegation of responsibility.* The skill of the ball player will never be developed, or his talents accurately evaluated, until he steps up to bat or handles the ball. A man needs to feel the weight of real responsibility. He needs to know the size of "the ball park." He needs an understanding of policies, procedures, and guidelines; but he shouldn't be told in minute detail simply to "pick it up here and put it down right over there."

The development of the executive can be advanced faster and with greater assurance if he is given an area of responsibility or a specific project with only minimum instructions. He will learn most by innovating, by formulating the best procedures on his own. Further, he needs authority to match his responsibility, accountability based on expected results, controls based on appraisal of progress, and coaching based on suggested improvement, if needed. This developmental process reveals to the man, and to the company, the magnitude of the position he is capable of handling successfully.

*Performance evaluation.* Management development assumes that both individual and company are concerned with the executive's advancement to higher levels of competency, responsibility, and compensation. It must be concluded that both are also concerned with improved performance and results. Even in the formative stages of learning and trying to discriminate between effective and ineffective procedures, the trainee must know how his performance is regarded by his superiors. In addition to being given actual performance standards, he needs to see in writing, or hear stated, his strong and his weak points. He needs to know how well he is doing in relation to standards and in the judgment of the individuals who will influence his future.

*Coaching.* Potential becomes contributing talent when it is appropriately coached. Almost to a man, superstar athletes give one or more coaches credit for their rise to stardom. In the management field also, star performers attribute much of their success to "a boss I had when I started out, who took me in hand and steered me right." And, interestingly, top executives, in reviewing long and successful careers, list the development of young men as their most satisfying achievement.

Both the individual and the company deserve and need the benefit of effective coaching. Too often, the superior is reluctant to interfere in areas where performance is considered negative or unsatisfactory. He hesitates to risk hurt feelings, broach awkward topics, or really level with the man. But consider the coach who wants to win ball games and produce all-Americans.

Does *he* ignore the weakness of any player? He levels in the most effective way for a given individual—whether with quiet counseling or public "chewing out."

Experience has proved that criticism should be administered promptly while the pertinent facts are still fresh, that coaching in general should be based on identifiable areas of performance, and that all comments should be translated into specific guidelines for change.

*Committees and special projects.* Service on committees and responsibility for special projects give the individual an opportunity to participate actively in company affairs and become better acquainted with the process of managing. He has a chance for interaction with others and learns how to function as a contributing member of the group.

Committee assignments often have the dual purpose of completing an assigned task while furthering the personal development of the individual. The key to the effectiveness of a committee is the manner in which it is chaired. Neophyte executives are seldom asked to chair committees; but, while serving as members, they may often demonstrate potential for future responsibilities.

Special projects, assigned to individuals or groups, may operate within the framework of an existing committee. An individual project provides a real moment of truth for the rising executive. A New York advertising executive, asked how to spot "really bright comers," replied that executives basically do maintenance work most of the time, but occasionally a special project must be developed. Some men, he said, will handle such a project routinely and achieve only routine results. The real comer will view it as a great opportunity; he may work on it day and night and on weekends; and his results will represent his best efforts and often make a real contribution to the company. This man is likely to continue this type of performance when given increased responsibility.

*Multiple management.* The basic purpose of multiple management, popularized by the McCormick Company of Baltimore, is to provide executives with opportunities to study, observe, and experience the responsibilities of more advanced company levels. Multiple management often involves junior boards, senior boards, and even plant or other special-interest boards. Each has an assigned area and level of responsibility. Typically, the junior board receives matters requiring decision, conducts investigations, and makes recommendations to the senior board. These boards do not run the company; and certain areas, such as salaries, are not appropriate matters for board consideration. Nevertheless, the boards do have tremendous value in developing the executive, at various stages of advancement, in the techniques and processes of management. He learns that management is not "they" but "we." He understands why it is not possible for the company to do all the things that certain employees or executives may consider desirable. And he becomes familiar with the goals of management and the criteria used for decision making.

Charles P. McCormick himself stated that the purpose of multiple management was

> a firm concept of putting people first. The plan operates through a combination of auxiliary management boards, participation, sponsorship, merit rating, and two-way communications between all employees and management. A major aim is to eliminate one-man rule in business and to train and develop young executives in accordance with their merit, rather than their age. The real secret of its success is participation; it offers administrative outlets for our basic needs as workers. (14)

Since the primary purpose of the development program is to improve performance on present jobs and qualify men for the climb to higher positions, multiple management is an ideal development vehicle. It uniquely serves the needs of the company and the desires of the individual to participate.

The most important condition for the success of any one development technique or the entire list in combination is an environment conducive to individual growth. Elaborate programs can be devised and implemented, but they will fall woefully short of their goals unless the environment nurtures the seeds that have been planted. Purposeful development can occur only where there is opportunity for modification of performance that can be translated into greater results achievement. Given the necessary climate, the sky is the limit for continuing executive education. Not only is the opportunity greater than ever before, but so is the need. An engineering professor has stated that "no engineer is ever more than half-educated. Half of what he knows now will be out of date in five years, and half of what he will need to know in five years hasn't even been discovered today." Almost the same thing can be said about the dynamics of professional management. Management techniques can become outmoded just as quickly as production or computer processes. The challenge to top management in the area of developmental training must not be limited to initial programs but should recognize the correlation between the company's profitable growth and the effectiveness with which management processes are continuously updated and improved.

In view of the fact that most major companies now have management development programs, individual executives might be pardoned for assuming that their development is a company responsibility. This belief, however, could be fatal insofar as the rise to top management is concerned. It should be remembered that each man will receive approximately the same training from the company—but that the company expects, from this common pattern of uniformity, the emergence of some uncommon superstars. The odds are that these individuals will view company programs as merely a starting point. They are likely to complete outside courses, ask to participate in company-sponsored programs, read extensively in related fields, and chart their own goals and programs for achieving them. The growing executive always realizes that his growth is far more important to him than it is to the company. The company is likely to survive and possibly even prosper whether he is promoted, remains in the same job, or fails completely.

### Promotion, Retention, and Separation

There are three categories of managerial employees: the aggressive contributors who will be promoted, the "status quo's" who will merely be retained, and the failures who must be separated. Top management can realistically expect to have all three types and should endeavor to handle the resulting problems in the best interests of the company. It should be recognized, however, that no company can tolerate conditions where many executives are standing still. When this occurs, *the company is standing still,* and this could be disastrous.

*Insuring the retention of outstanding talent.* It has been stated previously in this chapter that executive talent is the most important resource the company possesses, that it is in short supply, and that it is expensive to recruit and develop. These facts are well known not only to you but to your competitors, who are experiencing the same problems and casting covetous glances in the direction of your executives. Executive recruiting firms, sometimes referred to as "head hunters," have sprung up by the hundreds in most major cities and are aggressively seeking to assist companies in finding executive talent and executives in finding the right job. The individual executive knows very well that he can easily register with such a firm, or otherwise seek enlarged opportunities on his own initiative, if he becomes dissatisfied about his present situation.

It is only during recent years that researchers have centered their attention on the problems of retaining executives and keeping them motivated. An article in *Dun's Review and Modern Industry* suggests taking a second look at executive personnel policies since there are far more jobs than executives to fill them and about a half-million middle managers change jobs every year. The "up or out" philosophy is considered by many fast-growing companies to be one solution, because "knowing that there will be no long-tenure human obstacles in the way of promotion encourages capable executives to stay." (15) However, if this policy is adhered to too aggressively it will cause anxieties which will, in turn, influence some good men to escape the pressure-cooker atmosphere for opportunities more to their taste elsewhere.

Lack of communication, even among executives, is frequently cited as a significant reason for executive unrest. In order to remedy this, many companies are turning to regularly scheduled discussions of corporate goals or periodic feedback sessions.

Walker L. Cisler, of Detroit Edison, in commenting on the "care and feeding of executives," has stated: "We strongly believe in using our people's judgment and experience. We give them as much responsibility as they can take and a free hand to use it." (16) Executives seem to be happiest when they have an opportunity to face and successfully meet challenges. An increasing number of companies, among them Du Pont and ITT, follow this practice as a means of increasing executive effectiveness and reducing executive turnover.

*Business Week* has examined the corporate problem of "Finding the Right Silver for the Executive Palm," (17) and *Newsweek* offers advice on "How to Lure Executives: Cash Is Now in Vogue." (18) If executives are to be retained, they must be paid in accordance with their contribution to the company. The executive, like the professional athlete, has only talent to sell; and he will often sell it to the bidder who is willing to pay the highest price.

The total operating environment—including a man's interrelations with other executives and the confidence he has in the company—ranks high on the list of factors which influence his decision to leave or stay. In fact, if it can be assumed that his pay is reasonably in line and the company provides an effective operating structure, the decisive element seems to lie in this delicate area of personal relationships and basic feelings.

When too many executives leave the company, it can be assumed that something is amiss with management policies or with compensation practices or both.

*Identifying and promoting star performers.* The problem that management faces regarding promotions is just what this heading implies—identifying those most deserving. The first team tomorrow will be composed of those who are doing a good job today. Make too many mistakes in identifying this group and tomorrow's team will win too few ball games.

Most authorities agree that the identification of future management potential begins even before the man is employed—that patterns of performance and leadership are indicated by grades, extracurricular activities, summer employment, and spare- or part-time jobs. Roy Walters expresses it by saying, "The person I want to hire is the one who recognizes that school was his job and that everything he did there was a way to improve himself." (19) Several top personnel executives in banking have used such statements as these to describe the way they detect management potential:

"A man should be smart, sharp and hungry."
"A person capable of individual thought."
"A high energy level is essential. He must have a sense of going somewhere—a drive to succeed."
"We don't want people who fit into an easy mold. He should have independent ways of thinking, an ability to analyze a problem in a different and successful way." (20)

Douglas W. Bray (21) has found a significant relationship between future potential and the man's first job assignment and performance. The first contact with an industrial organization creates a lasting impression. Success in it is likely to be followed by a high level of performance later, even in relatively dull jobs; the young manager who is not challenged by his first job is likely to be handicapped throughout his career. Dr. Bray's work emphasizes that attitudes about the company and top management, work habits, and performance patterns which are formed early in executive careers have a profound and lasting influence. All the more reason, then, for keeping the beginner interested and productive in preference to standing around looking on, even during job rotation.

*Promotion based on performance results.* Vigorous, successful companies identify management potential and base promotions on job performance. Although they have some interest in personality, appearance, and other niceties, their value systems consider a man's contribution to the company team—his batting average—not his classic stance at the plate. Psychologists have concluded that patterns of behavior are established early in life, and management experts generally agree that while planned training and development can alter and improve the individual, basic patterns, energy levels, and commitment to maximum results are relatively fixed. The man most likely to produce the best results in a big department is the one who achieved the best results in a small one.

Identification of executive potential and promotion based on job performance depend on the proper use of other professional management techniques covered in this book: position descriptions, job performance standards, and accurate appraisal of results in relation to standards. It is only when the individual executive is operating within this framework that both he and his manager can determine, on an objective basis, the quantity and quality of the job performance in relation to expectations and the performance of others. Promotion based on actual performance enables all concerned to know that a particular choice has been fair—as when a production manager said, "I didn't get the district supervisor's job, but I've known all along that my record was not as good as George's. I'm sorry I didn't get it, but one thing I know for sure—it was because of production results and not because the president doesn't like me."

When it becomes necessary to hire a manager from outside the company, there can be no secrets as to the reasons why. If you are going to say with one major company, "We don't hire managers from the outside; we train and promote managers," you must follow this policy in actual practice. If you do, you may find that you seldom lose an executive through resignation to take other employment.

The feasibility of promotion through the ranks without weakening the present organization or the future position of the company is dependent on competent manpower planning, effective recruitment and placement, adequate management development programs, and a results-oriented system as described here. In addition, the company must maintain an accurate and up-to-date inventory of all executives qualified and available for promotion as well as a central listing of positions to be filled. Promotions are too often restricted by artificial barriers to limited areas or limited numbers of units. The resulting waste of leadership and profit potential is tragic.

The company may of course find it necessary to eliminate bottlenecks along the way—bottlenecks or obstacles in the form of other executives who either are satisfied where they are or fail to qualify for promotion, thus preventing those below from advancing. For this reason the chief executive officer should review the promotion picture regularly. How many of the present executive group (not counting professional specialists) were brought in from the outside as experienced rather than beginning-level managers? How long, on the average, does it take a reasonably capable manager to move up to the next level? What is the extent of executive turnover? How many promotions are actually occurring in the company? The chief executive who can't readily answer these questions might ask any young executive—chances are he has the answer to every one of them.

## Compensating Executives on the Basis of Performance

"Compensation is no longer considered only a device for attracting and retaining capable executives. Modern managers see a company's executive compensation program as an important tool in guiding and motivating their executives to achieve more challenging growth objectives and improved company profits." In these words, Sam Flanel, manager of the Controllers Congress of the National Retail Merchants Association, expressed the modern purpose of executive compensation, (22) whose use of financial incentives to maximize development and profitable job contribution goes far beyond limited salary ranges or delayed compensation programs.

No attempt is made here to minimize cash as a primary incentive, but the evidence indicates that money alone is insufficient to sustain executive performance at maximum levels for extended periods. After-tax compensations must be linked with attractive nonfinancial considerations. It is this mix of financial and other factors—such as opportunities for promotion, interesting and challenging work, and satisfactory environment—that influences a man's decision to stay or to accept a job elsewhere. When executives say they are well paid but are working below their true potential, we see that money alone will not suffice.

On the other hand, "Money is the most important single factor in recruiting, keeping, and motivating young adults." (23) More and more companies, says General Electric's John S. Morgan, are avoiding the "silence is golden" theory where salaries are concerned; they are bringing the matter up and talking about it. As company work time is shortened, outside interests become more dominant and the company becomes less the center of executive existence. It is at this point that compensation becomes an indicator of what the company thinks of him and what he, in turn, gets from the company. As he gains more and more of his intangible satisfactions from the world beyond the job, salary becomes more and more important. Compensation becomes the burning question for most employees, Mr. Morgan believes, for four reasons:

1. Money motivates directly.
2. Money gives security.
3. Money reassures.
4. Money gives status. (24)

Executive compensation presents one of management's most difficult challenges. Its administration must be fair to both the individual and the company in establishing the value of each position, measuring job performance, motivating to maximum levels of performance, and appropriately using monetary and nonmonetary rewards. The success of the system seems to rest largely on management's ability to match reward to contribution. The chief executive who seeks to maximize the total effectiveness of his company's executive compensation program should consider the following:

1. Practices and programs of comparable companies.
2. The total cost of executive compensation.
3. Evidence of the effectiveness of the program in bringing about exceptional effort and results, self-motivation, and merited promotions.
4. The effect of compensation on recruitment, morale, and turnover.
5. The appropriateness with which all forms of executive compensation are blended.
6. The overall competence of the management team and the results it achieves.

Perhaps few other areas of managing by design are as exclusively the responsibility and prerogative of top management as that of executive compensation. It can attract, motivate, and retain the leadership on which the success of the company rests. It is a vital function that can be neither delegated nor avoided without imperiling the achievement of company objectives.

## NOTES

[1] Marvin Bower, *The Will to Manage*, McGraw-Hill Book Company, Inc., New York, 1966, p. 156.

[2] Jerome W. Blood, editor, *The Personnel Job in a Changing World*, American Management Association, New York, 1964, p. 215.

[3] Bower, *op. cit.*, p. 159.

[4] Ralph S. Novak, "We're Wasting Our Management Resources," *Personnel*, May–June 1966.

[5] Frederick R. Kappel, "Where Are Tomorrow's Leaders?" *Reader's Digest*, November 1965, p. 123.

[6] Samuel Feinberg, *How Do You Manage?* Fairchild Publications, Inc., New York, 1965, p. viii.

[7] *Ibid.*

[8] "Help Wanted—and Very Badly," *Business Week*, April 2, 1966, p. 101.

[9] "Business Lectures Professors," *Business Week*, July 10, 1965, pp. 65–66.

[10] Richard J. Wytmar, "How to Find the RIGHT Executive," *Sales/Marketing Today*, March 1966, p. 20.

[11] Wayne J. Foreman, "Management Development Methods: What Large Companies Are Doing," *Training in Business and Industry*, August 1967.

[12] Feinberg, *op. cit.*, p. 82.

[13] John W. Gardner, *Self-Renewal*, Harper & Row, Publishers, Inc., New York, 1964, p. 77.

[14] Charles P. McCormick, *The Power of People*, Harper & Brothers, New York, 1949, p. 15.

[15] Jaala Weingarten, "How Do You Keep Executives?" *Dun's Review and Modern Industry*, July 1966.

[16] *Ibid.*

[17] "Finding the Right Silver for the Executive Palm," *Business Week*, July 22, 1967, p. 90.

[18] "How to Lure Executives: Cash Is Now in Vogue," *Newsweek*, June 20, 1966, p. 88.

[19] "A Recruiter's-Eye View of What It Takes to Be Boss," *Changing Times*, May 1966.

[20] "Battle for Bankers Fierce," *The Charlotte Observer*, Charlotte, N.C., July 30, 1967.

[21] "How Do You Pick an Executive Winner?" *Business Week*, March 5, 1966, p. 109.

[22] Sam Flanel, in James T. Powers, *Executive Compensation in Retailing*, National Retail Merchants Association, New York, 1966.

[23] John S. Morgan, *Managing the Young Adults*, American Management Association, New York, 1967.

[24] *Ibid.*

# 12

# Activating and Channeling
# Human Effort

THERE is a kind of ability that takes ordinary resources
and talent and converts them into extraordinary energy and results. It activates and blends into group effort both human and physical potential. It
turns all power components "on"; moves goalward at machpower; and leads,
directs, and motivates all concerned to the end that results are achieved. This
ability—this almost indefinable knack that separates the successes from the
failures—is what constitutes true management.

*Managerial Leadership Activates Total Energy*

Marvin Bower, in *The Will to Manage,* tells about a Swiss educator who
had discovered a significant reason for America's rapid industrial growth. He
said:

> The love of you Americans for industrial organization is not love of wealth but the pleasure of achievement. You take delight in producing bigger and better things, in inventing more ingenious contrivances, in discovering ways of harnessing nature. No wonder there is such a close association between industry and culture in your country. (1)

The dedicated and achieving manager views his accomplishment as the creative artist views his completed painting. It represents, not a tedious chore, but an exciting opportunity to engage in competitive leadership that brings many diverse elements together into a unified, programmed, and smoothly blended whole.

This type of dynamic management is far from mere "maintenance" and "just letting things happen." It means actively taking charge and making certain that the right things happen to the degree that will insure success. It is the type of management that creates the right environment and the right systems and then activates the company's total resources.


## A Management Balance

Management is most effective and achieves maximum results when it maintains an appropriate balance. This balance is the crux of the managerial task. It is not a "top down" concept or a consensus of popular opinion. The most effective technique is that of consultative or participative management, which is based on the recognition that "command" authority has relatively limited acceptance or value today.

Participative management assumes that productive effort is largely a voluntary response. It is not generated in satisfactory amounts by compensation, fringe benefits, threats, or complete self-government. The conclusions that are gradually emerging from the studies of the behavioral scientists support the belief that the individual will not contribute maximum effort for the achievement of company goals or management's objectives and quotas alone, but will do so if he can equate these with his own personal goals. The achievement of personal goals then parallels the achievement of company goals. But company goals become individual goals only when they have been arrived at through the involvement of the individual by means of consultation and participation.

Management is constantly searching for, testing, and experimenting with leadership skills that will produce this coalescence of company and personal goals. The response to ordering people to perform is not only unsatisfactory but often negative. Nor does a system of penalties—such as loss of pay, dismissal, group disapproval, frowns from one's superior, and curtailed promotional opportunities—often produce maximum effort. The human spirit accepts and responds more generously and effectively when the negative attitudes associated with "someone else's" program have been eliminated. Management will be well advised to capitalize on the benefits that result from including every individual in the development of objectives and procedures with which he will be involved. If the individual is to feel that his effort is necessary to the successful achievement of objectives, he wants his opinions considered in their initial formulation and in the plans made for action.

## Management Roadblocks

Productive effort is the result of two types of forces: pushing from behind and decreasing resistance in front. The force that lifts an airplane is not increased air pressure on the bottom of the wing or the angle of the plane as it moves through the air, but decreased air pressure on the top of the tailing half of the wing because of the flow of air created by the shape of the structure. Similarly, management can create more productive "lift" by eliminating or minimizing the obstacles ahead than by increasing the push from behind.

The following management "danger areas" should alert the executive to possible problems and trigger the elimination of these potential hindrances to productive effort.

*Failure to manage.* The boss must be boss. The overly democratic boss, or the one who believes that all problems can be solved through consultation (valuable though this technique can be), is often inclined to carry things too far. He is tempted to think that he can manage without being in control—deluded into believing that to be effective he must be popular, and that in order to be popular he must refrain from being firm. Douglas McGregor wrote of this need to be in charge in very personal terms:

> It took the direct experience of becoming a line executive, and meeting personally the problems involved, to teach me what no amount of observation of other people could have taught. I believed, for example, that a leader could operate successfully as a kind of adviser to his organization. I thought I could avoid being a "boss." Unconsciously, I suspect, I hoped to duck the unpleasant necessity of making difficult decisions, of taking the responsibility for one course of action among many uncertain

alternatives, and of making mistakes and taking the consequences. I thought that maybe I could operate so that everyone would like me— that "good human relations" would eliminate all discord and disagreement.

It took a couple of years, but I finally began to realize that a leader cannot avoid responsibility for what happens to his organization. In fact, it is a major function of the top executive to take on his own shoulders the responsibility for resolving the uncertainties that are always involved in important decisions. Moreover, since no important decision ever pleases everyone in the organization, he must also absorb the displeasure, and sometimes severe hostility, of those who would have taken a different course. . . . Good human relations develop out of strength, not out of weakness. (2)

*Management obsolescence.* One of the most serious handicaps faced by many managers is obsolescence on the part of their superiors. If the cost of obsolete management could be computed, it would be astronomical. Consider the large numbers of executives who must be forced to retire early, downgraded, "kicked upstairs," or otherwise moved from strategic positions in order to avoid permanent damage to the organization—including the loss, to other companies, of impatient younger men.

Managerial obsolescence is no respecter of persons or organizations. It can affect both. It can strike the president or the first-line supervisor at any age. The principal reason for it is failure to keep abreast of trends, techniques, and managerial approaches capable of producing the expected results. It can be a matter of abilities or of attitudes.

Obsolescence may come on abruptly, as when the installation of a computer eliminates or drastically changes managerial requirements. Or the onset of obsolescence may be almost imperceptible; the requirements change slowly, and the manager fails to change accordingly. He is afflicted with "hardening of the managerial arteries," a disease fatal to sharp, effective leadership. In extreme instances, entire companies or industries become out of date.

How does the enlightened manager identify and guard against this threat to managerial effectiveness? He should keep his ear to the ground for rumblings of change, his eyes peeled for its visible manifestations. He should be cognizant of what is occurring throughout his industry in new products, new techniques, and new forms of competition. He should surround himself with bright, energetic, almost annoying innovators to keep him on his toes. He should continually appraise his own managerial performance, developing a specific schedule of activities aimed at keeping him up to date with what he needs to know. He should deliberately press for new experiences and accept new challenges (possibly off the job). And he should consciously broaden horizons and seek opportunities for further growth and improvement.

*The "command post" mentality.* Some executives view the executive position as a command post. It is this, to some extent, but the application of strict military principles is seldom appropriate. Harold P. Koenig, a retired naval officer, has drawn parallels between military and business management in the areas of objectives, planning, intelligence, economy, simplicity, offense, readiness, and morale. (3) The analogy can be instructive for industrial "commanders." Many of the disciplines and tactics required for military leadership can prove extremely beneficial to the business leader, but he must recognize that he is subject both to more limitations and to more freedom than the military field commander. He does not have absolute control over his "troops," outside influences are different, and missions often extend over a longer period of time.

The business executive should think twice before attempting to give orders in the way that is possible, and often necessary, in a military environment. Excesses of this sort may prove more harmful than almost any other errors. Once again, a balance between the two extremes is much to be desired.

## Building Blocks for Results

In management, as in the construction of a building, the finished product is the direct result of the guides and the materials used. And the first and most important of the building blocks is the builder or manager himself.

The manager has the job of creating something that is greater than the sum of its parts and more valuable than the sum of all the resources required for its creation. It is his essential task to employ these resources in such a manner as to produce the greatest possible increase in value. He accepts, rejects, and utilizes activities, systems, techniques, and controls in accordance with this stated purpose. This concept affords an objective look at the problems which confront him as a manager.

Much has been said regarding the influence of thinking on action and subsequent results. Appropriate thought precedes almost every instance of outstanding performance. The coach dwells at length on the team's mental attitude. The office manager talks about morale. The sales manager calls it self-confidence or enthusiasm. Whatever his field of interest, the executive who accepts the importance of thinking to performance will develop his own thought patterns most favorably. Because the executive's self-confidence is increased by believing that he can manage successfully, he should upgrade his thinking about the obligations and responsibilities of management. He should supply, for himself and others, that mental stimulus that will promote action suited to the purposes of the enterprise.

The real puzzler to top management is the executive who possesses the knowledge, the skills, and the motivation to manage, yet fails to do so satisfactorily. What is lacking? It appears to be the "will" to become involved and committed to the limit of his full potential. He is content just to meet team standards rather than to be so outstanding that he becomes a star. Such a man needs to have his will intensified through increased self-confidence, thorough preparation, a sound operating framework, and the deliberate application of psychological boosters. Once total commitment is achieved, it becomes an inspiration for greater dedication to company objectives on the part of all the man's subordinates.

How efficient, really, is the effort of most executives? It is possible that the average rating would be pretty low. Why? Probably because the executive has never analyzed how he spends his time or made a deliberate attempt to establish priorities based on the relative importance of each activity to the success of his job performance. Yet another important building block for the manager is a new and objective look at his overall job and its component parts. He should forget that he is the incumbent and try to streamline his approach just as if he were the boss. Managerial time and effort have practical limitations; they should be used in the most beneficial manner.

## Structuring Effective Group Management

Management of a group often requires a technique slightly different from that employed in the person-to-person relationship. As in the case of civil authority, the subordinate surrenders a degree of his own job-related self-direction to the superior, who is thus given collective authority by both the company and the individual to direct his work activities. Often a key to the effectiveness of management is whether this right to manage is real or imagined. After James Hayes, head of the Department of Business Administration at Duquesne University, had examined a company organization chart, he remarked, "O.K., that's how it looks on paper and maybe that's the way it's supposed to be, but now tell me about the real power structure. Who really makes the decisions and gets things done?"

The continuing authority to manage, given freely or reluctantly by the group, depends largely on the type of service that is rendered to the group by the manager. A managerial title is not precisely a badge of authority; it should be viewed more as a hunting license, as merely the opportunity to produce results through the exercise of leadership. The extent to which the group agrees voluntarily to be managed will be in direct proportion to the beneficial service that results from the surrendering of authority. It is certainly true that the company delegates to the manager certain prerogatives. However, for this delegation to be truly effective, the manager must merit the respect of his subordinates. This he gains largely through the nature of his management and, specifically, the service he succeeds in rendering to the group. If that service enables the individuals in the group to attain their own personal goals, he will win the respect he needs.

The manager must develop strong individuals, but he must give equal attention to consolidating these individuals into a smoothly functioning collective force. There is an appropriate role for the "lone ranger," but a coordinated team is required to win the battles of production and competition. Building this winning employee and executive team demands quality management.

### Achieving the Competitive Edge

Will five runs win the baseball game? Will a score of 74 win the golf match? No one knows until it can be determined what the competition can achieve. Success is often relative. Management may follow all the rules and be considered excellent; but, unless it achieves a competitive edge, it may only create a false sense of accomplishment. It must not only strive for excellence internally but keep ahead of the competition externally.

To maintain peak performance, management must decide what it is—what conditions will exist, what standards will be met, what levels of achievement will be attained when excellence exists—and shoot for that mark. Peak performance is easier to attain than to maintain, yet this is precisely the challenge.

Peak performance obviously involves excellence in every phase of the operation. Unfortunately, however, the performance of some managers is analogous to that of the baseball catcher who is superior in every phase of the game except fielding bunts. Such a manager often has a dislike, or lack of zeal, for some part of his job; therefore, he neglects it. Yet peak performance is attainable only when every phase of the managerial game is thoroughly mastered and exceptionally performed. The manager cannot neglect his financial responsibility, his human leadership, his developmental role, or any other function essential to total job performance. Peak personal performance and peak subordinate performance should be sought as the only type of activity that will insure the executive and his area of responsibility the competitive edge.

Problems that stand in the way of progress can largely be eliminated by preventive management. However, when a problem does arise, the manager must solve it as quickly and smoothly as possible. The machine that is not operating makes no contribution to production. The advertising campaign that is not clicking is not adding to sales. The stenographer who is producing at only 93 percent of required quantity and quality needs supervisory attention. All such problems the manager should view as liabilities. Their magnitude, and the length of time they are tolerated before being solved, will have a significant bearing on the final operating statement and the likelihood of maintaining the competitive edge.

The manager, of course, has his eye on the competitive edge, and he knows that achieving it and maintaining it will require uncommon dedication and effort on everyone's part. He must therefore discover and utilize the dominant drives of his subordinates—those motivators that produce superior job performance. These are as varied as the individuals involved. In addition to monetary considerations, the following are relatively important to most individuals: prestige, status, social acceptance and belonging, and self-development or growth. The specific drive dominating a particular individual must be diagnosed before the prescription can be applied. The challenge to the manager is to discover it (often it is a combination of drives in varying degrees) and utilize it to obtain uncommon performance from that individual. How? By convincing him that his goals will be attained in proportion to his success in contributing to company goals.

Just as pilots are sensitive to the response of their planes, so must managers be sensitive to human response. People must be fully turned on, charged, activated, and stimulated in order to realize their maximum potential. This is a question not of manipulating people, but of understanding what motivates them—and encouraging them to motivate themselves.

Uncommon achievement can usually be traced to an ability to establish the kind of rapport that taps the full potential of the individual. It is seen in the coach who can take an average athlete and make a star out of him. It is seen in the manager who can take a mediocre company or unit and make it outstanding. It is the fine art of human leadership that coaches, influences, challenges, persuades, and elicits precisely the response desired. It is the alchemy of individual and group interaction through which the manager is able to maximize human commitment and effort.

## A Climate for Productivity

It is the seed and the climate that determine the harvest. It is human resources plus the working environment that shape the corporate harvest. Climate is the result of relationships, understandings, attitudes, and the sort of spirit that permeates every individual in the organization. It reflects a willing acceptance of high performance requirements and total dedication to their achievement. Climate is created by management through its personal character, its sense of fairness, its unwillingness to condone mediocre performance, and its practice of rewarding according to contribution.

Don G. Mitchell recommends the following guides to assuring a dynamic organization:

- *There must be a leader.* He must know what he is doing, and his team must have confidence in him.
- *There must be an organization.* This becomes the operating framework.
- *Every key member must know his place in the organization and what is expected of him.* Also, he should know every other key member's place.
- *There must be goals*—destinations, both near and far, and also the dream goal.
- *There must be checkpoints along the road to the goal.* Management committees or other adequate review procedures must function for this purpose.
- *There must be a climate in which a dynamic organization can operate*—an opportunity for full potential performance in accordance with "lowest possible level" decision making.

- *Each key man must be allowed to operate within his sphere of authority.* He should be left free to operate in that sphere and held accountable for results in it.
- *There must be incentives to get the job done.* Incentives become the "payoff" for response to the dynamics of the organization. (4)

The implication is explicit: A dynamic organization is composed of certain specific ingredients which constitute the operating foundation for management. These must be linked properly and must function as a coordinated whole.

Glenn D. Clark, director of management development for the Whirlpool Corporation, states that the lack of an appropriate climate "imposes a twofold burden on the company. If one of these burdens is cost of less than optimum performance by people who are task- instead of responsibility-oriented, the second and even greater burden lies in the failure of managers at all levels to realize their potential capacity to shoulder broader responsibility." (5) At Whirlpool, Mr. Clark states, every effort is made to create a favorable climate through agreement between the superior and subordinate on—

- Specific areas of responsibility of the subordinate's job in terms of end results.
- The expected standard of performance in each area of responsibility.
- A work plan for achieving the desired results in each area of responsibility, always in accordance with the overall objectives of the company.
- A periodic review of how standards are being met and the extent to which revisions are needed in work plans, standards, and/or areas of responsibility. (6)

Again, the emphasis is on an appropriate organization and dynamic management leadership. It is on these that climate and operating environment depend.

### NOTES

[1] Marvin Bower, *The Will to Manage*, McGraw-Hill Book Co., Inc., New York, 1966, p. 223.

2 Douglas McGregor, "The Boss Must Boss," in W. G. Bennis, *et al.*, editors, *Leadership and Motivation*, M.I.T. Press, Cambridge, Mass.

3 Harold P. Koenig, "Clausewitz and the Corporation: Applying Military Principles to Business Management," *Personnel*, May–June 1967, pp. 8–15.

4 Don G. Mitchell, "Assuring a Dynamic Organization," a speech delivered before various AMA top management briefings.

5 Glenn D. Clark, "Creating the Conditions for Growth on the Job," *Personnel*, January–February 1961, pp. 9–10.

6 *Ibid.*, p. 11.

# 13

# Increasing Management Results

# Through Delegation

I⊤ is likely that most managers and subordinates have shared the feelings of Prime Minister Winston Churchill when he once told the House of Commons, "I am your servant, and you have the right to dismiss me when you please. What you have no right to do is ask me to bear responsibilities without the power of effective action." (1) No task can be performed unless the individual who must do it has been given the opportunity, the right, the authority, and the resources to get it done.

The authors of *The Art of Delegating* state:

> Survival in today's highly intricate world of business—a world complicated by new and dynamic methods of production, transportation, marketing, and communications—depends upon the successful utilization of employee ability.

> The manager cannot "do it all" himself. If he is to be a successful manager, he must get his work done through others. He must define organization objectives, ensure that they are understood, and fix responsibility for their achievement; in short, he must delegate. (2)

In the same vein Frederick R. Seltzer, of the J. C. Penney Company, has emphasized that "the critical point in the careers of many young management people is reached at the stage where they must learn either to delegate or cease to grow in scope and responsibility." (3) And Charles Percy, while president of Bell & Howell, explained his phenomenal success by stating, "I gave my managers real power for the first time. Responsibility brings out the best in people."(4)

Delegation is one of the most important skills a manager must acquire if he expects to continue up the ladder of management. Although it is often confused, neglected, misused, and maligned, it can be learned and effectively practiced. Use of this management technique is essential to the growth of both the individual executive and the company.

## The Impact of Delegation

Delegation means sharing management with another. It involves entrusting some of your own responsibilities and functions to a subordinate. The process includes identifying the parts of the job that can best be passed along, ways for getting others to accept these portions of the job, and ways for checking and controlling the related activities. Delegation transfers responsibilities, authority, and accountability: responsibility for a portion of the work; authority, or the power needed to carry out the responsibility; and accountability, or the obligation to get the job done in accordance with established standards. Standard Oil of California has defined responsibilities as "the duties of a position." For Boeing, authority is "the right to originate, direct, act, decide, and control," while Jones and Laughlin Steel Company terms accountability "the obligation to account for and report upon the discharge of responsibility or use of authority." (5)

Delegation is the basis for the organization of modern corporate enterprise. Authority vested in the owners or stockholders is delegated to a board of directors. They elect a president and delegate to him; and he, in turn, delegates to subordinate levels of management and supervision. Wherever the position load is too great for one individual, a portion is delegated to subordinates. This chain of interlocking responsibility, authority, and accountability, from top to bottom and back up, provides the dynamics for getting the job done.

The true impact of delegation is best realized when it is recognized as being indispensable in today's multimillion-dollar, multiproduct, giant-size corporations. Many businesses have simply faded into oblivion because the founder or his heirs failed to delegate and did not measure up personally to company needs.

## The Consequences of Failure to Delegate

Three kinds of robbery have been said to occur when the superior fails to delegate:

1. You have robbed yourself of the time in which you could do more interesting and important things, such as planning.
2. You have robbed your subordinate of his or her opportunity to grow.
3. You have robbed your employer of the difference between what it cost for you to do the work and what it would cost for your subordinate to do the work. (6)

Everyone suffers a loss when delegation is not practiced effectively. Failure to delegate commits the superior to a hectic schedule and ties all activities to his availability and willingness to make decisions. The whole work process is bottled up; often jobs either are never completed or are done less than adequately.

Delegation is one of the surest methods for getting everyone off the bench and into the game. Lacking the willing support it makes possible, the manager will incur additional costs for the company in lost results, lost compensation, and missed promotions.

## Working Versus Managing

Every executive is both worker and manager. He is working when he himself does a part of the job—paperwork, planning, or anything else for which he is personally responsible. He is a manager when he gets a portion of the work done through others. The higher he goes in management, the less work and the more managing he should do. In fact, he is almost totally dependent, as a manager, on delegating and then making certain that what he has delegated is done. Time places practical limitations around what he can accomplish as a worker; but as a manager, delegating to and through others, he is virtually unlimited.

Effectiveness of delegation is a very accurate indication of the ability to manage. When a manager is able to delegate responsibility and be reasonably confident that it will be properly carried out, he is showing confidence in his people, confidence in his operating framework, and faith in the training that people have received.

*The indirect approach.* Operate on the basis that the subordinate knows you expect him to have an answer, a plan, and a recommendation to discuss with you. Your purpose is to make him think, analyze, propose alternatives, and tax his own managerial abilities. When he talks a problem over with you, you have an opportunity to clarify exactly what and how the task in question should be done. In turn, he has an opportunity to gain insight into the responsibility being delegated and how he is to carry it out. The more willing he is to confront and solve problems—gradually gaining skill and improving his results—the more you are freed to attend to other matters, thus increasing your own managerial effectiveness.

*Appropriate questioning can improve delegation.* A veteran supervisor was heard to remark, "The best boss may be, not the one who gives the clearest orders, but the one who asks the best questions." Intelligent questions can tell you exactly what the subordinate understands concerning his assignment. You learn where he needs additional clarification, where further training is necessary, and what you must do to improve the delegated portion of the work for which he is being held accountable. Appropriate questions throw the ball to him and enable you to see how well he catches it and what he does with it. Questioning also is one of the most effective techniques for soliciting his active involvement in carrying out the functions of the job.

*Delegation significantly increases initiative.* You must have confidence in a subordinate before you make the decision to delegate responsibility to him. Subordinates begin to think constructively on their own, instead of duplicating your thoughts, when you can safely let them "take over the wheel." Responsibility, intelligently delegated, spurs initiative and keeps enthusiasm alive. The type of delegated leadership that the subordinate receives communicates the degree of initiative that he can exercise. Appropriate delegation not only encourages initiative but actually demands it, since the subordinate is being held accountable for the initiation and completion of the tasks assigned.

*Delegation compels a subordinate to plan.* An axiom of professional management is that every decision should be made at the lowest level possible. This is the essence of delegating "all the way down." Likewise responsibility for planning should be delegated down to the lowest level at which it can be effectively discharged. The superior who trains his subordinates in the skills of planning is encouraging their initiative, developing their abilities, and greatly increasing their capacity for accepting and effectively discharging delegated portions of the work.

### Obstacles to Delegation

Managers are often puzzled when delegation doesn't work out according to plan—especially when "I've followed the rules very carefully." It is doubtful that delegation itself is at fault; but, like most managerial techniques, delegation is only as effective as the manager by whom it is being applied. When he analyzes the reasons for his failures, he is likely to discover one or more of the following errors.

*Failure to delegate enough.* This is a common error—the manager has resolved to be a good delegator; but, because he has misgivings, he decides to delegate just a little. This little is not enough to enable the subordinate to get the job done.

*Failure to make delegation stick.* The task is delegated, but before long it ends up on his desk again. The subordinate is too willing to seek help, and the superior gives it too willingly and freely. In order to guard against this possibility, the superior should invite the person to whom the task has been delegated to discuss it, but remind him that it is his job and he should seek assistance only when he has exhausted all reasonable resources.

*Failure to define or identify the assignment adequately.* What is the individual really supposed to do? What is he supposed to accomplish, not in generalities, but in terms of results? Hasty, off-the-cuff assignments are seldom viewed as real delegated assignments. The more clearly the assignment is understood, the greater the likelihood that it will be completed in accordance with the superior's expectations.

*Failure to keep up with progress.* What headway is being made? How long has it been since the boss was in touch with the subordinate regarding the assignment? There is a strong possibility that the subordinate needs some guidance.

*Unwillingness to make allowance for errors.* The opportunity to make the right decisions is also the opportunity to make the wrong decisions. Don't expect the subordinate to do the job exactly the same way you would do it. If he is just learning, it can be expected that errors will occur. They should not be overlooked or condoned, but a coaching approach—talking them over and seeking to correct them—will steer the subordinate in the right direction and probably help him to avoid future mistakes.

*Failure to keep the communication lines open.* Delegation can function smoothly only so long as there is a constant flow of information between the delegator and the individual given the assignment. Delegation is doomed when a subordinate is so infected with fear of failure or reprisal that he is discouraged from coming back to the superior to seek additional guidance. Or the subordinate may be so independent that he feels he should not have to keep the superior informed. There should be a sufficient flow of communication both ways to insure the success of the assignment.

*Failure to appraise the results of the delegated assignment.* It might be a single-shot project or a continuing responsibility. Probably both the superior and the subordinate have benefited from the experience; in any case, appraisal will enable them to share their thinking and pinpoint those aspects of performance that have been most—and least—acceptable. The subordinate will then be able to put the new knowledge to use; and, since it has been reinforced by the superior's approval, it should contribute to improved results in the next assignment.

## Sign of the Superior's Confidence

An often-heard complaint is: "I would get things done around here if it were my job—especially if I had the authority." But what causes the superior to make his decision to delegate? In all probability, it is the confidence he has in the ability and willingness of the individual to do the job. And the chances are that his judgment concerning these two factors is based on his previous experience with the individual.

In a well-organized company, each position has a certain amount of authority assigned to it. Both the incumbent and the supervisor recognize this authority. It should not be true, although it often is, that delegated authority is like water seeking its own level: It is given to individuals who have proved they are capable of handling it, no matter what the job description may say. In many cases the untried incumbent must earn delegated authority.

The factor exerting the most weight for most managers is competence. If a subordinate is judged competent to receive and handle an assignment, authority is likely to be delegated in direct proportion. The individual interested in being given more authority and more opportunities to try his hand at larger tasks should strive to strengthen the competence factors which determine the superior's confidence in him.

## Making Delegation Work

Despite many difficulties, delegation does work and is one technique that will enable the manager to manage successively larger and more varied operations. Attempts to delegate authority will fall on more fertile soil when one or more of the following conditions are present:

1. Workloads are too heavy for a single individual. When a man can remark, "If I delegate too much of the work, there won't be enough left for me to do," something surely is wrong. The job is too small, the incumbent doesn't want to grow, or the process of delegation is completely misunderstood.

2. The security of the organization is assured, the jobs are established, and the boundaries of authority are well known. Where guidelines exist for nearly all activities, delegation becomes almost routine.

3. The assigned goal is attainable. An individual accepts a delegated task reluctantly unless there is a feeling that it can be handled successfully.

4. The delegator has a sense of personal security. The insecure person, who is uncertain of his authority, isn't likely to delegate much of it. But, when an acceptable measure of security exists, the threat of competition is largely eliminated and the fear of making mistakes is minimized.

5. The organization, climate, and management systems of the com-

pany emphasize development and growth, which can occur only through delegation.

6. There is a sizable measure of mutual trust among all individuals involved in the delegation process. This type of confidence promotes the free exchange of ideas that lays the foundation for continuing delegation.

David S. Brown, professor of public administration in the George Washington University School of Government and Business Administration, (7) suggests 12 requirements for effective delegation.

1. *An adequate understanding of the conceptual base on which delegation works.* The manager must understand why delegation is not only desirable but necessary if both he and the organization are to be successful. The subordinate should have a comparable understanding of this purpose and necessity. Delegation is not a mysterious potion, but a systematic division of labor. It is the willingness of various levels of the organization to accept and support the decisions and the actions taken by others one or more levels below them. The delegator does not surrender his own prerogatives, but remains continuously involved in the process as guide, leader, and sharer of the responsibility.

2. *Specific goals and objectives.* It is essential that understanding on the part of all concerned be achieved. This includes what is to be done, how well, when, by whom, with what resources, and in what manner.

3. *A thorough and accurate understanding of the subordinate's capabilities and characteristics.* What is your prediction of the subordinate's performance in relation to the delegated assignment? This is essential knowledge before the superior can accurately determine what and how much to delegate.

4. *An understanding with one's own superiors.* It is important that the supervisor reach an agreement with those above him. They will be involved in the delegation and its consequences. They are entitled to know, and be consulted, where significant changes are taking place regarding delegation.

5. *Agreement on standards for the performance of the delegated task.* The subordinate must understand the expectations of his superior. Standards should be specific, but should have sufficient latitude to encourage individual initiative, creativity, and organizational loyalty.

6. *Agreement on areas of no delegation.* There are certain areas and responsibilities which should not and cannot logically be delegated. A general manager of one large company reserved the right to approve all pay changes throughout the organization. It was his prerogative not to delegate his respon-

sibility, and he chose not to do so. The subordinate needs to understand what is not being delegated—precisely where he can begin and where he must stop.

7. *Planning for training and overall development.* Delegation, like other management skills, requires competence on the part of both the superior and the subordinate. It must be determined that the subordinate knows how to do what will be required. There should be sufficient feedback for the superior to determine whether the subordinate has this adequate understanding.

8. *Interest in the delegated work activity.* Does the action of the superior demonstrate that he is interested in the work? Subordinates expect this interest and interpret it as support of what they are doing. It reinforces their self-confidence and efforts.

9. *A measuring of results.* Systems of reporting, as well as personal observation and conversation, provide ways for gauging results. Results as compared with expectations become the guide for future delegating relationships.

10. *Continuous correction and improvement.* Errors will occur. Future performance depends on how effectively they are corrected.

11. *Rewarding where appropriate.* Money talks, but subordinates expect to be "paid" in other ways as well. These may include recognition, approval, and other intangibles necessary for the affirmation of the individual's needs. The appraisal determines how well the job has been done, and this is followed up with appropriate rewards, all correct experience thus being reinforced and repetition encouraged.

12. *The ability to live with differing points of view.* This may prove to be the most difficult part of delegation. After all, the subordinate will not carry the task through in exactly the same manner as the boss, and perhaps he shouldn't. Achieving satisfactory results, but in a different manner, still may be perfectly acceptable, provided they are achieved within the broad operating framework of the company. A willingness to live with these differences requires tolerance on the part of the superior and may even require some adjustment of his attitudes. A large dose of objectivity and orientation toward goal achievement, instead of personalities or methods, may be beneficial.

## The Subordinate's Role

In discussing delegation, attention is usually focused on the responsibility of the manager; but it should be remembered that the subordinate has a vital role to perform before the process will function effectively. Consider some of the reasons subordinates give for shunning acceptance of delegated responsibilities:

- The feeling that it is easier to ask the boss.
- Fear of criticism for making mistakes.
- Lack of necessary information and resources.
- A heavy overload.
- Lack of self-confidence.
- Incentives inadequate to motivate the acceptance of the additional work that may be involved.

Delegation plans and efforts should take into account that some or all of these reservations may be held, in varying degrees, by the individual to whom work is to be delegated. If they do exist, ways must be found to eliminate or compensate for them.

## Results Dependent on Controls

Delegation often involves neophytes performing a task for the first time. Even though training and instructions have been thorough, the situation is ripe for errors. The manager is faced with the problem of keeping these to a minimum.

The cardinal principle for avoiding mistakes is to follow all appropriate guides for effective delegation. The results will be no better than the quality of delegation skill and leadership. As a means of minimizing errors, it is recommended that delegation be delayed until it can be determined that the recipient knows how to perform the task effectively. If possible, the subordinate should be fed authority in gradual and reasonable doses. In the early stages, too, the superior should check carefully and frequently on both understanding and performance. This checking should be continued until it is certain that the delegated job is being done in accordance with acceptable standards. Finally, there should be sufficient initial and continuing controls to provide targets, checkpoints, and comparisons of results to let superior and subordinate know how well the work is progressing or to what extent goals have been achieved.

Too many managers believe that general guides or rule-of-thumb procedures are the only ones that can be established. It is for this reason that a few often-neglected factors in delegation are listed here by way of further assistance.

1. *The significant influence of others.* More people than the subordinate and his superior are involved in delegation and its success. The person to whom the responsibility is delegated must often rely on the contribution and cooperation of many others. It is difficult to show this relationship on the organization chart or to describe it fully, but its understanding is essential to effective delegation. Teamwork must flourish if delegated goals are to be reached. Both the superior and the subordinate should be cognizant of the need for bringing others into the delegation process.

2. *Company policy.* United Air Lines is an example of the many companies that believe that while policy should be formulated by top management, it is the duty of every manager to interpret this policy to his subordinates with clarity and conviction. Top mangement delegates to lower-level managers the authority not to change this policy but to transmit it. Each is held accountable for compliance with policy within this unit. Policy provides established guides which cannot be changed. Delegation involves knowing what the manager has the authority to change and when, and what he should transmit unchanged.

3. *Degree of delegation.* How much authority can be delegated? The only sensible answer is that this depends on the situation, company procedures, and the individuals involved. Most executives find it desirable to delegate details and routines which are performed daily in the course of business. The magnitude of the tasks delegated is gradually increased on the basis of successful experience. Certain responsibilities for policy, discipline, and accountability for the overall operation cannot be delegated.

4 *Responsibility for coordination.* Responsibility for coordination also cannot be delegated. The timing and integration of activities are prime responsibilities of the manager. In most instances, only the top man is in a position to know, assess, and reconcile all the interests involved.

5. *Delegation as a prime motivation tool.* A continuing challenge to every superior is to initiate and maintain peak motivation throughout his unit. Delegation can serve this purpose effectively by increasing interest, involvement, and satisfaction in addition to the obvious improvement in results that it makes possible. Sharing authority unifies the group, promotes the sharing of motives, clarifies expectations, and provides compensation, both tangible and intangible.

In delegation, one comes face to face with differences in goals and values among individuals and with differences in the interpretation and understanding of organizational objectives. Delegation success often hinges on the degree to which these differences can be resolved and total effort solidified in accordance with plans.

No manager can keep a finger on every detail of every job for which he is responsible. If he expects to continue to grow, to make a continuously greater contribution to the enterprise, he must be willing to delegate and be skilled at delegating effectively. The growing manager gives more than lip service to it. He implements it through the development of his own skills and the competence of his subordinates. He practices it for the continuing benefit of subordinates, himself, and the company.

## NOTES

[1] As quoted in *Women's Wear Daily*, August 18, 1967.

[2] John N. Davis and Neely D. Gardner, *The Art of Delegating*, Doubleday & Co., Inc., Garden City, N.Y., 1965, p. 1.

[3] Frederick Seltzer, "The Art of Delegation," *Stores*, July 1967, p. 31.

[4] "The Art of Delegation," a guide prepared by the American Management Association.

[5] Ray F. Boedecker, "Why Delegation Goes Wrong," *Supervisory Management*, February 1964.

[6] Seltzer, *op. cit.*, p. 31.

[7] David S. Brown, "Why Delegation Works—and Why It Doesn't," *Personnel*, January–February, 1967, pp. 48–51.

# ⌘ 14

## Mastering the Management Skills
## of Decision Making
## and Problem Solving

Don't just stand there; make a decision." "Solve a problem." "Wave a magic wand and bring order out of chaos." This appears to be the layman's stereotyped concept of an executive in action. He is seated behind a battery of telephones, answering several of them at the same time and all the while carrying on conversations with a host of subordinates in the room. Or he is out trouble shooting in the plant or calling on important customers, miraculously detecting and solving problems and making decisions that have eluded hard-working but less perceptive subordinates. Since he is a "manager," he is thought to possess unique decision-making and problem-solving powers. And, too often, it is assumed that these special powers are innate, that they cannot be learned, and that the manager cannot be trained in the techniques of better decision making and problem solving.

At times, the experienced manager is inclined to believe these myths about himself. It may prove beneficial, however, to take a more objective and diagnostic look at the problem-solving, decision-making manager and the techniques and possibilities for improving in these areas. But "telling an experienced manager how to make decisions seems, to some businessmen, as presumptuous as instructing a master plumber in the use of a pipe wrench." (1)

Many leading corporations believe decision making to be the critical test of management. In their opinion, finding the right decision in a given situation, the courage to make that decision, and the talent to persuade others to accept it constitute the three unmistakable marks of management leadership. The decision-making process is based on objective, factual information and, in this regard, is scientific; but subjective judgment must be substituted where facts are unavailable. Decision making, then, becomes a management art based on scientific data.

## Decisions and Problems

What is a decision? Why is it necessary? Chester I. Barnard pointed out in his classic book *The Function of the Executive* that the essence of the executive function lies in making selective decisions: "The fine art of executive decision consists in not deciding questions that are not now pertinent, in not deciding prematurely, in not making decisions that cannot be made effective, and in not making decisions that others should make." (2)

A decision in its simplest form is a selection of alternatives. It may involve a crisp yes or no answer. It may encompass the selection of one of many possibilities—the lesser of several evils or the preferable of various favorable solutions. Decision making becomes more difficult as solutions become less obvious and additional information and analysis become necessary. The speed and accuracy with which a decision can be made depend on the nature of the alternatives and the ability of the manager.

Decision making requires the same systematic analysis as problem solving, and the decision is arrived at by similar processes. In the case of a problem, the field is narrowed until the deviation can be attributed to only one cause. Decision making, which looks to the future rather than the past, narrows the field of possible action until nothing remains but the best way to achieve the objective. Problems require decisions for solution. Decisions determine which pathways will be followed in solving problems.

## Tactical and Strategic Decisions

Tactical decisions involve less important, routine, current problems of a one-dimensional type. They normally apply to the kind of situation that experienced executives untangle quickly and with relative ease. The requirements are usually evident and typically involve the most economical adaptation of known resources.

Strategic decisions are relatively more difficult, have far more impact on the future of business, and often involve the entire unit or company. They include decisions on business objectives and the means of reaching them and decisions concerning production, sales, capital expenditures, major operating changes, plant layout, and long-range manpower development programs. These decisions often require the commitment of major economic resources for extended periods of time. This commitment, often contractual in nature, is nonretrievable. Therefore, if the decision is a poor one, the enterprise may suffer a serious loss.

It is not enough to find the most expedient decision; it is often necessary to discover whether the decision is appropriate and whether it will prove successful, leading to effective action. Objective and results-oriented management is less concerned with the decision itself than with its outcome. Strategic decisions, particularly, are of no value to the company if they are filed away or quietly sabotaged by the individuals who have to implement them. Managerial decision making is not complete until all the results are in.

## Current Decisions for Future Results

The professional football coach's decision to draft and sign a college player is made with an eye to the potential contribution that player will make to the specific strategy to be used by the team. The coach makes current decisions the results of which will extend over a period of years. The effective decision maker must be able to think in short-range terms regarding current problems and in long-range terms on strategy.

It is the need for current decisions for future results that distinguishes the manager from the mere operator. The operator can put out fires, handle emergencies, and make decisions for the moment. Too often, he becomes frustrated and ducks the analytical discipline required for decisions which involve major commitments and have implications for the future. When he reaches the point on the management ladder where major decisions must be made, he begins to level off and peak out. Higher levels of management require skills and scientific methods which some executives are unable or unwilling to master.

The establishment and implementation of company plans involves a collection of systematized decisions. It should be obvious that these decisions will be made not by the enterprise itself, but by individual executives. If the present and future fate of the enterprise hinges on these decisions, then the quality of the decisions becomes, when translated into action, the future of the company. Recognizing the importance of decision making to managerial job performance and to the economic welfare and perpetuation of the company, many of the nation's leading corporations have sought ways to improve decision-making techniques. Seminars, workshops, books, and management consultant firms have this stated purpose. Special attention has been given to the ingredients of decision making, simulated techniques for developing related skills, and the implementation of decisions.

## Consequences of Decision Failures

Decision failures fall into two general categories: wrong decisions and no decisions. Major damage may result when wrong decisions are made or when necessary decisions are not made.

It is perhaps consoling that the cost of squandered resources, wasted human potential, and lost competitive position caused by decision failures cannot be calculated accurately. This can, however, be estimated sufficiently to reveal the staggering consequences of poor decision making.

In the 1967 World Series, Boston manager Dick Williams was asked why he left the pitcher in after four runs had been scored. He answered, "I thought that the next batter would bunt, but I guessed wrong." The game and the series were lost. And, to cite another example, a store manager was heard to remark a couple of years ago, "My store is good enough for the town. I know the area is growing, but they'll keep coming to me. It won't be necessary to expand or modernize." The "For Sale" sign on the building two years later, after the shopping center had been built, eloquently advertised that decision failure. This was a do-nothing decision, which is probably more costly than a wrong decision. In many instances, the manager even fails to recognize that a decision needs to be made—that it is actually being made by doing nothing.

If an executive is to manage, he must make decisions. He moves forward only on these stepping stones. If he ignores the impact and realities of market dynamics, new products, electronic data processing, environmental economics, and other decision inputs, he is in essence deciding to jeopardize the profits and future survival of the enterprise. The overly careful, certain-to-avoid-mistakes, solidly conservative manager should be shocked into reality by the possible consequences of his approach. Effective, results-producing managers learn to achieve a high batting average of right decisions, and they make certain that decisions are action-implemented. They do not delay and thereby pass the buck of responsibility for decision making to future years and future managers.

## Decision-Making Difficulties

Decision making calls for the gathering of information, its assembly into logical patterns, the appraisal of relative values, and the deduction of logical future action. All this requires certain elements of pure creativity—and creativity is a rare managerial quality.

Decision making also involves differences in conditions as compared with the ideal. This is frustrating. In extreme cases, the indicated decision may involve basic changes in the concepts and philosophies of the company, which top management may refuse to countenance. The pressure of other responsibilities and the fear of wrong or unpopular decisions cause procrastination. "Bombarding" situations, requiring major decisions, are downright arduous. It takes time, concentration, and often the cooperation of other people to complete the decision process.

The burden of decision making is often more than the manager is willing to shoulder. Small wonder that decision making is an area in which more excuses for delay can be found than in almost any other. The situation may change, additional facts may come to light, resources may not be available, or it may be difficult to justify action. These are very plausible, but they may well lack foundation. The weak manager's perspective is distorted by these ever present uncertainties; he sees his fellow managers make decisions which history proves wrong, and he decides that inactivity is the best course to follow. One Edsel, to him, means no new ventures. His is the sort of gun-shyness which misses out on the Mustangs and Xeroxes.

## Problem Solving Versus Decision Making

A problem is a deviation from the expected norm, serious enough to require correction. This emergency type of decision making is more typical of the lower levels of supervision, which are basically charged with the responsibility of insuring conformity to established standards. Higher levels of management concern themselves with decisions which are less problem-oriented and relate more to future direction. Regardless of the level or quality of management, however, problems inevitably occur. They often originate in the outside environment or in internal areas where they are difficult to anticipate.

The types and magnitudes of problems confronted by the manager are as varied as the functions of his job and the population of his work group. Problems may arise from almost any source and will constitute obstacles to progress until solved. Only when they are eliminated can activity proceed normally toward established goals.

A capable manager has a way of converting problems into opportunities to improve procedures, increase results, and make the operation more efficient. A customer complaint, for example, becomes an opportunity to get better acquainted with that customer and focus on customer relations in general. And a department which chronically runs out of supplies affords an opportunity for establishing a more effective system of maintaining inventories and initiating reorders.

## A Search for Order

Westinghouse Electric's specially designed "Problem Solving and Decision Making" workshop for internal use concentrates on:

1. Identifying, classifying, and fact finding.
2. Problem diagnosis.
3. Creative development of alternative solutions.
4. Selecting the best solution from alternatives.
5. Arriving at a decision.
6. Application of the decision to the problem.
7. Overcoming difficulties in problem solving–decision making. (3)

Most companies and experts recommend basically the same steps. Solving a problem is a search for order. Many solutions will not be completely satisfactory; they may be temporary and change with time. And certain problems may even have to be accepted as insoluble and lived with. Almost every privately owned company and many public ones have certain philosophies or operating policies which, for one reason or another, are being retained. Managers in these companies have learned to accept and live with the resulting problems.

Still, when an impasse is reached in attempting to solve a problem, the unconventional solution may hold possibilities. For example, the problem may be reversed, thereby creating new means of approach. The classic case in point is Henry Ford's great contribution to the industrial world. He realized how time consuming it was for men to move from one place to another in order to perform their limited tasks over and over again on each car. He couldn't see how they could be speeded up; so he reversed the problem and began figuring out how the cars could be brought to the men. The result was the assembly line, which ushered in the age of mass production.

Dr. Sidney Parnes, of the State University of New York, identifies three general types of problems: (1) *fact-finding* ("Do I have the necessary qualifications to join the XYZ organization?"); (2) *decision or judgment* ("Should I take on that new line or territory?"); and (3) *creative,* those calling for ideas ("How do I stimulate my employees to take more interest in their work?"). Managers, he states, fail to find solutions to these problems because they fail to use their imagination. And Alex F. Osborn suggests that problem solving can be stimulated by adapting, modifying, magnifying, minifying, substituting, rearranging, reversing, combining, or eliminating the normal process or product or putting it to another use. (4) There are two alternatives: solving the problem in the same way others have or solving it in a completely new and creative way for which no historical guide exists.

Just as proper maintenance of machinery prevents breakdown, managing by design—appropriately executed—eliminates many potential problems and reduces the severity of those that do arise. The manager who is quick to pat himself on the back for his ability to deal with emergencies should ask himself why the problems arose in the first place. Instead of awarding himself bouquets for his managerial prowess, he might be wiser to determine how often he may be guilty of managerial failure.

For some managers, life moves along with few crises. They have done their homework well and kept their house in order. They have set objectives, planned, clarified jobs and relationships, established standards of performance, and installed continuing programs for the improvement of performance as needed. These are the best problem solvers because they are first of all problem preventers. The economy of their approach is obvious.

## Techniques of Decision Making

Most decisions are the result of facts plus judgment. The president of one large company has said: "Every businessman has to take the unknown into consideration. Of course, you try to reduce the size of the unknown as much as possible by chopping away at it with facts, but you always have to do a little guessing. Columbus knew the world was round, and he had done his best to figure out its size, but his calculations were off. If he had waited until he had all the facts, he would never have discovered America." (5) The quality and certainty of decision making can be improved if all the available facts are taken into account. The purpose of both quantitative and qualitative research data is to reduce the dependence of the decision on judgment. Major decisions are seldom based on precise scientific or mathematical formulas, but it is reliance on reasonably accurate data, combined with the experienced judgment of the manager, that produces contributory decisions.

Decisions can be categorized a dozen different ways, but for the purpose of illustrating decision-making techniques, let us consider two types only: off-the-cuff and planned decisions.

*Off-the-cuff decisions.* To mix metaphors, off-the-cuff decisions involve "shooting from the hip." Managers like to brag about this kind of quick decision, but in reality there is seldom any difficulty in making it. In fact, the uninformed manager may find it extremely easy because he doesn't even understand the problem. The too hasty decision often is made before the problem is fully stated. It may also be made with inadequate facts or on the basis of unsupported personal feelings. It may not be oriented toward the purposes of the enterprise at all.

Experienced, mature managers seldom make such amateurish errors. They may have indulged in hasty decision making during their neophyte days, but they know this is not the sort of management expected of them now.

*Planned decisions.* The planned decision is based on the facts. It weighs every reasonable solution, selects the best alternative, and follows it up with action. The first step is *definition of the problem*. The decision maker has a clear, detailed understanding of exactly what requires a decision or is causing trouble. This alone often makes the solution clearer.

Next *sufficient and pertinent information* must be obtained. Accurate decisions cannot be made with inaccurate data or based on the sum of all the available details until these have been thoroughly studied in light of the problem to be solved. For instance, the decision regarding which make of truck to purchase will require a different type and magnitude of information than the decision regarding the layout of a proposed new plant. Comparative information may be readily available regarding various trucks; but market statistics, figures on present production capacity, and an extensive list of other data will have to be gathered and appraised in depth before making a commitment to build the new plant.

Also essential is *an analysis of the problem and related facts*. This analysis is not always easy, since factual information and relationships have a way of becoming ambiguous and hazy. Some of this vagueness may be eliminated by classifying the problem to determine who must make the decision, who must be consulted in making it, and who must be informed once it is made.

A more objective evaluation of the facts occurs when they are compared with the standards established for the activity affected by the impending decision. With these standards in mind, what do the facts reveal about the problem? What course of action do the facts seem to indicate?

Since the manager will eventually have to make a definite decision, his search for facts and his evaluation of them must come to a halt at some point. And, if the information available to him is still incomplete, he will have to do some educated guessing. Even the best diagnostician is not always right, but he keeps alert to changing conditions and adjusts his diagnosis accordingly. A manager can do no less; he must determine where inadequate analysis or knowledge is forcing him into a guessing situation and endeavor to minimize the "unknowns."

Which course of action will make the greatest contribution to goals? Which involves the most profitable investment of resources? The *selection of the best solution* may not be clear-cut; it often involves compromising and choosing the best features of several possibilities.

The consideration of alternative solutions is the only means of bringing basic assumptions up to the conscious level, forcing examination, testing, and appraising their validity. Moreover, decisions that demand change often incur the displeasure and even hostility of those affected. If this should prove sufficiently severe, it may dictate the selection of an alternative that involves less or more gradual change.

The manager has to weigh the risks of each course of action against the expected gain. What is the ratio of risk to gain? Which of the alternatives will give the best results with the least expenditure of resources? If the decision is of great urgency, it may have to be dramatized to get quick action.

In short, if action is called for, get on with it. Although the thinking-through process is the most difficult step in decision making, *the transformation of the decision* into effective action is usually the most time consuming. And nothing really happens until the decision is implemented. A decision made is merely the determination of the action, not the execution of it.

Converting the decision into action requires additional decisions. Who has to know about it? What specific steps must be taken? What do people have to do, and who will be doing it? Consider the typical consequences of not following through, of not communicating the decision to those who need to know about it.

A major manufacturer of industrial equipment decided to discontinue a model that had for years been standard equipment in a line of machine tools, many of which were still in use. It was decided to sell the model to present owners of the old equipment for another three years as replacement, and then to stop making and selling it. Orders for this particular model had been going down for many years. But they shot up immediately as customers reordered against the day when the model would no longer be available. No one had, however, asked, "Who needs to know about this decision?"

Consequently, nobody informed the purchasing clerk in charge of buying parts for the model. His instructions were to buy parts in a given ratio to current sales—and the instructions remained unchanged. When the time came to discontinue further production of the model, the company had in its warehouse enough parts for eight to ten years of production—parts that had to be written off at a considerable loss. (6)

The recommended procedure is to structure into the decision sufficient action commitment for execution. The decision is not completely made until the planning and execution have been carried through.

Procrastination, fear of criticism, the possibility of resistance, and the natural desire to avoid the unpleasant often cause hesitation or even harmful delay in action. Effective managers recognize this sort of delay as unsatisfactory job performance. They follow through on all aspects of their decisions at the most appropriate time.

*Persuading Others to Accept and Respond*

The final decision must be made by the manager who is responsible for the results. When he makes the decision, it must be sold—up and down the line. All the available resources must be applied to successful implementation. There must be adequate feedback on the degree of acceptance which the decision is having and any adjustments which may increase its acceptability. Also, it is important that monitoring and reporting devices be provided in order that testing, measuring, and comparison with expectations will be on a continuing basis. Planned, well-organized intelligence, preferably based on established control points, should give the executive the facts he needs for determining the effectiveness of his decision. Reports will help, but even though these may be accurate and thorough, the executive will still find it highly desirable to get out into the factory and the field, talk with people, and personally find out how things are going.

The swing is from autocratic, arbitrary decisions and action to the more effective consultative approach. Group involvement is the key to making the right decision and having it put into practice once it has been made. Often a committee or other group serves the function of involvement and communication more realistically than that of the actual decision making. In decentralized operations, where considerable local autonomy exists, consultative decision making is the most effective way to insure acceptance of decisions.

A large wholesale organization had 20 offices throughout an eight-state area. Each office was a profit center, and each manager ran his own show. He was responsible for operating expense and for markdowns on unsold merchandise. His bonus was based on the profit of his unit. Because of these operating responsibilities, he exercised a decisive voice in the selection and purchase of merchandise and in the choice of sales promotion methods. The executive vice president in charge of these two functions for the entire company was very knowledgeable about the market and knew which items and promotions each local office should have. But he and his key associates were wise enough to use committees, including the branch manager or someone designated by him, to assist with the final selection of merchandise and the design of the sales promotion package. This involvement in decision making meant acceptance of "my merchandise and sales promotion." Because he had participated in a decision, the local manager understood it and was prepared to put it into immediate practice.

One of the nation's largest department store groups, the May Company, with headquarters in St. Louis, has installed "participative management" from the president down to the lowest level. The underlying reason for this shift was a recognition that command authority no longer exists in our industrial and business society; that involvement, commitment, and self-development have replaced it as the most effective means for getting things done through people.

This is particularly true in the areas of making and implementing decisions. The individual subordinate is reluctant to accept or act on the "packaged" decision of the superior but will accept and respond to the same decision when he has participated in its formulation. Managers recognize that in complying with government regulations, for example, they will be wise to accept decisions and guides exactly as written. In other cases, however, they want to be consulted, have an opportunity to present their own ideas, be able to influence the final decision and its implementation because it affects them, their operations, and their compensation.

Consultative decision making and implementation does take more time, but it also involves fewer mistakes, encounters less resistance, and usually results in better decisions. It does not imply taking a vote or necessarily incorporating into the decision all the ideas of everyone concerned. The responsible manager must make the final decision; but, when he has consulted those concerned with the effects of the decision, he then has the benefit of their thinking and experience. And, by way of benefits, he probably will have achieved greater rapport, better team spirit, increased confidence, and a heightened sense of commitment to mutual goals.

## The Test of a Decision

How do you know when a good decision has been made? Is it necessary to wait for months or years before its correctness can be measured? How well is it being received, and how much improvement is it making in operations?

Perhaps the most immediate test is how you justify your decision to your superior. When he asks why you made it, how convincing will your answer be? Suppose you have decided to go along with a new advertising plan. It will involve considerable additional money, a reorganization of the advertising department, the employment of new talent, and the relocation of some accounts. Now your problem is to justify your decision. Was it based on sufficient facts? Research data? Established need for a change? Trends in the market? The experienced judgment of a knowledgeable manager? If it was the best alternative available, if it was selected in a valid manner and there are sufficient facts to support it, then its defense should be relatively easy.

## Training in Decision Making and Problem Solving

Can managers learn the techniques and skills involved in decision making and problem solving, or is this an intuitive art? The answer lies in an understanding of the process involved. As discussed in this chapter, decision making involves basic principles, techniques, and processes. These can be identified and their use made more effective through greater understanding and deliberate attention to their improvement. Decision making and problem solving lend themselves as readily as any other management functions to study and practice.

David G. Moore, of the Graduate School of Business Administration at Michigan State University, (7) suggests that the executive finds the role of decision maker the toughest he has to play. Professor Moore identifies some of the difficulties involved as follows:

- *Important decisions always involve judgment of values.* Values, in turn, are concerned with psychological and social phenomena, multiples of values, conflict of values, and the burden of placing a priority on values.
- *The sheer complexity of modern business must be reckoned with.* Consider the complexity of a modern-day corporation, with interlocking companies, products, markets, research and development, and financial structures. Commitment decisions often involve tens of millions of dollars. Take the decision-making burden of the managers of a worldwide shoe manufacturer as compared with the neighborhood cobbler of little more than a century ago. Decision making is not simple because the environment, the activities, and the size of the commitment are not simple.
- *Decisions are of necessity based on imprecise information and future unknowns.* Information on which decisions are based is often fragmentary and distorted—the manager has no X-ray perception of reality aside from certain obvious facts and experienced judg-

ment. The facts on which decisions have to be based are anemic representations of realities. Often the information received from subordinates is beclouded by personal opinion and self-interest. The decision maker's world is not as precise or orderly as that of the mathematician.

■ *There is a built-in time lag surrounding decisions.* Significant decisions almost invariably involve a span of time before their consequences can be fully assessed. Decisions which involve predictions about the future might look rational today, but appear pretty ridiculous in retrospect. Yet the management decision must be tacked up in public view for all to see and take pot shots at.

These uncertainties make training in decision making difficult. It is a far cry from skill training and job instruction. "How to do it" manuals are conspicuously absent, and handbooks are sparse.

One promising development has been the "in-basket" approach to training managers in the skills of decision making. In its simplest terms, this technique simulates decision-demanding situations. The participant makes the decisions on the basis of information given him and his own judgment, and the results are appraised by a team of experts. Felix M. Lopez, Jr. states that the concept involved is grounded in the following principles:

Experience is the best teacher, and the best predictor of future performance is past performance. Truisms though these are, they are useful guides to managers when they must make decisions that affect executives who have worked before on jobs closely similar to the one to be filled. Frequently such conditions are not present, however. Experience is not always readily obtainable, and performance may have been in activities too unrelated for good prediction, although both continue as factors to be considered. What alternative approaches then might be used? . . .

The idea that the actual job is the best teacher and the best predictor of future performance has prompted the question: Why not simulate the job for which the executive is being trained or for which a selection must be made, and use the resulting performance for training or prediction purposes? Assuming that a realistic job situation can be set up, that performance can be described accurately and evaluated consistently and in a way that relates to future success on the actual job, the situational technique has exciting possibilities. (8)

Research on the in-basket technique has been pioneered by IBM, the Bell System, the Air Force, General Electric, Port Authority of New York, Harvard Business School, University of Michigan, and many others. Extensive experimentation has gone into the construction of models designed for specific types of business in addition to specific managerial skills. For example, there are models for Sears, Roebuck and completely different ones for the Air Force.

Since its inception, the in-basket technique has been used in a sufficient number of situations to enable some conclusions to be drawn concerning its value. These indicate that it can provide management with significant information about a prospective manager's ability to function in an administrative situation. The exercises can be scored in a manner sufficiently systematic and objective to yield fairly reliable and meaningful descriptions of the performer's administrative characteristics.

It is certain that overall decision-making competence is of such crucial importance to management that experiments will continue in the search for training methods in this area. Most companies are still using the more obvious methods, which too often require that the student learn by apprenticeship, classroom study, or plain osmosis. Newer techniques like the in-basket offer exciting possibilities for greater effectiveness in improving and predicting managerial performance as it relates to decision making.

## The Major Decisions

Peter Drucker suggests that the key decisions are those concerning the very nature of business; the company's specific excellence; and the priorities assigned to various activities by the company. (9) These decisions involving the future of the company are the most important ones that management must make, relating, as they do, to the commitment of resources and the selection of those opportunities that seem most promising. These major decisions must represent management's best judgment, made on the basis of objective data.

Big-league decision making demands the utmost in professional competence. It is not for the fainthearted, the mentally confused, the immature, or the uninitiated. Every officer and employee, every customer, and everyone with a financial interest in the company has a stake in it. The decisions made must both accelerate the achievement of mutual goals and, insofar as possible, insure the future well-being of the enterprise.

## NOTES

[1] "Charting Pitfalls of Decision," *Business Week*, June 5, 1965, p. 65.

[2] Chester I. Barnard, *The Function of the Executive*, Harvard University Press, Cambridge, Mass., 1964, p. 194.

[3] As reproduced in Elizabeth Marting, AMA *Encyclopedia of Supervisory Training*, American Management Association, New York, 1961, p. 230.

[4] M. O. Edwards, "Tips on Solving Problems Creatively," *Systems and Procedures Journal*, January–February 1966.

[5] As quoted in James Menzies Black, *How to Grow in Management*, Prentice-Hall, Inc., Englewood Cliffs, N.J., 1957, p. 100.

[6] Peter F. Drucker, "The Effective Decision," *Harvard Business Review*, January–February 1967.

[7] David G. Moore, "What Decision Makers Need," *Nation's Business*, November 1960.

[8] Felix M. Lopez, Jr., *Evaluating Executive Decision Making*, Research Study 75, American Management Association, New York, 1966.

[9] Peter F. Drucker, *Managing for Results*, Harper & Row Publishers, Inc., New York, 1964.

# 15

# Leadership and Persuasion: Key Management Skills

$\mathbf{W}_{\text{HAT}}$ is leadership? Harvey A. Stackman, research economist at the University of South Carolina, says: "In the literature of management during the past forty years, more has been written about leadership than about any other topic." (1) But has the subject been exhausted—the riddle solved? Not at all. Major errors in attempting to understand, isolate, identify, refine, and improve it are committed over and over because of its very nature.

Leadership must always be viewed as an integral part of functions, activities, and people. It is the electrical current that powers the motor; the ingredient that energizes the battery; the force that transforms chaos into order; the insight that converts despair into hope and changes half-hearted endeavor into superior performance.

Leadership can be understood, then, only in relation to what it does. It exists only to the degree that it influences individual and group enterprise.

## No Influence, No Leadership

The measure of leadership is the degree to which it influences the behavior or job performance of other people. Where there is no influence, there is no leadership. Conversely, where there is no leadership, there is no influence. This premise can be debated, but our concern here is with that type and quality of leadership that makes the right things happen and prevents the wrong things from happening.

This test can be applied in almost any type of organized environment. The amount of influence exerted is the measure of leadership in the military and certainly in loosely knit volunteer groups such as community organizations. And it becomes the key criterion in the industrial corporation.

Perhaps reluctance to accept this principle is caused by the lack of a clear concept of the manner in which this influence makes itself felt. It is not dependent on force, oratory, or economic sanctions. It is the product of everything the leader is and does, including his ability, his experience, his personality, his communication skills, his capacity for gaining respect, and his success in creating a willingness on the part of others to follow his lead. Finally, influence can be favorable or unfavorable—good or bad.

It should be emphasized here, as it has at other points in this book, that influence is not intended to imply the manipulation of human lives. The leader's principal aim is to stimulate intelligent self-interested response. The subordinate accepts the guidance and service of leadership for his own benefit and enlightenment.

The statement has been made that "the manager belongs to one of the world's scarcest species: the leaders. Everyone on his staff has a practical stake of the most concrete kind in the quality of his leadership." The follower or subordinate recognizes that his own job performance and personal achievements are significant byproducts of this leadership.

## Contribution to Management Goals

What does leadership contribute to goal achievement? The most descriptive answer to this question is that "leaders lead"—contribute the ingredients to the corporate mix that lead or move all resources toward established goals in the quickest, most economical, and most profitable manner. Leadership's contribution is the conversion of potential into actuality. It is the service of making every individual more productive, more loyal, and better satisfied with his job performance and with himself. It is the service of making every process more efficient and profitable and maximizing the value of resources and return on investment.

A leader is a man of action. He doesn't stand around waiting—he creates and initiates. His subordinates trust him because he has shown them, through persuasion and action, that they share the same goals. Leadership contributes a minimum of tangibles, but it makes concrete the object of its influence. Almost without exception, group achievement varies in direct ratio to quality of leadership, as is illustrated by the following comparison:

| *Department A* | *Department B* |
|---|---|
| People well trained. | Inadequate training. |
| High morale. | Low morale. |
| Attractive department. | Cluttered, confused department. |
| Low employee turnover. | High employee turnover. |
| Expenses in line. | Excessive operating costs. |
| Goals achieved. | Short of goals. |

*All factors identical except one . . . leadership!*

In addition to the intangibles of morale and training, the two lists indicate differences in tangible, statistical areas. Also, note that all conditions and all influences on these two departments are identical except one. The only ingredient that is different is leadership, yet it is obvious that Department A is contributing results and profits while Department B is a liability in almost every respect.

A recognition of this decisive role of leadership in the performance picture should accelerate management's search for and maximum development of the leadership ingredient. Without it, corporate purpose is doomed to failure.

## Conditions and Sources of Leadership

One group of authorities contends that the *situation* produces or at least provides the environment conducive to the emergence of leadership. The other contends that appropriate *leadership* shapes the situation and molds the environment in accordance with needs and objectives. Although situation-produced leadership may occur in political or other crises, it cannot be relied on to get the corporate job accomplished. This depends on an abundance of the type of leadership that can initiate and implement action designed to achieve the specific goals of the enterprise.

This dependence of success on leadership has caused management to seek diligently to identify its qualities and characteristics; to analyze its influence; and to develop and improve its effectiveness. Research has thus explored the conditions most favorable to its exercise, the sources of its authority, and the psychology of its practice.

*Favorable conditions.* Not all environments provide the same opportunity for the exercise of leadership. The system that produces the most favorable conditions is that system organized to take full advantage of professional management by design. Creating favorable conditions requires certain specific preparatory procedures and activities. It means tilling and preparing the soil before the seed is planted. It involves fertilization through motivation and the constant care that promotes maximum growth and eliminates the weeds of interference.

Leadership must function within the four-walled "box" formed by superiors, subordinates, associates, and the public. Leadership opportunities must be created and maintained in relation to these influences. The conditions of leadership are significantly affected by the objectives, policies, plans, organizational patterns, and procedures of corporate management.

Top management must therefore promote leadership throughout the organization, at every level, not only through the employment and development of leadership potential but through the creation of conditions that will provide maximum opportunity for its exercise.

*Sources of authority.* The authority to lead is derived from two principal sources: (1) the nature of the position involved and (2) the quality and style of the incumbent. Although authority is assigned to every executive position, this seldom automatically bestows with it the mantle of leadership.

In the church, the state, and the military, authority traditionally has been clearly identified and represents reasonable continuity from incumbent to incumbent. It is in fact desirable that every position have some sustaining sanction of authority—that of title, uniform, or office. In the corporate environment, however, neither the authority assigned to the position nor the title assumed by the individual guarantees leadership. These merely provide the opportunity for the individual to develop and practice purposeful leadership. Although authority is inherent in the position, its value depends on what the individual makes of it.

*Psychology of leadership.* Leadership is based on the psychological relationship existing between the superior and the subordinate. This relationship is influenced more by subconscious feeling than by logical thinking. The subordinate seldom decides to respect and follow the leadership of the superior because he has listed the pros and cons, applied a slide rule, or deduced that it is to his advantage to do so. The actual decision is almost never expressed in words; and, in most instances, the subordinate is not aware that he has made it. Evidence that he has indeed made it is, however, implicit in his job performance.

The psychological basis of leadership is the result of every moment of association between the two people. It has evolved from every accumulating influence—spoken word, frown, smile, kindness, sarcasm, rumor, helpfulness, firmness, recommendation for pay increase or promotion, disciplinary action. Its status at any given point in time is the answer fed to the conscious motor reactors from the knowledge-feeling bank. The same principle applies here as with the computer—the answer is totally dependent on the data fed into the system. If the superior knows and can evaluate what has gone into the subordinate's "computer system," he should be able to predict the response. The implication is clear: If the superior expects to lead from a strong and favorable psychological base, he had better make certain that contributory influences are being fed constantly into that system.

As a means of identifying some of the areas in which this superior-subordinate relationship may exist, the following guides are recommended:

1. Show that you care about your subordinates as people.
2. Show your subordinates that you are willing to learn from them.
3. Keep everybody informed about the changes that they think might affect them.
4. Learn to avoid those things which cause you to think emotionally.
5. Understand that production can be increased most by attention to people, not output.
6. Show that you have confidence in your associates.
7. Set an example of personal respect, diligent effort, and an expectation of success.
8. When you give instructions, check the understanding of the listener.
9. Beware of appearing to play favorites, granting special privileges, or "blowing hot and cold" on a decision.
10. Realize that the subordinate-supervisor relationship is actually

the reverse of popular belief—the subordinate is not an inferior working for the superior. The follower is the only one who can make the manager successful. (2)

## A Leadership Profile

Every book and article on leadership has at least one section on the qualities of the ideal leader. However, these efforts to identify a model and to develop leaders to meet the complex demands of modern life provide ample evidence that the subject has not yet been exhausted and that no satisfactory conclusions have been reached.

In answer to the question, "What makes a good leader?" Gordon L. Lippitt, George Washington University professor and president of Leadership Resources, Inc., offers four historical answers:

1. *The great-man theory.* This assumes that a leader is a great man —that leadership qualities are inborn.
2. *The trait approach.* It is the traits of great leaders that make them different from the followers. The theory is that if these traits can be identified and duplicated, leadership will result. This supports the suspicion that leadership consists of certain chromosomes and genes, physical characteristics, intellectual abilities, and personality traits.
3. *The behavioral approach.* This theory assumes that leadership is based on what the leader does. He may be primarily a problem solver or decision maker, may perform an advisory or information-giving function, may function primarily as an initiator or as an advocate of some plan or proposition.
4. *The situational approach.* This theory assumes that there are certain traits which bring forth leadership in one situation, but may not in another. The premise is that it is the situation which promotes or minimizes the emergence of leadership. (3)

It can be accurately stated that, historically and currently, leadership has been all these things to some extent. Great men have been powerful and effective leaders because of innate greatness if not the accident of birth. Leadership has been influenced by the traits and behavior of the leader. Leadership has also been substantially affected by the situational environment in which it operated. In reality, however, leadership penetrates deeper into the fabric of the organism of which it is a part.

If leadership is not to be considered an inherent quality, it must reflect the development of acquired environmental experiences. Certain abilities, traits, and disciplines appear to favor the emergence of leaders, just as of athletes, journalists, or craftsmen. It is readily acknowledged that forceful leadership exists to challenge every rule and stereotype that could be mentioned. However, the clusters of traits and qualities that seem typically characteristic of effective leaders argue strongly for the probability of their being duplicated through training and development by those who would be similarly effective.

It should not be falsely assumed that the mere possession of similar characteristics will necessarily produce leadership. There are many different patterns from which leadership can emerge: Not all military generals are as small in stature as Napoleon; not all political leaders are as peaceful as Gandhi; and not all corporate officers are carbon copies of the puritanical, clean-living, hard-working, poorly educated, aggressive industrial barons of the last century. But, in spite of transitory patterns, new models, and exceptions, it should be beneficial to examine constructively the characteristics thought to typify those corporate leaders who have achieved recognized success.

There are many lists of such qualities. One authority describes the leader as a man of action, knowing what you want as well as what he wants; a man with the ability to supply answers; a man characterized by dependability, thoroughness, and calm; a capable organizer and delegator of authority who can handle people and quarterback a team; a man who is humane, fair, and honest, has good judgment, is tolerant but expects results, respects the rights of others, is generous by nature, knows how to teach and is eager to learn, has vision, is progressive, and works hard.

Again, leaders are men with the ability to look ahead; those who are steady at the wheel regardless of the many cross-currents, whose spirit is buoyant, whose personal morals, ethics, and sense of responsibility are such that they command respect; those who unmistakably possess courage, will power, mental flexibility, knowledge, and integrity. (4)

## Result-Producing Leadership

Although it may seem like putting last things first, a better way to evaluate the qualities and characteristics of leadership is to focus first on objectives and desired results, then on the specific types of activity. Leadership's role is to make certain that these do occur, and in appropriate quantity and quality. The leadership qualities and characteristics that are essential are those that influence job performance sufficiently to produce the appropriate activity. Leadership under these circumstances is the result not of a rigid pattern, but of a flexible, dynamic process that reacts to the specific challenge with which it is confronted.

It is certainly valid to assume that many of the qualities and characteristics of leaders that are desirable and valid in a given situation will also be desirable and valid in others. The athletic ability, mental discipline, and emotional control that produce an outstanding baseball player are basically the same qualities required for the development of an outstanding basketball player. Analogously, those qualities that have met the needs of leadership in one business environment will, in most instances, be the same as those needed in other companies. The trick is to judge what specific influence may be needed and to provide it.

There are exceptions. Leaders who were effective in one position have failed in others because they lacked sufficient discipline to adjust to the requirements of the new challenge. Providing leadership for a million-dollar company may be quite different from managing a multimillion-dollar department.

### Suggestions for Improved Leadership

The following pointers have proved helpful to experienced leaders. Their usefulness to others will depend on the nature of both the individual and the circumstances in which he finds himself.

*Involve yourself.* Leadership functions only to the extent that it becomes involved. This active involvement may focus on management or on long-range planning, to cite just two important corporate activities. It implies being a part of the group to the extent of making certain that the right things are happening.

*Meet the situation.* Gordon L. Lippitt suggests that "leadership is the effective meeting of the situation—whatever the situation. And this meeting comes through confrontation, search, and coping." (5) The leader faces up to the situation; he doesn't run away or ignore what exists or what has to be done. Also, he must search for understanding—of the situation and of the people involved. (Much of his subsequent leadership will depend on this understanding.) He then copes with the situation by making decisions, providing guides, and stimulating the individuals concerned to move forward toward their goals.

*Be neither autocratic nor democratic.* This is a problem that every leader confronts with his first opportunity for leadership, and it remains with him throughout his leadership life. The temptation is to be either too rigid or too flexible; however, most leaders discover fairly early that neither extreme will suffice. The leader has to be tough-minded enough to insist on standards of performance and disciplines that will guarantee success, but he must at the same time be democratic enough to give everyone a sense of participation and a feeling that the leader is understanding and that his performance requirements are beneficial to all concerned.

*Achieve response to your leadership.* The most severe test of leadership is the response it obtains—the extent to which the people who are supposed to be following it commit themselves. Napoleon achieved this response of leadership in one way; Churchill, with a completely different approach. Leaders operate in a great variety of ways, but they must discover their excellence and capitalize on it. The follower's response may be the result of the leader's personal magnetism, his superior mind, his creative genius, his organizational talent, or his persuasiveness. In any case, the leader who achieves response is providing something which the follower finds so desirable that he is willing to respond in order to acquire it or enjoy its benefits.

*Set an example.* The leader who is most effective is the one who leads by personal example, whose performance sets the pattern for the entire group. He is at the front of the advancing ranks. "Pattern your own performance, adherence to company guides, and commitment after my own," he says. "I will not expect performance or effort beyond what I myself am willing to give."

*Think like a leader.* Effective leadership is the result of positive thought and attitudes. Negative attitudes, particularly with regard to cooperative effort, will prove detrimental to the purposes of leadership.

In other words, leadership is the result of thinking like a leader. And the leader thinks in terms of results, balancing long-range values with short-range gains, utilizing his mental faculties to understand and to evaluate, bringing all his resources to bear on every issue and activity. The leader recognizes that leadership means employing the full capacity of the mind. He focuses on the target and is constantly devising the fastest and most effective ways of hitting it.

*Leadership is dependent on communication.* Leadership implies interaction between two or more people—understanding, influence, conviction, and response. This interaction becomes possible only to the extent that communication makes it possible. The follower responds only insofar as he "understands." Leadership does not function until it communicates sufficiently to achieve a satisfactory level of response. The superior gets work done through others only when they understand what he wants done, how he wants it done, when he wants it done, and how well he wants it done. They gain this understanding through the effectiveness of his communication skill.

*Be willing to follow and understand your followers.* Leaders are basically disciplined followers. This does not imply that they should follow blindly in the same rut or neglect innovation and initiative. But leaders are cooperating members of the team. The manager who is a true leader knows how to work effectively with others. He knows the importance of the company framework and guides as represented by its systems and procedures. He seeks to change, to improve, and to speed up, but he does not attempt to destroy the framework's usefulness.

Willingness to follow is based on self-interest. The leader makes a dedicated effort to understand those whose loyalty he must have in order to get the job done. They will not respond to his expressed self-interest except as he relates it to their needs. He understands his subordinate and builds on this understanding for the purpose of collective goal achievement.

Leadership is no respecter of age or place. It may be born of crisis or incubated in the deliberate quietness of an isolated human mind. It is capable of flowering or fading under almost any circumstances. It represents qualities, characteristics, and techniques which, when appropriately used, produce the results the leader demands.

## Persuasion: A Key Leadership Skill

It is generally accepted that the ability to persuade others to your point of view and to have this acceptance translated into a satisfactory response is the real test of leadership. This implies change, improvement, increase—not merely maintenance of existing levels and conditions. The type of motivation produced through persuasive leadership is the catalyst that produces a forward thrust, superior effort, and resulting excellence.

The coach talks with the team, collectively and individually, before the game. He does the same thing between the halves. His purpose is to inspire, motivate, and produce improved performance. He assumes he has something to offer that will achieve this purpose. He assumes the players will accept what he offers and will attempt to respond, because they too want improved performance.

There can be no effective motivation unless goals have been established, statistically identified, and communicated in understandable terms. The leader's primary challenge at this point is to convince the group of the validity and integrity of these goals, enhance their desirability, provide the program or means for reaching them, and urge a total, goal-oriented commitment of resources—primarily time and talent. This high level of motivation is essential in today's corporate environment, in which survival is often dependent on superior commitment and effort.

Vince Lombardi stated it simply in football terms: "My job is to produce a better individual and team performance." The purpose of motivation and persuasion in the corporate ball park is improved individual and unit results.

## Increasing Individual Commitment

Thomas B. Macauley asserted that "genius is subject to the same laws which regulate the production of cotton and molasses. The supply adjusts itself to the demand. The quantity may be diminished by restriction, and multiplied by bounties." This may be a slight overstatement, but it illustrates the importance of individual belief and effort even at the genius level. John W. Gardner, commenting on the mysteries of individual motivation, says:

> We are a long way from understanding the complexities of individual motivation. We understand very imperfectly, for example, the inner pressures to excel which are present in some children and absent in others. We really don't know why, from earliest years, some individuals seem indomitable, while others are tossed about by events like the bird in a badminton game. (6)

In spite of these mysteries, the corporate manager must confront and seek to improve results through increased individual motivation. In doing this, he attempts to understand what the motivators are for each individual; their relative importance from individual to individual; and the ways in which they can be related to job performance. The real key to success seems to lie in the degree to which the superior is able to convince the subordinate that his personal goals can be achieved as a direct result of the contribution his job performance makes to corporate goals.

The leader should have no illusion that he is capable of exerting an omnipotent influence on the physical or mental productivity of other human beings. He must recognize that inner forces, influences, and self-will exert a far greater influence than any that can be brought to bear externally. The most severe challenge he faces is the unleashing of this inner potential and its direction into channels beneficial to the purposes of the enterprise. The highest aim of the leader should be the development of personal excellence in himself and in those who look to him for leadership.

What is the nature of this excellence? To quote John Gardner once more:

> Taking the whole span of history and literature, the images of excellence are amply varied: Confucius teaching the feudal lords to govern wisely . . . Leonidas defending the pass at Thermopylae . . . St. Francis preaching to the birds at Alviano . . . Lincoln writing the second inaugural "with malice toward none" . . . Mozart composing his first oratorio at the age of eleven . . . Galileo dropping weights from the Tower of Pisa . . . Emily Dickinson jotting her "letters to the world" on scraps of paper . . . Jesus saying, "Father, forgive them; for they know not what they do" . . . Florence Nightingale nursing the wounded at Balaclava . . . Eli Whitney pioneering the manufacture of interchangeable parts . . . Ruth saying to Naomi, "Thy people shall be my people." (7)

Every individual has a potential for excellence. It may be for excellence in making shoes, leading an army, rocketing to the moon, preaching a sermon, sewing a seam, teaching a child, selling a dress, driving a truck, supervising a department, managing a business, or tending a machine. It is fundamental that every manager believe that every subordinate is capable of excellence. It is equally central that the individual accept and respond to Thoreau's statement that "man was born to succeed, not to fail." When an individual becomes willing to make a commitment to excellence, the leader is fulfilling his motivation responsibility.

## Developing Leadership Competence

How does an organization generate the impelling type of leadership essential to its success? How can it structure into its development and management programs what Field Marshal Montgomery calls "the capacity and will to rally men and women to a common purpose"? Or what General Mark W. Clark calls the leader's "exceptional confidence, energy, sense of timing, clarity, skill, tenacity, boldness, concern, faith and morality"? (8)

The following guides are recommended for the development and practice of effective corporate leadership at all levels:

1. Identify precisely the goals of each unit or control component.
2. List the activities that must be engaged in by individuals and the group in order to reach these goals.
3. List the influences, the skills, the knowledge, and the standards of performance necessary to engage in these activities.
4. Formulate the best available program for developing these specific leadership attributes.
5. After specific skills and techniques have been mastered, integrate the individual components into a well-coordinated whole that can function like a coordinated golfer—never requiring undue analysis while in action. Leadership then becomes as natural as Arnold Palmer's swing.

Leadership functions most effectively when it is the natural outpouring of the leader's developed attitudes and skills. His performance should not be strained or forced; rather, it should be fluid, natural, and spontaneous. It is this type of leadership that develops the greatest thrust and trust. Fabricated leadership is easily detected. It is not trusted. It lacks the ring of personal conviction and therefore fails to convince others. Leadership functions best when it is founded on sincerity.

It is both possible and practical to develop sound leadership within the corporate framework. The capacity to learn implies the ability to acquire leadership qualities and improve their use. It must be emphasized, however, that leadership does not consist solely of knowing a set of rules. The possession of a set of golf clubs does not imply a championship round. The true test is in the selection of the right skill at the right time, of knowing its special assets and limitations, of being able to judge the human environment and develop the right approach shot and the right mental conditioning for the next putt.

## Tomorrow's Leaders: Styles in Transition

John J. Smith, of the Sparton Corporation, is quoted as saying:

The managers and executives of American manufacturing must be broad in their thinking to appreciate the problems confronting American industries. They must draw upon all of their training and experience because no longer can top management or intermediate management be indifferent or lackadaisical and still remain competitive. More than ever the alert, well-educated and aggressive supervisor will be the one who will get first call for promotion and advancement. In selecting for promotion, top management will be discriminating. (9)

Yes, leadership styles are in transition. "Lone rangers" who shoot from the hip will find no market for their talents tomorrow. This type of leadership will be phased out and replaced with the professional leader who can produce results systematically. He will utilize every resource to its fullest potential in conformity with the established policy. He will achieve goals in a firm and consistent manner but with maximum consideration for individual prerogatives and goals. He will do all this through the development of human potential, more effective management, and the improvement of all processes. He will maximize the excellence of his company and the talents of its people. He will encourage maximum self-development as the most promising source of goal-oriented activity.

## Standards of Leadership Performance

Those conditions should be clearly described that will prevail when the leadership job is being performed well. The specifics may vary with each position and with different levels of responsibility, but standards should be clearly identified and written down. For example, the leadership performance of the plant manager will be considered satisfactory when

1. All production quotas are met.
2. Production costs, including payroll and raw materials, are kept within budget maximums.
3. The cost of all employee benefits, including safety, contests, and employee health programs, does not exceed 20 percent of payroll.
4. The number of lost-time accidents does not exceed two per 20,-000 man-hours worked.
5. Cost of maintenance and machine replacement does not annually exceed 10 percent of the total amount invested in such machinery.

6. Cleanliness and safety scores average at least 90 percent as evidenced by plant inspections.
7. Working conditions and employee morale are being maintained at a high level as evidenced by an employee turnover rate of less than 7 percent, absences not exceeding 5 percent of the total number of days worked, productivity not dropping more than 2 percent below standard for any one week, and periodic morale surveys indicating a minimum score of 90 percent.
8. Quality is controlled to the point that no more than 2 percent of all items produced are either rejected at the time of production or returned by customers.
9. At least 20 percent of supervisors at all levels have reached the stage of development where they merit and are recommended for promotion.
10. Community relations are kept at a favorable level as evidenced by the receipt of no more than five justifiable complaints at the company home office per quarter.
11. The plant operation shows at least a 6 percent improvement in profit and production for the year.

Leaders should welcome such a set of standards; they provide targets and guides; they require that management measure up to its assigned leadership role.

The ultimate measure of leadership is a simple one—either goals are reached or they aren't. Standards of performance are exceeded or they aren't. When targets have been reached or exceeded, the final judgment will be "well done." When results have fallen short of goals, the implication is clear that changes and improvements in leadership are needed to insure that the next targets will be reached.

## Notes

[1] Harvey A. Stackman, "The Psychology of Leadership," *Business and Economic Review*, Bureau of Business and Economic Research, University of South Carolina, as condensed in *Advertiser's Digest*, June 1967, p. 17.

[2] *Ibid*.

[3] Gordon L. Lippitt, "*Changing Concepts of Managerial Leadership*," IMC *Bulletin*, January 1967.

[4] J. Keith Louden, "Leadership," an address delivered before various top management briefing sessions.

[5] Lippitt, *op. cit*.

6 John W. Gardner, *Excellence*, Harper & Row, Publishers, Inc., New York, 1961, p. 104.

7 *Ibid.*, p. 130.

8 General Mark W. Clark, "What It Takes to Be a Leader," an address delivered while president of The Citadel, the Military College of South Carolina.

9 *Leadership on the Job*, edited by the staff of *Supervisory Management*, American Management Association, New York, 1957, p. 38.

*Part IV*

# *Keys to Human Understanding and Response*

# 🏮 16

# Communication:

# Focusing on Action Response

LAWRENCE A. APPLEY has pointed out how many times people in positions of great influence have said that "the greatest need in this world is for better communication between people. It is extremely difficult to understand why, in a time when communication is most needed and when the facilities for attaining communications are the greatest in history and developing rapidly, human beings are paying less and less attention to and becoming less and less skilled at accomplishing effective communication." (1)

Yes, the problem of communication has always been with us and remains a serious challenge in even the most modern and efficiently organized companies. At a recent meeting where discussion centered around the subject, one participant turned to the man next to him and remarked, "Your company must have solved its communication problem. When we hear about new techniques, it's usually you people that are mentioned." He replied, "Yes, we *have* worked hard at communicating, but we still have a long way to go. We sometimes wonder whether we're really gaining on the problem."

## The Importance of Communication

Just how important is communication to the management process and to corporate success? Marshall K. Evans, of Westinghouse Electric Corporation, answers with these words:

> The explosive growth of management's need for information and the simultaneous mushrooming of information-handling technology leave many of today's executives worried and perplexed. They are worried about being swamped in a flood of paper and information that has to be assimilated, stored, and factored into operation decision and action. (2)

Yet: "My job is mostly talking with people," said a company president in a *Fortune* survey. It has been calculated that the average manager spends up to 90 percent of his time communicating by one means or another. (3)

The primary purpose of communication is to motivate a response. It produces the activity which is most appropriate for the achievement of established goals. The communication involved in the newspaper advertisement or the TV commercial is designed to motivate action: a purchase. Safety communication seeks to minimize accidents and injuries through a change in work practices. The sales manager communicates—by means of charts, diagrams, visual aids, and enthusiastic oratory—with the single purpose of motivating the response that will result in increased sales.

Motivation, persuasion, influence—all management activities that seek to elicit greater dedication or more effort are almost totally dependent on the flow of communication. No matter how varied the activities or how specialized the skills involved, the job of the manager is, ultimately, communication.

## The Biggest Obstacle

Consider the limited contribution to the overall battle plan of a ship at sea with no means of communication. And, on the positive side, the significant change in U.S. fortunes during World War II when the Japanese code was broken and the Allied forces were able to intercept and understand Japanese messages.

These examples could be duplicated thousands of times. Communication contributes to the success or failure of every human activity. Large corporations in particular, because of their complex multidivisional setup and the trend toward decentralized operations in recent years, would be helpless without their communications networks for cooperation, coordination, and overall utilization of resources. Such networks may employ computer systems, teletype, telephones, visits, meetings, written messages, and a variety of other means of dispersing information and influence. Efficiency and results, both for individual units and for the organization as a whole, depend on communication.

Belk Stores' problem of communicating adequately with more than 400 units in 18 states seems at times almost insurmountable. Conventions, conferences, bulletins, workshops, booklets, films, visits, telephones, established policies and procedures, and many other methods are used. But too often the flow of communication reaches a break in the pipeline and the message never gets beyond this gap. The clear understanding of purpose and procedure hoped for by the initiators of the communication is filtered out and lost before it reaches those expected to respond. Bulletins are often found stacked on the manager's desk, unopened and unread. Employee morale is damaged when the boss neglects to pass along details concerning benefits.

Such are the costs of inadequate communication—perhaps the most significant obstacle in the way of growth and profit.


## A Basis for Eliciting Results

The following ten basic rules provide a realistic guide for achieving results through effective communications.

1. Clarify ideas, information, policies, changes, and requests before attempting to communicate them.

2. Determine the true purpose of each communication. What is it expected to accomplish? What will be improved? Identify the most important goal and then adjust the communication to elicit the response that will achieve it.

3. Communicate with an awareness of the total physical and human setting in which the information will be received. Picture the place of work: determine the receptivity and understanding levels of the receivers; be aware of

social climate and customs; question the information's timeliness. Ask what, when, and in what manner you would like to be communicated with if you were in a similar environment and position.

4. Be cognizant of the fact that original intent is sometimes distorted. Remember that overtones, subtleties, shades of meaning, and special words can cause misinterpretation and therefore must be evaluated as a vital part of communication planning.

5. Make every effort to convey something helpful or beneficial to the receiver. Consider the other person's needs, interests, and desires. Remember that he has the option of blocking out the information and refusing to respond until he believes that there will be benefit for him.

6. Aim communication at tomorrow as well as today. Although it may focus primarily on today's problem, it should plant the seeds of constant growth and improvement and minimize future problems.

7. Check the results of communication. Was the message received in the manner in which it was intended, and was the response appropriate? Ask questions. Determine the understanding and reaction of the receiver. Seek sufficient feedback both to ascertain whether the communication has been acted on and to make adjustments, if necessary, to insure the expected results.

8. Be as interested in understanding as you are in being understood. In order for two-way communication to work, you must take the time to listen and be receptive to what the other person has to say. If the superior is not interested in the upward flow of communication, the subordinate interprets this as disinterest. He, in turn, becomes less receptive and responsive to messages from above.

9. Be as careful in planning communication as you are in planning other management functions. If necessary, consult with others in making plans—ask for their suggestions. Bring the recipients of your intended communication into the picture. Explain the nature of the problem and the results desired. Ask for their suggestions regarding the composition, transmission, and probable reception of the intended messages.

10. Be certain that your action supports your communication. This is simply a rewording of the old cliché about "practice what you preach." The most persuasive communication is not what the superior says or writes, but what he does—the example he sets. If he is trying to communicate the importance of good management and good organization, then he must practice it. For every manager this means good supervisory practices—such as clear assignment of responsibility, adequate delegation of authority, fair rewards for effort, and consistency in policy enforcement.

The key to obtaining a satisfactory response to a communication is the care with which it is planned and implemented. The fact that communication can take dozens of forms and still be as simple as a man-to-man conversation misleads many into thinking it is so easy and obvious that it does not require the most meticulous caution, forethought, selectivity, and follow-through.

## To Communicate or Not to Communicate?

This is *not* the question. Communication occurs whether it is intended or not. In many instances, the unintentional communication is more effective than the intentional. This the superior must acknowledge. If he is willing to accept the larger definition of communication as "the flow of information and influence," it will be easier to accept the fact that it is occurring all the time. He will realize that communication is much broader than he thought and extends far beyond the boundaries established by his formal communication program, which may consist primarily of written memos, talks, bulletin boards, and other structured media.

Accepting the premise that communication is anything and everything that influences a person or group creates a whole new role in communication for the manager. In this larger context, he soon discovers that influence will not wait for him to initiate it; that it is not limited to his formal and deliberate utterance or action; that unintentional, as well as intentional, communication is occurring at all times. If he does nothing, communication will occur—possibly of a negative variety. If he neglects to communicate the right information, it can only be assumed that the wrong information will be communicated. If his attempt at communication is not properly planned and executed in accordance with the previously listed ten guides, he should not expect response in accordance with expectations.

The manager, then, has but one communication choice—that of taking charge of the whole communication spectrum; of focusing on response and result; and of guiding all potential influences into positive and contributory channels.

## Information: Its Effective Presentation

The speaker has labored long and tediously to arrive at that climactic moment when he delivers the punch line of his story. But, when the words are out, nothing happens; the audience doesn't laugh or react in any visible way.

The advertising department has spent months in planning an elaborate and expensive campaign. But, when the opening guns are fired, nothing happens. The excitement fails to materialize. Sales do not increase. The only sound is a dull thud.

The plant manager has planned the perfect, all-encompassing program to reduce costs, increase production, improve quality, and better the climate of employee relations. Consultants are called in. New forms of communication are devised. Everything proceeds in accordance with the carefully outlined schedule. But there is no response. Results do not materialize.

These three examples of communication failure pose a serious and unavoidable question: What does it really take to elicit response? The answer to this question embodies: (1) basic communication principles, (2) what the recipients want to know, and (3) what management wants to achieve.

*Principles.* Let's look first at a few key communication principles.

- There is no magic formula for bringing men's minds and feelings into rapport.
- Communication must reflect a complete sincerity of purpose before an impact can be made on the recipient.
- Communication must be repetitive, not sporadic, to be effective.
- Communication must have a positive, beneficial, long-range, constructive purpose and not be limited merely to putting out fires.
- An analysis of all potential influences on communication, environmental factors, and concerns of the recipients should be part of the communication program.

*The recipients.* What do subordinates want to know? Imagine that you are a plant foreman, a warehouse manager, the sales manager for the Midwest territory, an office manager, or the vice president of finance. What do you think your people want to know about the company? What information do they need in order to want to give their best to their jobs and the company?

J. H. Fles, president of the Associated Truck Lines, Inc., lists the following needs:

- A need to be convinced and feel that the company is truthful and sincere in its contacts—the need for straight talk and information.
- The knowledge that the superior is really interested in the sub-

ordinate, beyond the limitations of what he can get out of the subordinate.

- A need to know what the company is doing. After all, the subordinate works for the outfit and has a stake in its future.
- A desire to share with management and associates his achievements —both on and off the job. There is a need to be able to share the "little triumphs" with the "gang" and to know more about what the others are doing.
- A need to have a person available to listen when the subordinate has problems, "beefs," or ideas on how to run the company. The subordinate is certainly not receptive to communication from a superior who snarls at him every time he opens his mouth. (4)

*Management's expectations.* What does the boss expect from communication? What does he seek to convey to his subordinates. The list may include:

- An understanding that the company must continuously offer more efficient service through production, sales, and customer relations.
- Information that lets the subordinate know what makes the wheels go round. He must know that making a profit provides the only means for growth and survival.
- An understanding that the whole "family" needs to be drawn closer together. The "family" feeling increases pride in the company, improves work attitudes and results.
- An awareness that the company is interested in educating the subordinate to the facts of economic life in order that he may know and appreciate what makes the American business system tick.
- The knowledge that the company encourages and supports service to the community in which the subordinate is located. As the subordinate becomes a better citizen, the image of the company and the industry is upgraded.

Perhaps true rapport is achieved only when the subordinate comes to understand and believe that he is more than an economic, social, and emotional creature to management. When he feels that he represents an ethical and spiritual being, he knows that the company is deeply interested in him. With this added dimension, the matter of communication takes on quite a different character.

## Creating an Atmosphere of Acceptance

It is almost impossible to suddenly create an atmosphere of acceptance or a dramatic change in the human climate existing in a group. The difficulty here is analogous to the difficulty of changing individual attitudes and behavior. Atmosphere or climate is the byproduct of months and years of personal experience.

So far as acceptance of communication is concerned, atmosphere has been and will continue to be shaped by everything that influences relationships between the subordinate and his supervisor and between the subordinate and the company. As mentioned in other connections, this includes trust, respect, fairness, integrity, and a record of promises kept. It should be remembered that acceptance is often more an attitude or feeling than a rational decision.

Managers should be constantly aware of the importance of atmosphere to the ultimate effectiveness of communication. At all times they should strive to keep it favorable and to avoid such psychological roadblocks to receptivity as these:

- Locked-in stereotypes that influence us to interpret information on the basis of preconceived attitudes.
- The tendency to ignore the message when we suspect the motives of the communicator; that is, to evaluate the source rather than the information.
- The tendency to ignore information that we feel we already know or that we know we already oppose.
- The making of comparisons on the basis of our own system of values.
- Individual emotional states that condition our acceptance, our understanding, and our response.

Psychologically, most of us seek to create a sort of jamming device to shut out those truths that we don't want to hear, messages from people we don't like, and information that may be difficult to understand and respond to.

Communistic countries, which are unable to prevent broadcasts from the free world, try to prevent their reception by means of jamming devices. These conditioned reception-rejection devices become decisive in the communicating process. It is extremely difficult to gain acceptance against the will of the other person.

Receptivity, understanding, and response obviously depend on clarity of communication. The individual must receive the message, but he will not receive it unless its words, symbols, and meaning are comprehensible to him. Here are some examples of communication errors that make clarity problematical.

*Fuzzy words and meanings.* When President Woodrow Wilson was a young man, he would submit much of his writing to his father for judgment and approval. After reading the material, the elder Wilson would often ask, "What do you mean by that statement?" Young Wilson would then explain to his father in direct, simple language what he meant. To which his father would reply, "Well, why didn't you write it that way in the beginning?"

Words can be sharp precision instruments, but they are also capable of being misinterpreted. Use words that convey a single vivid picture. If the word or exact symbol is not available, explain yourself—state what meaning you are attaching to your words. The language of communication should be simplified, reduced to the lowest common denominator, rather than formalized up the ladder of high-sounding generalities.

*Failure to clarify the differences among fact, inference, opinion, and value judgments.* In the case of facts, the subordinate is being asked to accept information as stated. Inference, opinion, and value judgments require justification so as not to confuse the recipient. Separate the two. When a person becomes confused, he is no longer willing to accept even facts.

*The careless use of generalized or abstract terms.* What do such terms as "big business," "the American Way," "Wall Street," and the like mean to the average person? If you're not sure, don't use them. Failure of communication is often failure to establish common grounds for understanding.

*Lack of attention to the generation gap.* The New York Times carried an advertisement, on June 28, 1966, which contained the following statement:

> Too many of our college youth think business is "dull," "soulless," "conformist," "noncreative," "money-grubbing," "for the birds." Above all, they believe business has failed to commit itself to the human issues of our time. . . . To many of this new generation, business seems to be living in a paper world of profits. Business, for them, is removed from the mainstream of social and moral responsibility. (5)

This sort of thinking ignores the billions of dollars contributed by corporations to the public good, not to mention their other services to the community. But the tragic fact is that business has failed in its responsibility to communicate to the half of the American public that is now under the age of 30. This group likes to say, "Don't trust anyone over 30." Too often, however, the over-30 group exhibits the same lack of confidence in the under-30 group.

The problem of communicating with customers and employees in the two population groups that are increasing most rapidly—the under-30's and the over-65's—presents a serious challenge. A national association recently sponsored a one-day seminar to instruct its members in the art of recruiting and managing youth. Attractive brochures had been written and distributed. The procession of speakers and their messages was little short of brilliant. Then, when it came time for the discussion, a college professor arose and pointed a finger at the "experts" on the stage. "The trouble with this whole day," he declared, "has been that it was planned and carried out entirely by adults. Adults wrote these brochures. If we want to learn about youth, why don't we talk with youth? Why weren't they asked to write or at least evaluate the brochures? Why were they not invited as speakers today? We are trying to find out what young people are thinking, what they want, and what they will respond to—yet no one has taken the trouble to ask their opinion."

*Failure to overcome the status barrier.* Unique to top management is the problem of "executive isolation"—the difficulty in finding out what's going on. One retiring chief executive said to his successor, "Yesterday was the last day you heard the truth from your subordinates." (6) Why is communicating such a difficult problem within the higher reaches of management? In a Washington speech, C. Virgil Martin, president of Carson Pirie Scott and Company, identified the "status barrier" as the communication gremlin. He added:

> I was young once, and I know what my attitude was towards the boss. I could not sit down and talk to the president of the company when I was a junior, any more than juniors today can really sit down and be at ease in talking to me. This is one of the realities that top management must recognize. . . . I have never kidded anybody about my door being open. My door can't be open. It is simply a physical and practical impossibility. (7)

Many organizations attribute their success to strong, informal personal contacts. Yet, with growth, there comes that inevitable time when the head is no longer closely connected to the arms and legs of the organization.

## How Management Can Get the Message

Management must take the initiative in order to hear the ungarbled word. It may be next to impossible to get the absolute truth in every instance, but effort must be exerted to get the best possible approximation of it by seeking as many perspectives on it as practical. Management can make clear that it expects information in the least distorted form; it can build mutual trust between itself and its associates; it can put a premium on integrity; and it can get out of the isolation of the office and find out for itself. As John W. Rollins, chairman of Rollins Leasing Corporation, Wilmington, Delaware, puts it: "I've found that too many memos and too many formal meetings leave too much of a barrier between myself and my staff. I like to visit a man in his office, where the domain is principally his and where he can feel more relaxed." (8)

Keith Davis, of Indiana University, lists the following reasons for emphasis on communication at the management level:

1. Management communication is a prerequisite to worker communication.
2. An appropriate flow of information is necessary before management can make the proper judgment and decisions.
3. The scope of management's influence is typically greater than the subordinate's.
4. Management communication deserves emphasis because it represents most of the links in the chain. There is only one link between the first-level supervisor and the worker, but there might be many layers of management communication flow between the president and the first-line supervisor—more opportunity for foul-up and distortion.
5. Managers, as employees, have the same need for communication as every other member of the group. If they don't get the word, they might assume, "If I don't know what's going on around here, why should I worry about what happens?" (9)

Robert N. McMurry (10) suggests the following guides for the chief executive:

- He should seek to identify and overcome those barriers to the "knowledge of what's going on" in the middle and lower echelons of his organization.
- He should seek to rectify those errors which hinder his management ability owing to communication errors.
- He should implement those remedies which are appropriate to

his situation for the improvement and correction of communication weaknesses.

- He should resolve the personal conflicts which interfere with communications throughout the organization.

So long as serious vacuums and errors exist, there will be failures in upward communication which will seriously jeopardize management's opportunity to manage effectively. If information should be willfully or maliciously inaccurate, it may reflect discredit on the manager, hide weaknesses, and cause him to make the wrong decisions concerning the present and future operation of the company. The acceptance of misinformation can also result in the institution and perpetuation of ill-advised policies and practices; loss of contact with customer, public, and employee; and misinterpretation of their attitudes toward the company.

## Techniques for Producing Response

The techniques listed here are suggested as means of improving the effectiveness of communication and influence flow for the purpose of eliciting the desired response.

*Strive for an understanding of what is communicated.* A survey of 100 firms attempted to determine how much of what top management has to say is actually understood. The results:

- Men at the vice-presidential level understand about two-thirds of what they hear from the top.
- Men at the general supervisor level get 56 percent.
- Men at the plant manager level get 40 percent.
- Men at the foreman level get 30 percent.
- Men on the production line get 20 percent.

The following recommendations may improve or check this spillage to successive levels: Ask the person receiving the information to state it in his own words. When disagreement regarding the information is possible, be especially careful about completeness and clarity. If the information appears overly interesting or exciting, watch out for exaggeration in meaning. On the other hand, if it appears boring or uninteresting, guard against errors of transposition. Finally, concentrate on the unfamiliar ideas, words, phrases, and information contained in the communication.

*Promote the practice of careful listening.* Some companies call their supervisors together for meetings in which higher management listens to their problems and asks them for possible solutions. Management thus demonstrates its willingness to listen and, at the same time, educates the various levels of supervision in the techniques and importance of listening as a vital link in the communication chain.

The reception of information is, ideally, a deliberate act. When it becomes this, the individual is making a conscious effort to hear, to understand, and to respond when conviction merits it. Being in the presence of verbal or written information is no more indicative that influence has been effected than the fact that the communication existed in the first place. The test is not exposure but the degree to which information has been received and acted upon.

*Remember to use questions effectively.* Questions reveal the superior's real understanding of what he proposes to communicate. Questions provide the best means available for gauging reception. They also reveal how the recipient intends to act on the information. A good question should be personal, constructive, single-purpose, selective, involving, clear, and brief. (11)

*Influence communication flow.* Educational Designs, of Westport, Connecticut, states that communication within the group can be influenced in anyone of the following four ways:

> *Control.* The superior can exercise most of the control and influence.
> *Develop.* The superior can use his influence and the subordinate's to solve the problem. He seeks to develop the best thinking and interaction of ideas on the part of all concerned.
> *Relinquish.* The superior can relinquish the influence and thus permit the subordinate to carry the communication ball.
> *Withdraw.* The superior can withdraw completely. He thus seeks to stay uninvolved and neither exert nor respond to influence. (12)

It is obvious that the superior has a decisive voice in the initiation and flow of influence, especially where ideas and processes are involved. He should be aware that communication is not restricted to the formal verbal and written variety but can emerge, just as effectively, from interaction within the group.

*Communication and Professional Management*

The deliberate intent of this book is to promote the systems and benefits of professional management. This type of management can permeate an organization only through the process of communication. All forms of communication should be employed in instituting and implementing the functions of goal setting, planning, organizing, controlling, delegation of responsibility and accountability, personnel development, problem solving, and so on. If professional management is the aim, it must be programmed into the communication system.

Managers must devote the same careful, systematic, and thorough attention to communication that they devote to any other phase of the management job. This is extremely important, since communication constitutes the network that links the disjointed activities and interests into a coordinated whole. The primary responsibility for communication should be assigned to a single individual or position, and accountability for results and standards of performance should be established for the function. But this will not relieve anyone of his own proper role in communication any more than the presence of a training executive relieves the individual manager of his responsibility for training.

The following guides are recommended for the improvement of the company communication network:

1. Make a realistic appraisal of current communication practices and their effectiveness. It may be advisable to seek outside experts to conduct this appraisal.
2. Identify the responses and results desired and design a communication program that can achieve them.
3. Arrange for whatever training, orientation, and skill development are necessary to install and manage the program. Include everyone from the president down.
4. Structure constant feedback and control points into the program in order to appraise results and make appropriate adjustments.
5. Plan for the continuing updating and improvement of the entire communication program.
6. Recognize the value and necessity of repetition. In order to be effective, communication must be continuous—provide for a constant building of atmosphere, relationships, and channels for

a response-producing information. No one paid much attention the first time he heard the slogan "Winston tastes good. . . ." But this simple, direct statement has been repeated so many times and in so many ways that enough people responded to make Winston a best seller. So—communicate as often as is necessary to elicit the response required to achieve desired goals.

The guides and ideas suggested in this chapter should prove of value to the manager in his continuing role as a communicator. It is a great thrill to overhear subordinates say, "The boss really says what he means, believes what he says, and lives what he believes." When he hears remarks like this, he can rest assured that his company is on the right road in the matter of communicating in such a way as to elicit result-producing response.

## NOTES

[1] Lawrence A. Appley, "Understanding Communication," *Management News*, September 1967.

[2] Marshall K. Evans, "How to Get the Right Information, in the Right Place, at the Right Time," *Management Review*, August 1966, p. 33.

[3] Joseph M. Dooher, and Vivienne Marquis, *Effective Communication on the Job*, American Management Association, New York, 1956, p. 13.

[4] J. H. Fles, "Employee-Employer Communication," *ABWA Bulletin*, The American Writing Association, University of Illinois, Urbana, Illinois, 1967.

[5] As quoted in John S. Morgan, *Managing the Young Adults*, American Management Association, New York, 1967, p. 174.

[6] Robert N. McMurry, "Clear Communications for Chief Executives," *Harvard Business Review*, March-April 1965.

[7] C. Virgil Martin, "Top Management Criticizes Its Own Communications," *Stores*, January 1967.

[8] "The Dangers of Executive Isolation," *Business Management*, October 1966.

[9] Keith Davis, "Communication *Within* Management," *Personnel*, November 1954.

[10] McMurry, *op. cit.*

[11] "Questions—Key to Communication," *The Hillsdale College Leadership Letter*, September 1962.

[12] "Developing Communication Skills," *Educational Designs*, Westport, Connecticut.

# 17

# Verbal Exchange:
# Bridge to Human Interaction

THE vice president in charge of production for the Precision Auto Parts Company had been trying for three months to improve production and quality control at the Summerville plant. The plant was located 275 miles from the central office, and he had tried to solve the problem by telephone, memos, and visits by his assistant. After all his efforts, production was still running 6 percent behind and complaints about quality were twice the number received at similar plants. Eventually, the president received a complaint himself and decided to review the Summerville record. What he discovered sent the vice president scurrying to make a personal investigation. He toured the plant, talked with production supervisors, and had a lengthy conversation with the manager.

During these discussions, the vice president discovered that the raw materials being received were below standard. This not only slowed production but accounted for low quality and, consequently, the complaints. The plant manager had attempted to correct the situation; he had talked with the supplier and repeatedly called matters to the attention of the purchasing agent. In fact, the plant manager felt he was doing everything he could without going over somebody's head. As a result of his on-the-spot inspection and the give and take of his lengthy fact-finding conversation with the plant manager, the vice president of production was able to initiate the action necessary to improve the quality of the raw materials received. Within days, production was on schedule and complaints were returning to normal.

Hundreds of similar examples could be cited to support the contention that verbal exchange is the best method of solving problems, achieving rapport, instituting change, and bringing about desired results. This exchange can range all the way from a spontaneous, short conversation to an elaborate presentation before an audience of thousands. Effective verbal communication is the bridge to effective management and productive performance.

## The Transmission of Ideas

The manager seeking to transmit an idea has in his mind a mental picture, an understanding, a concept, an attitude, and a prescription for action. Transmission is complete only when the person (or group) addressed has an identical mental picture, understanding, or concept. The difficulty arises when the initiator has an out-of-focus picture of what he wants to communicate and therefore is not able to transmit a sharp, clear picture. As in reproducing a photograph, the print cannot be any sharper or contain any more detail than the negative.

Skill in transmission depends on the effectiveness of the communicator in finding appropriate words, symbols, or other media for the accurate, undistorted transfer of ideas from one mind to another. Even if he does have a clear picture of how a project should be carried out, for example, he cannot obtain the support of others until he can make them see the same picture. And that includes its purposes and his feelings about it as well as objective facts.

## Continuing Need for Oral Exchange

Compare the number of times the manager interacts with subordinates and superiors in writing as opposed to the amount of oral exchange that takes place. The latter usually adds up to about ten times the other.

The importance of oral exchange can best be visualized by reviewing the daily activities of a busy executive. Imagine his limitations without oral communication. Consider the time that would be lost in written communication—the delays, the misunderstandings, the higher costs, the greater opportunity for error, the almost nonexistent chance for immediate feedback, and the general frustration. Talk is as indispensable to goal achievement as any technique at the manager's disposal.

The significance of oral exchange of course lies, not in mere speaking, but in the interaction that takes place. Interaction, by its very nature, implies a two-way flow; it amounts to the opening of a pipeline. The manager, the employment interviewer, and the production foreman must all understand that interaction provides the opportunity to be influenced, to be acted on. It implies listening, asking questions, explaining, answering questions freely, and soliciting information from the other person.

## Opportunities in Conversation

Although oral interaction may take many forms, this chapter will be concerned with the three that are most important in management. The first of these is conversation.

> Today scientists are rediscovering what wise men have known since Plato—that talking with people is not only fun; it's good for you. . . . The formal word "dialogue" is now widely used in business and government to refer to the dynamic verbal process that clarifies issues and solves problems.
>
> . . . When people talk together honestly and intensely, the human spirit is lifted and refreshed. Problems are solved; mental blocks disintegrate. Minds touch each other and allow themselves to be influenced and changed. (1)

A simple, warm, sincere conversation between two people is the most powerful and, at the same time, the most neglected tool in the manager's kit. If the boss were only to realize what a conversation centered around the interests of the subordinate could do for his morale, sense of belonging, and sense of importance, he would be amazed. It never hurts for the subordinate to recognize that the boss is human and that the manner in which he is regarded by his superior is important to his future with the company.

One supervisor remarked proudly to a colleague, "Say, do you know whom I was just talking with? The president." The other responded, "Well, what was wrong? What did he chew you out about?" "No," the first supervisor said, "you've got it all wrong. He didn't bawl me out about anything. He just stopped by to talk with me. You know, he seemed genuinely interested in what I'm doing—seemed to know all about it. He even asked about my family and said he was sorry he couldn't spend as much time in the plant as he used to. It's really great to have a president you can actually talk with."

This president probably didn't have any particular subject in mind when he stopped to talk to the supervisor. He didn't need to, and perhaps it was better that way. Conversation must not be "canned" or insincere. Unless it can be a genuine, friendly exchange, it shouldn't be attempted. Doing nothing, in this context, may be preferable to doing the wrong thing. But, if an executive has the capacity for engaging in genial conversation with his associates and subordinates, he can break down more barriers and create more rapport than a barrelful of "morale builders." When a subordinate can feel that this state of rapport exists, a whole new climate is created for the release of his productive effort.

## The Interview: All-Purpose Tool

An interview is often more formal than a casual conversation, and it is usually initiated and structured to achieve a specific purpose. It is an activity in which the typical manager spends a sizable portion of his time and which accounts for more decisions than all the conferences and committees combined. Interviews affect decisions to employ, discharge, change, purchase, announce, appoint, approve, improve, transmit, check.

The manager initiating an interview should remember that its primary purpose is to provide—

- An exchange of ideas, opinions, and information between two people.
- Benefit for both parties.
- Insights and understanding for better decision making and action.
- An opportunity to recognize the eternal "dignity of man."
- A chance for the person being interviewed to express opinions, ask questions, seek clarification, and convey feelings.

- The attainment of a specific purpose—employ, negotiate a change in procedure, determine reasons for failure to meet production standards.

Hand a canvas, a set of brushes, and a set of oils to an uninitiated amateur and ask him to paint a picture. But don't be surprised at the resulting mess. Be assured, too, that almost the same kind of "mess" occurs when the amateur tries his hand at interviewing. Although every operating manager handles a substantial share of his management activity through interviews, he is basically untrained and unskilled in what is very nearly an art. Yet the results of his interviews are of just as great consequence to the company as the interviews of the personnel manager or employment specialist. Therefore, it is just as important for the operating manager to understand the techniques of effective interviewing.

The three basic types of interviews involve certain disciplines, techniques, and practices. These can be identified and their mastery significantly improved with deliberate effort and practice.

1. *The directive interview* is one in which the interviewer has specific topics on which he wishes to get or give information. He is in control of the interview at all times, directs its course, and moves forward to achieve the planned purpose.

2. *The nondirective interview* generally does not seek to ferret out answers to specific questions, but rather provides the interviewee with an opportunity to talk about the things that interest him. In many instances, the interviewee has requested or initiated the interview in order to state his opinions and voice his complaints or grievances. The interviewee has more to do with the direction of this type of interview, and the subject matter, than does the interviewer; it can take almost any direction. It is this type of interview—one that is initiated by the subordinate and takes considerable time—that the average line manager often is too impatient to handle effectively.

3. *The structured or patterned interview* is one that has been worked out, presumably with great care, in advance. It usually involves a set of questions or guides, which the interviewer expects to follow. This type is especially helpful when one is just learning to interview or when the same information must be covered with many individuals. Typical are individual interviews

in which managers review employee benefits, announce changes in policies and procedures, or convey other essential information. .The skilled interviewer can use the set of questions or pattern in such a way that the structured uniformity isn't obvious.

Each of the three types of interviews serves its own unique function, and each should be mastered by the manager who expects to be versatile enough to handle all interview situations. Surprisingly, the nondirective interview is the most difficult to master. Too often, managers are tempted to plunge right into the directive interview; they are generally conscientious about planning the items to be covered and the most effective manner of presentation, so that they have a guide of points to follow. The structured interview provides a guide or pattern, and the manager has only to master the technique of using it. But in the nondirective interview he seldom has made preparations and has no pattern to follow; he must rely on his own ingenuity and nimbleness of mind. Unless he is experienced in the skills of interviewing and the art of patience, the result is not likely to prove satisfactory for the interviewees.

*Essentials of an effective interview.* Failure to plan for the interview is frequently the cause of partial or complete failure to achieve the intended purpose. The manager-interviewer should always be aware that—

- The interview's purpose and its reasons for being conducted will affect the outcome.
- The situation that initiated the interview, as well as factors influencing both parties, must be taken into account.
- The interviewer wields the most decisive influence on the nature and outcome of the interview.
- The reaction of the interviewee depends largely on his previous experience, his attitude, and his expectations.
- There must be sufficient planning to insure the availability of facts and figures that may be needed. Also, the pattern that will be followed and the order in which ideas will be introduced should be anticipated.
- All facts and circumstances bearing on the subject of the interview should be investigated.

*Developing sound interviewing skills.* Since the interview is an exchange between two people in which both react and interact, what counts is not the impression that each hopes to make, but the one which is actually received. It is what comes out of the exchange pipeline that determines the response of the other person. The following points represent skill areas which require practice for maximum interview effectiveness.

1. The interviewer must begin with the *knowledge of his own attitudes and feelings* concerning the situation and the person to be interviewed.

2. The most *appropriate time and place* for the interview should be selected. The interview is often more difficult if it is unduly delayed.

3. The easiest and most effective interview features the *"Ping-Pong" technique*. This consists of short exchanges, with each person gauging and reacting to what the other says, in contrast to the "touchdown" technique in which one participant tries to carry the ball throughout the interview. Such speech making is more likely to create problems and confusion than anything else. It all but eliminates the opportunity for questions and free discussion. The manager will be well advised to learn to make short statements, often in the form of questions, and then give the other person a chance to react. If he is alert enough to listen carefully, he will often be given a clue as to what his next statement or approach should be.

4. The interviewer should be *"tuned in."* He should know what the other person is saying, what he is not saying, and his reasons for saying or not saying the things he does. And he should be willing to accept and consider information offered by the interviewees.

5. The interview should be kept from becoming argumentative. The interview is *no debating forum*. Calmness, established facts, and experienced judgment should set tone and content. The interviewer must refuse to be trapped into argument or into agreeing with a statement contrary to fact.

6. The interviewer should try to *see the interview as the interviewee sees it*. What would your question be? Your reactions? Your judgment of the results? Plan and conduct the interview with the other person's point of view in mind.

7. The interview should move forward to accomplish its *intended purpose*. All the pertinent information should be presented, and significant facts should be repeated for clarity and reinforcement.

8. The *opening and close* of the interview are often decisive. The opening sets the climate and emotional base, and the close should include a recapitulation or summary of what has been covered, the understanding that has been reached, and the action expected. The interviewer should clearly state that he has full confidence in the other person, and the session should end on a pleasant, encouraging note.

9. Before the interview is completed the interviewee should be given *an*

*opportunity to present ideas and ask questions.* He should be asked whether he understands everything that has been covered. He might also be encouraged to state his understanding of what his response is supposed to be.

10. The interviewer should "go to school" on every interview—in some cases, literally arrange for *playback.* How effective was the discussion? What part was least effective? Was the purpose accomplished? What changes in technique might make the next interview better?

Interviewing results will significantly affect employment, job performance, human relationships, employee attitudes, and most other results-oriented activities. Its decisive importance to the success of the enterprise justifies dedicated effort to refine and sharpen the techniques involved.

## The Executive as a Public Speaker

There are few really outstanding public speakers. This is obvious all the way from the pulpit to the sales conference. Many businessmen are unable to speak on their feet, as the saying goes; they read a prepared speech in a dull, inaudible drone or flounder unintelligibly.

Yet who can be expected to speak for American business and the free enterprise system except the men who know the system best and appreciate its advantages most? Who will tell the story of your industry and your company to civic clubs, educational groups, and professional and special interest organizations except you, the knowledgeable "authority"? Who will inform and inspire subordinate executives in your own company except you and your associates in top management, who are in the best position to know all the facts and whose thinking influences the future of every man in your audience?

The manager, by the very nature of his status and responsibility, has an inherent responsibility to speak up. His effectiveness as a manager and his value as a company representative are significantly influenced by his public speaking ability. His refusal to speak up, to gain acceptance for company objectives internally and enhance the company's image externally, does a disservice to his position. One simple, unavoidable fact cannot be argued away: The executive who masters the art of public speaking is a more valuable representative of his company than the otherwise competent man who does not.

Kenneth McFarland, often listed as America's No. 1 public speaker, has stated: "For a variety of reasons 'men of affairs' are becoming intensely interested in effective public speaking. Some of these reasons are as elemental as the law of self-preservation. . . . We are going to have to develop the same effective public speaking skills as those who seek to discredit free enterprise or there isn't going to be any management." (2)

Why are tough production managers, alert sales executives, and top decision makers, with a missionary zeal for the profit system and an almost religious dedication to company philosophy and goals, reduced to incoherent mumbling on the platform? Is it that courage in one arena is cowardice in another? Are the requirements or skills so different? Is the public rostrum such a strange milieu that the operating executive who finds himself facing a sea of unfamiliar faces must immediately lose his self-confidence?

Let the following facts set the record straight:

1. The chief executive is the logical spokesman for the company—both internally and externally. Others can and should assist him, but he can no more abdicate this obligation completely than he can any other portion of his responsibility.
2. Managers can increase the dynamic aspects of their performance through effective public speaking.
3. Speaking before groups of whatever size—committees, departments, the assembled workforce, the Community Chest rally, the annual industrial association convention—entails specific skills and techniques that can be identified and improved.
4. There are no short cuts, no secrets, and no magic formulas for effective public speaking. It requires painstaking preparation, knowledge of one's subject, practice, and observance of the rules of good delivery.
5. The executive can be as self-confident and effective as he is willing to be.

In short, almost anyone can become a forceful public speaker—almost anyone, that is, who can read, think, organize, and carry on an intelligent conversation. Appearance and the voice are not nearly as important as message and delivery. (One of the most effective and sought-after speakers in America today has a high, rasping voice.) Effective speakers come from every walk of life, in all sizes and ages, and they can talk on as many subjects as there are categories of knowledge. They can be as eloquent as William Jennings Bryan, as emotional as Adolf Hitler, as clever as John F. Kennedy, as homespun as Will Rogers, or as intellectual as Adlai Stevenson. But they *must* have something to say, a style for saying it, and the ability to gain and hold attention.

## Guides for Successful Public Speaking

The following guides apply with almost equal validity to the neophyte who is still at the "wishing" stage, the occasional speaker who gets to his feet only when forced to, and the real pro, who is always waiting at the gate and will start speaking at the drop of a gavel.

*Every talk starts with the audience.* Remember that the purpose of the talk is not to give the speaker a platform for exercising his vocal chords but to give the audience something it wants or needs to hear.

*Make certain the subject is appropriate* for this audience and for you. Employees are primarily interested in those things that affect them. Interest is high when a speech relates to their jobs, their pay, their benefits, their future. It begins to fade when the speaker moves too far afield. Moreover, they will listen only to a speaker with the authority to speak on his chosen subject—authority based on position or his acknowledged expertise.

*Be an authentic expert on your subject.* Your qualifications should be evident throughout your talk. Gather information from all available sources. Talk with others. Clip ideas and illustrations from current publications. Find out what others have said about the subject. Even though you are the expert, you can't know everything there is to know about anything.

*Begin organizing your speech with an outline,* including an introduction, a body, and a close. The body should consist of the major points of the speech—preferably three to seven. Keep the whole thing simple and short.

*Fill in the outline.* This puts the flesh, the color, and the substance on the skeleton. Each major point will probably be a premise or statement that will need justification. The purpose of the speech is to explain these statements and prove them—with facts, illustrations, quotations, and so on.

*Write out the speech.* This is especially important for the beginner. The first draft may read well, but when delivered as a speech it is likely to sound formal and stilted. Often words are too intellectual, sentences are too long, there's not enough variety, and the organization is too complex. Reread it in a way that sounds natural and direct—changing the written copy as you go. Don't be afraid to make changes—or even start over. Every time you improve a phrase, insert a stronger illustration, and improve the structure, you increase your confidence in the effectiveness of your speech.

*When you make your presentation, don't read from a complete manuscript.* Well, hardly ever. If it is a technical paper or is of such strategic importance that a slip of the tongue would cause embarrassment or repercussions, it may be advisable to stick to the script. Even in these instances, some of the inspirational fire will be lost. Preferably, use only the briefest outline while speaking. By this time, you should be so familiar with it that you won't need the manuscript.

*Make certain that all environmental conditions are favorable.* Maybe you shouldn't depend on the chairman to make satisfactory arrangements. Arrive ahead of time in order to familiarize yourself with the mike, the podium, the size of the room, and any handicaps that you are likely to encounter. Minimize "separation" from the audience. The chairman can ask people to come forward, to move their chairs closer. Or, if the mike is too high or the flowers are in the way, you can tactfully try to make a change.

*Be ready.* If visual aids or props are to be used, make certain that they are in position and operative. Know what changes or rearrangements you expect to make before beginning to talk.

*Begin strong, continue strong, and end stronger.* Give the speech your best effort—not necessarily in loudness, although you must speak loudly enough to be heard easily, but in terms of delivering a forceful message to this audience at this precise time. There is no unimportant audience or unimportant speech.

*Remember that variety is the spice of listening.* A monotonous diet, whether of food or of words, breeds disinterest. Vary the tone of your voice. Use different types of illustrations. If interest appears to be sagging, change your pace. Keep a few aces up your sleeve for just such moments of crisis.

*Close while you're ahead.* The best meal is the one in which the last bite of food is savored and there is the lingering feeling that a few more bites would be good. The stuffed feeling is not nearly so enjoyable, and the same thing can be said for the audience-speaker relationship. Stop while the audience is still leaning forward to hear more—not after people have slumped back in boredom from overexposure. In any event, find out how long you are expected to speak and stay within the allotted time.

*Perform a "post-mortem."* What can you learn from the composition of the speech, its delivery, and audience reaction that can be used for improvement next time? Write it down and review it as appropriate.

*Retain all speech outlines and related material, properly identified.* These may prove useful for other speeches and other audiences. Perhaps even more important, you can avoid repeating the same points and illustrations if you appear before any members of the same audience again.

Improving Speech Composition and Delivery

The following tips may be helpful in dealing with specific problems:

*Priming the pump of self-confidence.* Your anxiety is not unique. Consider the ways in which self-confidence can be built. What do you need before you can feel complete poise when speaking before others? The best answer is, simply, speaking experience. Select subjects on which you are sure of your knowledge. Speak in your "official capacity." Believe that you have an important message to deliver. Be so well prepared that you know the speech will go well.

*To laugh or not to laugh?* If the audience has to think whether to laugh or has to force its response, then your attempt at humor has failed. Humor in a speech is desirable, but by no means necessary. It is the most difficult speech-making technique to master. If you're not good at humor, forget it—especially *borrowed* humor. You may not be able to pull off a story with the same finesse as its originator. Humor is usually supposed to support a speech, not replace it. If your purpose is solely to entertain, then pull out all stops—but you had better be a real artist before you try it.

*Learn to speak by speaking.* The only way to master any activity is to engage in it—to practice and to improve with each session. Accept invitations to speak, beginning with small audiences. Select topics that are uncomplicated, with which you are familiar. Keep adding numbers. As Kenneth McFarland advises, "learn to pitch one inning, then a game, and then the series." (3)

*Be willing to work for improvement.* The main reason speakers give amateurish performances is that they are not willing to follow the disciplines demanded of a professional. The superstar, the "naturally talented," the silver-toned orator, the born humorist, and the "lucky" ones didn't attain their status by accident. They owe their success to hard work, long hours of practice at the cost of other activities, and dedication to a goal.

George Bernard Shaw was noted for his rapierlike tongue. But behind each quick thrust were years of study, observation, and thought. He once explained, "I am the most spontaneous speaker in the world because every word, every gesture, and every retort has been carefully rehearsed."

*Be a copycat—learn from others.* A manager once remarked, "I know I'm not smart enough to think up all the ideas I need for running my business profitably. But I'm willing to learn from others." Read the great speeches of the masters, from Plato to Winston Churchill. Listen to today's outstanding speakers. What is there about them that makes them outstanding?

Don't attempt to give the same type of speech or imitate the mannerisms of others, but do learn from their successes. Join a toastmaster's club. Take a public speaking course at a local college. Read books on public speaking. Be willing to serve as chairman at meetings. Use a tape recorder. Make notes during talks and ask for copies of speeches.

*Live where you speak and speak where you live.* Vitality, indispensable to effective speech making, depends on an outpouring of one's own convictions, ideals, experience, and knowledge. The audience must be able to recognize the speaker as a genuine person. What comes from the heart is more persuasive than the product of the best mind. Effectiveness can be multiplied many times just by sincerity. What you have to say must ring true; it must be believable—believable coming from you! You don't have to be intellectual or fancy; simplicity is power. Big ideas often get lost in big words, but ideas come across big through simple word pictures that say exactly what the speaker wants to communicate.

E. C. Nance eloquently summed up the case for effective verbal exchange:

> Words can change the face of a city, build churches, schools, playgrounds, boys' clubs, scout troops, civic forums, civic clubs, little theaters, civic organizations, garden clubs, and better local government. . . . Words can engender self-respect, hope, and constructive ambition in a friend, acquaintance, or employee; or words can discourage and frustrate.
>
> The force of words is great, good, glorious, or terrifying. . . .
>
> We will remain dependent upon speech. We need words that will make us laugh, wonder, work, think, aspire, and hope. We need words that will leap and sing in our souls. We need words that will cause us to face up to life with a fighting faith and contend for those ideals that have made this the greatest nation on earth. (4)

### NOTES

[1] John Kord Lagemann, "Conversation Can Nourish Your Life," *The Rotarian*, June 1966.

[2] Kenneth McFarland, *Eloquence in Public Speaking*, Prentice-Hall, Inc., Englewood Cliffs, N.J., 1961, p. 7.

[3] *Ibid.*, p. 67.

[4] E. C. Nance, "The Power and the Glory of the World," *Vital Speeches*, April 1, 1957.

# ꂦ  18

# Planning and Conducting
# Worthwhile Meetings

W<sub>HY</sub> have a meeting? Are most meetings really worth attending? Do they justify the time, travel, equipment, and dollars invested?

- "The biggest waste of time in our company is our top management meeting on Monday mornings. We don't know where we are going or why, so we never know when we arrive. We do know that it is Monday, and we always meet on Monday," said one experienced executive.
- "Whenever the old man gets his dander up over something, he calls a hurry-up meeting," reported a young man in middle management. "It burns me to have to drop important matters which he has assigned to run to his office for an 'emergency session.' One will get you five that by the end of the day I will be combed for not getting the work done that he made me drop for his meeting."

■ "Last week I sat in on the full-day meeting with the top men," said a junior executive. "The ten men probably represented $400,000 in annual salary. But if I ran a meeting with my lieutenants as they did, I'd be back in the ranks. No real leadership, no suggestion of direction, no agenda, nobody took notes, there was no summary—no arrangement for action. I simply couldn't believe it. But they didn't seem distressed." (1)

Opinion is unanimous. "Time-consuming, unproductive, high-priced but indispensable—that's the average executive's opinion of most meetings. But no business organization could function without some form of internal communications, so the answer is not fewer meetings, but more effective ones." (2)

*The Basic Issue*

"In a society which finds its institutions and organizations increasing in size, scope, volume and numbers of people," it has been pointed out, "there must be more meetings than ever to keep the communications avenues open to get work done through people. . . . 'Once,' said the late Nathan Lurie, then president of the Wrigley Super Market chain, 'when my brother and I had a problem, we went behind the meat counter and worked it out. But how,' he asked, 'do you get 5,000 people in 100 stores behind the meat counter?'" (3)

Thus the meeting issue boils down to the two basic questions of how many and how effective. It has been estimated that middle managers spend approximately one-third of their time in meetings. If only ten managers with average annual earnings of $15,000 spend a third of their time in meetings, the average company—to figure it conservatively—is investing $50,000 in salary costs alone, and this reflects nothing of the loss in productive potential if the meetings fail to produce results.

How much time does the average higher-level executive spend in meetings? A sampling by Minnesota Mining and Manufacturing Company shows the proportion to be about 60 percent. Says B. Y. Auger, 3M's general manager for visual products:

Companies don't seem to evaluate the time their managers spend in meetings the way they do other parts of their business. The very outfits which send efficiency men around with clipboards to check on their factory people think nothing of letting their best-paid men spend hours in ill-planned meetings. Many executives don't consider the possibility that their own activities can be a source of waste. (4)

Management has an unavoidable responsibility for keeping the amount of time and talent consumed by meetings within bounds and, at the same time, a return-on-investment accountability to insure that every meeting produces maximum benefits in terms of results. Meetings represent a significant factor in the successful operation of the company—from the standpoint of both cost and decision making regarding its future. Meetings involve everyone, and for very significant periods. Therefore, the skillful conduct of meetings has to be a direct concern of every executive.

## Facing Up to the Problems

Many organizations are dealing forthrightly with their meeting problems. Mandall Kaplan, manager of a Consolidated Foods subsidiary, states, "We've cut in half the number of our committees, reduced the times the rest of them meet, and set an hour-and-a-half time limit on meetings we do hold. In my view, most meetings are held to avoid decisions or split up the responsibility for them. Now decisions are in the hands of individuals, where they belong." (5)

American Telephone and Telegraph Company abolished regular meeting dates for its standing committees a few years ago and instructed these groups to convene only when some definite business had to be transacted. (Still, "We probably have as many meetings as before," says an AT&T spokesman. [6]) Other companies have appointed meeting "referees," scheduled meetings near the end of the work period to keep them short, installed closed-circuit television, issued taped messages, and sought in many ingenious ways to lick the problem of the dangerously expensive meeting malady.

What, aside from the time required, are a few of the specific problems connected with meetings? Alfred J. Marrow, of the Harwood Manufacturing Corporation, lists these flagrant abuses:

- The agenda contains only trivial matters which could be handled by the executive without an expensive and time-consuming meeting.

- The items to be discussed are important only to the superior, but not to the subordinate.
- The meeting is called after the superior has already reached a decision and further discussion accomplishes nothing.

Dr. Marrow states that a meeting should not be called—

. . . unless the issue is important for the work of the entire group.

. . . to pass the buck to the group. If you're the only one concerned, make your own decision.

. . . just to approve, or share responsibility for, a decision you've already made.

. . . unless—and until—the group is informed about the subject of the meeting. (7)

Decisions regarding meetings should be made with the same tough-mindedness with which all other profit-related operating decisions are made. This approach will aid in deciding who should attend, how much time and money will be invested in staging the meeting, and who should be responsible for its conduct.

The evaluation of meetings falls in about the same category as the statement attributed to John Wanamaker concerning advertising: "We probably waste half of our advertising dollars, but we don't know which half." It is safe to estimate that half of the time spent in meetings is wasted—but how are we to determine which half? Management needs to answer this question. In the case of advertising, research techniques are being used to cut down on the wasted half. In the case of meetings, management can use the same approach. It can conduct surveys, test for ideas and information gained at meetings, and evaluate the amount of change that takes place as a direct result of the meetings.

Actually, there are few secrets about meetings—what makes them effective and why many are time wasters. Management by deliberate design should be able to predetermine the effectiveness of every meeting. If this cannot be done, then the purpose of the meeting, the agenda, the speakers, the method of presenting material, or some other factor is at fault. In that event, don't hold the meeting until the time wasters are identified and the problems are eliminated.

## A Realistic Management Approach

Attending more meetings but enjoying them less? It's a familiar refrain. But there are ways to get more out of meetings and to make certain that management is discharging its reponsibility in this area. The Belk group of stores has had its share of meeting problems. It started as a one-man operation and has grown into a 400-unit complex spread over a wide geographical area. Questions have had to be answered regarding the number of company-wide meetings or conventions to be held, the number of regional meetings, and the number and types of specialized meetings. In addition, someone has had to decide who will attend each meeting, what the agenda will include, and scores of other matters relating, literally, to hundreds of meetings each year. Management has worked hard at being more realistic about the number of meetings necessary and the people who really need to attend them, and an effort has been made to improve agenda, presentations, and scheduling. The following recommendations are based on Belk experience and that of many other companies:

*What is the primary purpose of the meeting?* In what ways will it benefit company performance? Decisions regarding the meeting should be based on objectives, *not* on the fact that a similar meeting was held at the same time last year. If the purpose is to increase sales by 10 percent, then list this as the objective. If the purpose is to reduce operating costs by 5 percent, then list it. Those who make the final decision concerning a proposed meeting should have before them a realistic, comprehensive statement of the goals.

If the meeting is to be small—consisting, say, of a manager and his subordinate supervisors—the manager will most likely think out its objectives on his own. But he still needs to follow the procedure described because, on a percentage basis, he can waste as much time in one departmental meeting as the president can in a companywide meeting.

*Is the proposed meeting the best solution?* Is it the most economical, effective, and realistic way to accomplish the purpose for which it is being proposed? If the meeting is to be primarily for communication, possibly a written memo or report will prove as effective and more economical.

*If the meeting is held, what will it cost in relation to the expected benefits?* Consider all the costs involved. Apply the same tests that would be applied to any expenditure. Will the meeting be a sound investment for the company in terms of improved job performance, morale, personnel development, and results? Management decisions in this area are basically no different from those in many other categories where sound judgment must be exercised.

*What specific steps will be taken to insure the maximum effectiveness of the meeting?* The individual or group that decides whether to hold the meeting must also answer this question.

## Responsibility for Meetings

Realistically, everyone concerned should be responsibile for meetings—especially for the ones he personally schedules. But, from a practical standpoint, the amount of time and money involved requires that someone be assigned direct responsibility for the scheduling and conduct of all major meetings in order to provide at least some protection against unprofitable results.

This seeming centralization of meeting control is not intended to restrict or censor activity in any way. It should, however, minimize conflicts—as when two meetings require the attendance of the same people at the same time—and it should help prevent overburdening the individual executive to the extent that he attends so many meetings he has no time left for other duties and responsibilities. Central scheduling of meetings also should make it possible to minimize out-of-town trips, travel time, and excessive expense. Result: better coordination of all meetings. At Belk, one-location scheduling and management of major meetings has brought considerable order to a rather disorganized activity. And Mr. Auger of 3M estimates that his company is saving $200,000 per year through the use of a "referee" to coordinate major meetings.

In addition to assigning overall responsibility to one individual or group, there still must be accountability for individual meetings. Somebody—an individual, a management group, or a committee—has to make certain that all essential activities are being carried out. Typically, responsibility for a meeting includes the selection of time, place, theme, attendees, subject matter, method of presentation, physical arrangements, notices, meeting conduct, budgeting and control of expenses, and follow-up. Too much is at stake to have all this handled in any but the most efficient and effective manner.

The man in charge of the meeting—the executive assigned the responsibility or the chairman of the meeting committee—has to be accountable for its success. He can assign and delegate, but he cannot avoid being held accountable for everything connected with the occasion and for the results.

## Advance Preparations

By the time the meeting starts it is too late to worry. But if the necessary "homework" has been done well ahead of time, lingering anxiety should be minimal. As with other management activities, planning is the key.

No matter who is in charge, it is usually wise to share the work of planning as widely as possible, though not to the extent of watering down either the purpose of the meeting or responsibility for it. Both superiors and subordinates should be involved. This builds interest and confidence in the meeting's value. First steps in planning should cover:

- Stating the theme and goals of the meeting—what it proposes to accomplish.
- Arriving at a strategy that will match the stated goals.
- Listing the improvements in skills, techniques, and knowledge areas that should occur as byproducts of the meeting.
- Listing the "carry home" benefits that each attendee should gain.

If the planner disciplines himself to take these preliminary steps, a target for the meeting will have been established.

It may be a matter of debate as to what order the details of meeting planning should take. Obviously, objectives, time and place, program, attendees, and notification are interrelated; each has a bearing on the rest. Let us consider them in order.

*Objectives.* If no purpose can be written down for all to see and understand, the meeting hasn't jelled.

Just a word in favor of *limited* objectives. Don't assume that one meeting can solve all the company's problems. Meetings are frequently doomed at the outset by overambitious programs. Putting too much into the pot causes confusion. It is usually advisable to keep within limited subject areas, to schedule fewer topics and cover each more comprehensively.

*Time and place.* Battle tactics recognize the importance of time and place, and meeting planners will do well to follow suit. There is perhaps no one best time and place for all meetings; however, careful consideration should be given to selecting the time and place most acceptable to those people who will attend. It would be wise to check dates with key participants, speakers, company leaders, and others whose presence is essential.

The time of the meeting should involve the least possible conflict with other activities, either inside or outside the company. The place should be the most convenient one that offers appropriate facilities and environment, whether it be the manager's office or a distant hotel. For a major meeting, such as a companywide convention, place considerations should include meeting rooms, food facilities, recreation, transportation, hotel rooms, staff assistance, and staging and exhibit facilities. Requirements should be personally checked before a final decision is made; pictures or someone else's description may not provide the desired information.

*Program.* What subject areas will be covered? The three primary resource areas for these should be the job descriptions of those expected to attend, the principal goals and activities of the company, and the objectives of this particular meeting. In many instances the question of subject matter will already be answered, the meeting having been scheduled for the sole purpose of covering a specific area.

Major conventions and conferences generally involve a reasonable balance of formal sessions, discussions, recreation, and other activities. The agenda should be shaped around the stated purposes of the meeting, including everything from arrival to departure.

*Attendees.* Again, this will not be a problem in cases where the meeting has been scheduled for a specific purpose or a specific group. Where the "who" is not quite so obvious, the following should be invited: those individuals who can be expected to benefit most; those who are needed because of the contribution they will be able to make; the company officials who should be there in order to show their support; and those individuals whose direct leadership will be needed to stage the meeting.

*Notification.* Notices should include more than just time and place. They should be sent out as far in advance as possible and, wherever appropriate, should include the exact reason for the meeting; specifics as to time and place, not forgetting arrival and departure times; information regarding dress, wives, transportation arrangements, and equipment or sports gear needed; information that the attendee should be prepared to furnish or advance preparations that he will be expected to make; and the minimal goals set for the meeting.

Any changes, after the initial notice, should be passed along promptly.


## Further Planning: Methods of Presentation

No matter what your favorite method of presentation may be, don't use it throughout the meeting. Variety is the price of interest. Only the truly exceptional speaker should stand before a large audience for longer than 30 minutes. The program or agenda planners are responsible for determining the most effective ways of handling the different topics and parts of the meeting. Here are just a few of the scores of available techniques:

- Featured speakers.
- A panel discussion; that is, short presentations by panel members followed by questions and answers.
- An unstructured discussion of anything that may interest those attending (not recommended for large groups).
- A structured discussion on topics that are announced ahead of time —and those topics only.
- Films, video tapes, demonstrations, skits, role playing, reports, and so forth.

With any or all of these methods, a wide variety of props can be used. It is usually advisable, where physical facilities allow and the speaker is trained in the necessary techniques, to use such aids. This creates interest, helps the speaker to get his message across, and increases audience retention. Remember, though, that when such aids are used amateurishly they are often a detriment rather than an asset. They should be simple, accurate, clear, and manageable. If they are too complex, inaccurate, too cumbersome, or impossible for everyone in the audience to see or hear, they actually detract from the effectiveness of the speaker and the success of the meeting.

Edith M. Lynch finds these overall guides convenient in planning presentations:

1. Be sure to match the subject to the audience's interest.
2. Don't let the meeting get too large unless you're planning a convention.
3. Choose leaders with know-how to lead the meeting.
4. Check with leaders ahead of time to see that they aren't falling behind in their preparation for the meeting.
5. Order all audiovisual or other special equipment necessary to make the chairman of the meeting happy.
6. Make sure that meeting facilities are adequate.
7. Be specific on the directions given to those who set up facilities, and follow through to see that they are followed.
8. Set up the meeting room in as much detail as possible a few hours ahead of time, and make a last-minute check on it.

9. Arrange for back-up resources in case the unforeseen arises.
10. If it is an outside meeting, or if the conferees don't know each other, arrange for some method of identification, such as badges. (8)

Preparation should also include a list of all the materials and equipment needed. These should be moved to the site well in advance.

## Briefing of Speakers and Leaders

For a large meeting, it is highly advisable to hold a one-day briefing session with all speakers, discussion leaders, chairmen, and others who will be expected to participate. These sessions usually cover all particulars concerning location, facilities, and arrangements. The entire agenda is reviewed, and the subjects to be presented are discussed in depth. This serves two purposes: (1) a clear identification of the subject area and role assigned to each participant, so as to avoid overlap or gaps in the presentations; and (2) insurance that all significant areas of the subject will be covered acceptably.

In addition, the time allotted for each program item is stated carefully. The availability of props and other paraphernalia is made clear. Deadlines are set for the completion of speeches, reproduction of materials, and preparation of slides, handouts, and the like. There is a certain amount of coaching in chairmanship and discussion leadership, with everyone receiving an outline of his duties and responsibility. Everyone has a chance to ask questions and clear up any uncertainties.

Experience shows that when an individual does not attend such a briefing session before participating in a meeting, he is significantly less effective in his role as speaker, chairman, or leader, and the results are often disappointing.

## The Care and Feeding of Outside Speakers

This chapter is concerned primarily with company meetings, and it assumes that most speakers and program leaders will come from within the company. However, outside speakers may be used from time to time and, generally, will require special attention.

The following communication checklist has been suggested: (9)

| Send to Speaker | Request from Speaker |
|---|---|
| __ Meeting theme. | __ Visual equipment needed in connection with talk. |
| __ Objectives of meeting. | __ Type of transportation that will be used; expected time of arrival and departure. |
| __ Size and type of audience. | |
| __ Confirmation of hotel reservations. | __ Biographical data for use in introduction of speaker. |
| __ Company annual report. | |
| __ List of company executives and meeting participants. | __ Glossy photographs for publicity. |
| __ Product information—methods of distribution and other pertinent information. | __ Verbatim copy or summary of speech. |
| __ Advance publicity and printed promotional material. | __ Any special requests, tours and so on, that would make his visit more productive and more enjoyable. |

Outside speakers are guests of the company and should be treated as such. They have something to offer, or they wouldn't have been invited to speak. A little extra graciousness will make each one a more enthusiastic and convincing participant.

## Physical Arrangements for the Meeting

What physical arrangements must be made to insure a smoothly functioning meeting? These notes, made at a top management briefing, indicate what is often desirable:

- Notebooks had been prepared and material inserted systematically.
- Name tags and table cards were prepared.
- Tables were arranged in a semicircle.
- A chalkboard and folding flannelboards were available.
- Large, clear cards had been preprinted for use on the flannelboards.
- A table in the back of the room held pertinent printed materials.

- An all-directional neck mike was available.
- Side spotlights made it easier to see the speaker and the visual props.
- Ice water and glasses were on all tables and were renewed regularly.
- Coffee was served on schedule and quickly.
- An expert was available to manage lights and visual aids, assist speakers, and avoid fumbling delays.
- Color transparencies, overhead projectors, pointers, flip charts, and a variety of other aids added interest to the presentations.
- A high revolving stool was used for the convenience of speakers, some of whom were before the group for several hours.
- A low lectern was used on a table, so that the speaker was not isolated from the audience.
- Masking tape was used on the floor to pre-position movie projectors and other equipment.
- Speech material was passed out after each talk.
- All sessions began and ended on schedule.
- Everything was in readiness when needed.
- The meeting was managed so as to maximize the speakers' effectiveness and the attendees' opportunity to hear and learn.

This will indicate the sort of comprehensive checklist that is useful in making certain that the physical environment will prove advantageous to both speaker and listener.

It is disconcerting to a speaker to arrive and discover that facilities and arrangements are not as requested or as promised. The chairman should not only comply with the speaker's last-minute requests, but should take the initiative in suggesting rearrangements that might improve the effectiveness of the presentation.

So far as the audience is concerned, creature comfort is the prime consideration. The size and length of the meeting will have a significant bearing on chairs, tables, breaks, provision for note taking, and so on. Lighting is especially important. Remember that an ill-lighted room usually results in dull interaction between speaker and audience. And, when specifying room temperature, remember that the room may seem chilly when the people arrive, but the average human body gives off heat equivalent to a 150-watt bulb; therefore, the temperature is likely to soar unless it is low at the beginning.

Every effort should be made to prevent interruptions in the orderly flow of the meeting. Ringing telephones, arrivals and departures, and any noise or activity not directly connected with the program are likely to be distracting. It is often desirable to hold meetings away from company offices simply to keep down such interruptions.

Materials to be passed out during or following a session should be handled with a minimum of delay and interference. If more than one item is involved, it is usually advisable to clip them together, put them in an envelope or notebook, or otherwise handle them so that very little time is wasted in distribution.

## The Role of the Audience

At companywide meetings in one organization each attendee receives in his folder a sheet stating the duties of a participant at a meeting—with particular reference to discussion sessions. This is an attempt to convince those attending that they have a vital role in the success of the meeting and that they are expected to contribute to it. They are reminded of the importance of arriving on time for all sessions and participating in accordance with the guides listed in the program.

Professor Harold P. Zelko, of Pennsylvania State University, has the following advice for meeting participants:

> Although you probably find yourself a participant in a meeting many more times than you are the leader or chairman, most advice on meetings centers on leadership. But the assumption that the participant is unimportant or that his responsibilities and skills can be taken for granted is anything but true. Any member of a business meeting faces problems, dilemmas, and adjustments. You can do a great deal toward making your participation more productive by adopting a cooperative attitude and by following a few basic suggestions:
>
> - Look for areas of agreement first.
> - Determine to what extent you agree with the speaker.
> - Restate his point clearly and fairly before you respond.
> - Start your reply in a pleasant manner.
> - State your position and support it with evidence and reasoning. (10)

The meeting chairman has a unique responsibility to make certain that the audience is prepared to participate and assume its proper role.

*While the Meeting Is in Progress*

Although by the time the meeting starts the die is cast, there are still many areas needing constant attention and "managing" to keep it on track and moving forward. If circumstances dictate, the man in charge should be willing to change plans. The chairman should always be prepared for emergencies and should have alternative procedures ready for use.

*Keeping on schedule.* The following guides should help:

- Begin the first session on time so that everyone will know you mean business.
- Make certain that all participants, chairmen, speakers, and associates have a carefully timed agenda—that each knows how much time he has been allotted and when he is supposed to start and finish.
- Screen speeches for length.
- Structure a few time gaps in the program for catching up if proceedings should fall slightly behind schedule.
- Leave habitually long-winded and time-abusing speakers off the program.
- Keep the meeting under control.
- If feasible, hold an extra session for material still not covered.
- If you are running slow and you have only one more session, rearrange the program so as to cover the most important material first.
- Shorten slightly the time allotted to subsequent speakers.
- Combine the neglected material with that to be covered at a later date.

The fact remains that if meetings are carefully planned and timed, speakers are adequately briefed, and all participants are properly oriented, each session should proceed on schedule.

*Small discussion sessions.* It seems extremely difficult to find people who can keep their opinions to themselves long enough to lead effective discussions. It is particularly difficult for discussion leaders to understand that their role is not speechmaker but "referee."

If discussion sessions are to be included in the meeting, the program chairman should be especially thorough in advising the leaders about their duties. Outstandingly effective public speakers are often not the best discussion leaders; if they are used, special restraint should be urged.

The discussion leader should understand that his function is to promote, control, regulate, and guide the conversation of others. He should prevent a limited number of individuals from dominating the discussion and should draw out those who are less talkative. He should be skilled in keeping the discussion on the subject and moving forward, as well as in keeping it lively and meaningful, and he must be able to manage the discussion without dominating it.

At appropriate places, the chairman may want to summarize what has been said, tie it together, and arrange it into logical patterns. He should make certain that each attendee has something beneficial to take away from the discussion. This can be done by asking members of the group to review useful ideas they have gained during the session and those they plan to put into practice.

*Follow-through for greater payoff.* Remember that the meeting started out with a theme and a set of objectives. The attendees were promised that they would receive certain benefits that would improve performance and results in their area of operations. Is the meeting making good on this promise? Assurance that it is can be gained through the following steps:

- Prevent time wasters and repeated distractions from robbing the sessions of their planned purpose.
- Provide the opportunity to discuss and evaluate the consequences of action to be taken.
- Test participants' receptiveness and mental commitment to the goals of the meeting. What major obstacles to action must still be overcome?
- Determine whether the participants have a complete understanding of the action to be taken and who is to take it. Do they understand what is to be done and when and how it is to be done?
- Review, summarize, and reaffirm mutual understanding of the plan of action prior to adjourning.
- Make a record of the conclusions and actions to be taken in order to minimize future misunderstandings.

No matter how successful a meeting appears at the time, it must produce results in terms of decisions made, action taken, and concrete accomplishments. In other words, the meeting is not finished when the gavel has fallen for the last time. The payoff depends on what follows. To encourage future action, give each attendee a sheet with the heading "Ideas Regarding This Session That I Expect to Take Back and Put into Practice." This will increase analytical thinking, careful listening and note taking, and the ultimate application of what has been learned.

Also, it is a good plan to have each session recorded or reported by an officially designated person for duplication and mailing to all attendees. This should motivate everyone to review his own notes and to put new ideas into practice.

A meeting appraisal form can be sent to each attendee after the meeting. This customarily asks for an evaluation of arrangements and facilities, food, service, subjects, speakers, methods of presentation, recommendations for the future, and—particularly—those sessions and speakers that were most beneficial. This appraisal sheet furnishes valuable information for planning future meetings.

The meeting chairman's responsibility continues until all details connected with the meeting have been taken care of: the payment of bills; the writing of letters of appreciation to all who participated; distribution of minutes or other promised material; and the orderly recording and filing of all pertinent information.

Finally, the chairman should keep an eye out for tangible results as evidenced by changes and improvements throughout the company. In view of the astronomical cost of meetings in most companies, he is clearly responsible for making that investment worthwhile.

## NOTES

[1] Laurence J. Taylor, editor, "There Will Be a Meeting Monday Morning," *The Hillsdale College Leadership Letter*, April 1962.

[2] "The Executive's Meeting Manual," *Research Institute Recommendations*, The Research Institute of America, Inc., New York, 1965.

[3] Taylor, *op. cit.*

[4] As quoted in *The Wall Street Journal*, April 4, 1967.

[5] *Ibid.*

[6] *Ibid.*

[7] As quoted in Elizabeth Marting, AMA *Encyclopedia of Supervisory Training*, American Management Association, New York, 1961.

[8] Edith M. Lynch, "Guides to Better Meetings," *Personnel Journal*, January 1966.

[9] Charles L. Lapp and Jack R. Dauner, *Conducting Sales Meetings*, Sales and Marketing Executives-International, New York, 1963.

[10] Harold P. Zelko, "How to Participate in a Group Meeting," *Nation's Business*, September 1964.

*Part V*

*Management's Unique
Challenges: Today and Tomorrow*

# 卍 19

# Moment of Truth:
# Profit and Expense Management

MAN does not live by bread alone," but neither can he live for very long without it. It is not accurate to state that the sole purpose of a corporation is to produce profit, but it is unrealistic to ignore profit—its basic importance to the company and everyone associated therewith as well as its role in society.

There seems to be an irresistible urge to "knock" success, especially the success of others. It is commonly agreed that the real reason there is so much anti-American feeling throughout the world today is that the critics are jealous. They envy the American standard of living and the success of the American system. The same thing can be said of most of our own internal critics of the free enterprise profit system, which has produced the most of everything for the greatest number in the history of mankind.

The system is not perfect. It needs to improve, to become more efficient, to render more service, to produce more goods, and to sell them more cheaply and more widely. It needs to commit more resources to research and development; to be more efficient in its use of time, human effort, and money; and to find better ways for people to achieve personal goals through their work.

But these very improvements are dependent on profit itself. Except for funding and growth through profit, companies have no resources for either self-perpetuation or growth and expansion.

## Profit as Corporate Purpose

If profit is not the sole purpose of a business, what other purposes does it have? Where does profit fit in? (We need not repeat here our earlier remarks on goals and objectives.)

Peter Drucker believes that the "contributed value concept" is the purpose of enterprise. He states that the objectives of production are "to increase the ratio of contributed value to total revenue within the existing process and to increase the proportion of contributed value retained as profit. For this means that the business has improved the productivity of its own resources." (1) He also stresses the fact that the ultimate purpose of the business must lie outside the business itself. "There is only one valid definition of business purpose: to create a customer." Regardless of company activity, its products or services, it exists and has reason for existence only as it creates and serves customers. It is the customers who determine what a business is. Customers and markets must exist in order to provide opportunities for the company to compete for business and endeavor to make a profit in the process.

Lewis Lloyd, economist for Dow Chemical, points out that "the company which sets out to make profit its primary objective is somewhat like the epicurean who seeks happiness as the ultimate goal." Dr. Lloyd believes that Henry Ford and other founders of great companies were more interested in developing greater efficiency, better processes, and better products than they were in profits. The latter was a byproduct. "The reason that profits received so much consideration," he maintains, "is that they provide a measure of success."

> They have so long been the label for effective contribution that we often confuse the label with the real factor. . . . Thus profits become objectives, results, criteria for measurement, guides, incentives and rewards. . . .

Profits are essential to the business because they are the capital for future growth, development, and expansion. With such capital, companies can build new plants, gain new markets, introduce new products—all of which can reduce risks in the future. (2)

Note that profit is only one (although the first) of the conditions that corporations have listed as essential to their success:

- Profit maximization and profitability.
- Productivity and efficiency.
- Survival and viability.
- Stability and continuity.
- Adaptability and flexibility.
- Innovation and improvement.
- Progress and achievement.
- Leadership and status.
- Excellence and quality. (3)

A business can change its organization, its products, its market, its services. But, if it expects to continue to grow, it must make a profit.

## Management's Stewardship

Professional managers recognize their responsibility for making a profit; they understand that the money and other resources committed to their care should yield at least enough increase year after year to cover the company's risks and maintain its capacity intact. In other words, managers are profit-oriented. Further, they believe that their leadership ought to maximize profits.

To make a profit means that revenues must exceed the costs of doing business. "Any organization—business, government, church, college, hospital, or labor union—must take in more money than it pays out. The difference is profit, and the source of the income does not change the profit-making responsibilities." (4)

Management has, inherent in its stated functions, profit-oriented motivators: methods improvement, quality control, avoidance of waste. The manager seeks to do the right things in order to insure the desired increase in economic value; at the same time he seeks through expense control to prevent those uneconomical expenditures that will minimize profit. The term "expense management" defines the manager's responsibility to administer expenditures with the same criteria that are applied to other managerial functions such as production and sales. Expense management may imply cost reduction, and it certainly does imply cost control; more specifically it requires the executive to test all expenses by measuring their contribution to the economic objectives of the enterprise.

## A Positive Attitude Toward Profits

American business has done, and is still doing, an inadequate job of communicating the role of profit to the public and, in particular, to the young managers of tomorrow. John S. Knight, newspaper editor and publisher, comments:

> It is fashionable these days to decry business as merely a money-grubbing pursuit. A study by the Harvard Graduate School of Business reveals that 88 percent of all college students would rather not embrace a business career. . . .

> [Yet] the onward march of progress began, not with government as such, but with inventive, imaginative and resourceful attitudes of business and industrial leaders. . . . If it were not for our free competitive system, the United States might still be an underdeveloped country—unable to support education, provide foreign aid or ever to support our government in both the essential expenses and its needless extravagances. (5)

It is high time business and industry declared, with Peter Drucker, that "profit is the result of the performance of the business in marketing, innovation and productivity. . . . Indeed, profit is a beautiful example of what today's scientists and engineers mean when they talk of the feedback that underlies all systems of automatic production: the self-regulation of a process by its own product." (6)

Every company and every manager must bear witness to this truth: It is the profit motive that disciplines business to produce only the things the public wants. It must demonstrate that profit regulates production at the price the public is willing to pay. It must remind its critics that management, in its urge to maximize profits, must constantly find ways and means of reducing costs; that this pressure acts as an incentive for the development of new processes and new machines in order to eliminate waste; and that this kind of incentive for greater efficiency, for new and better products produced more economically, does not exist in a nonprofit system.

To repeat: The entrepreneurial approach to profit is probably the economic system that will produce maximum profit and minimum waste. Individuals simply will not work with as much diligence and commitment for others as for themselves. The owner of the one-man service station and the proprietor of the 10,000-man factory understand the need for profit and the importance of careful expense management. The professional manager should develop this same "owner interest" and encourage the same commitment in all his subordinates. The result will be a true profit-expense orientation.

### Planning for Profits

Vital to overall company profit is the assignment of accountability for profit in accordance with managerial areas of responsibility. The manager *must* accept responsibility for the profitability of his unit or area, and he *must* have budgets, accounting systems, and controls for carrying out this responsibility.

The original idea behind the departmentalization of a store was better accounting, control, and profit management. In this way, the purchases, sales, operating costs, and profits for each department could be readily determined. If one department was not contributing its share of profit, management's attention quickly focused on it and corrective action could be taken.

Every department or other management unit, moreover, must have profit standards and goals just as it has production, safety, quality, and sales standards. For example: "Profit performance is satisfactory when an 8 percent gross profit is maintained throughout the year." Or: "The profit goal for the company is 9 percent annually." Such standards, clearly established and communicated, are the best guarantee of satisfactory profit achievement. They should be written into every managerial position description. Thus they should serve to keep the manager aware of his responsibility for profit and the fact that his job performance will be judged by the profit performance of his unit.

The manager must remember that he is supposed to plan to make the right things happen—including the right profit. ". . . In the crucial area of profit planning, the casual approach is still surprisingly prevalent. When it comes to profits, many top executives remain unconvinced of the power of planning. They will agree readily that profit planning is an exciting concept. They concede its logic. But in practice, they argue, it just doesn't seem to work—'at least not in our business.' " (7)

However, profit planning can and does work—dramatically—for many. The following questions suggest ways and means of making it work:

- Which of several alternative strategies would result in the greatest return on stockholder investment?
- What would be the profit impact of any of a host of possible changes in selling price, market share, distribution methods, consumption patterns, and product mix?
- What would be the potential profit impact of different operating and marketing policies?
- How would profits be affected if the company revised its required inventory practices and changed its inventory levels? (8)

Planning success demands broad involvement and participation. Each man must know exactly what is expected of him and the criteria that will be used to measure his profit performance. The following four steps are basic to effective profit planning:

- First, prepare and communicate in writing a comprehensive statement of overall strategy in terms of specific objectives and policy.
- Second, develop individual performance criteria for key positions.
- Third, insist on written plans that specify assignments, expected results, action steps, and deadlines.
- Fourth, test profit performance against targets. (9)

What is satisfactory profit performance? How well should the job be done? The manager needs answers to both questions, and both should be answered by his job performance standards. He and his superior must have the same understanding about profit expectations. They should agree on how well "the profit job" is to be done. The superior should realize that subordinate executives and managers are entitled to have quantitative profit standards to shoot for. As in the case of other goals and standards, these should be jointly established, and both superiors and subordinates must be committed to their achievement.

The professional manager's approach to his job, including his responsibility for making a profit, should produce consistently satisfactory profit results. Profit performance, he knows, is the ultimate test of managerial competence. Promotions, prestige, compensation—in short, the components of success —will be influenced more by profit achievement than by all other factors combined.

## Expense Management Is Satisfactory When . . .

Expenses are the bane of the average manager. "The boss is always on my back about expenses being too high," he complains. "Doesn't he know what's going on? Payroll costs have gone up 15 percent in two years, yet he expects me to keep operating costs at the same level."

How low is low enough where expenses are concerned? Probably, in the eyes of the president, they are never low enough, no matter what their level—or so most operating managers seem to feel. Don G. Mitchell has called periodic company economy drives "industry's equivalent of spring housecleaning." But, unfortunately, even faithful attention to expense management cannot quite eliminate the occasional need for drastic cost reduction—especially when sales are slumping or there is a decline in the economy. Even then, cost cutting is rationalized as just one phase of management's response to the emergency. Such statements as these are typical:

- "We are not tightening our belt. We are attempting to improve volume."
- "Capital expenditures have been reduced, but emphasis has shifted—rather than expansion we're working on efficiency."
- "We haven't made a crusade of it—we've just worked harder at the things we usually do, watching inventories and receivables."
- "We don't feel the situation is so urgent as to require an all-out crash program."
- "We've cut down handling the metal every place we could—each time you put it through a process it means scrap and that means money."
- "We are conducting a holding operation . . . a tightening process, looking for places where we have excess people or costs." (10)

The obvious fact highlighted by these statements is that profit-minded companies do not wait for economic declines or sales slumps before paying attention to expenses. It is a way of life in most companies. Management is constantly putting all expenses, both big and little, under the microscope to see whether they are justified.

*Deciding whether to spend.* The decision to purchase, to increase, or to invest should hinge on the potential long- and short-range contribution of the projected expenditure. Money saved by neglecting machine maintenance is false economy. The same may be true of the decision not to build the extra plant, buy the extra truck, add an additional salesman, or cut down on new product development.

The test ought to be the balance of short- and long-range return on investment or contribution to profit expectation. Money spent to purchase EDP equipment may save dollars and accelerate the growth of the company. The purchase of a new machine to replace the one that is uneconomical owing to high maintenance costs may be a profitable move. The shift to different and possibly more expensive raw materials may be a profitable investment if the additional expense is more than offset by increased production and reduced waste.

*Deciding how much to spend.* The fences of the financial ball park are expense budgets. Expenses are normally considered to be satisfactory when they are within budget limits. It is assumed that the budget has a structured margin for profit; therefore, when the manager operates within budgeted expense, he should also be making a profit.

In preparing the budget, it is essential that a margin for profit be programmed in as an identifiable category. For example, if profits are supposed to reach 8 percent, then an 8 percent profit margin should be included in the operating budget.

These expense-accounting tips should prove helpful:

- Categories of expenses should be sufficiently distinct and numerous to provide for the management of all significant expense items.
- Expense management should normally be decentralized to the lowest practical level but centralized for purposes of administrative control.
- Expense accounting should provide for a sufficient number of different types of accounting controls to spot deviations quickly and facilitate appropriate management action for correction.
- Expense accounting must make it possible to check an expenditure against budget before it is made and to compare it with budget after it has been made.

- The expense-accounting system should provide the needed guide for daily financial operations and for appraising expenses in relation to budget.

## Overall Guides to Expense Management

There is as much variation in expense management as in any other management activity. Different managers work with the same budgets yet achieve significantly different results. Here are a few recommended guides.

*Expense responsibility.* Someone has to be responsible. There should be no question about who is authorized to spend money, for what, and in what amounts. The manager must assume the responsibility for costs within his unit. If he delegates any of that responsibility, both he and the recipient must have a clear understanding of the latter's authority. In addition, every employee in the department should be made to feel responsible for operating costs. Accounting for expenditures is relatively simple compared with the job of making everyone economy-minded and savings-conscious.

*Cost effectiveness.* "All levels of management are constantly faced with the problem of allocating the organization's resources in ways that will maximize the return to the company. When both the resources and the return can be measured in monetary units, standard cost-revenue techniques will satisfactorily answer the usual questions about optimum product mix, breakeven point, and similar economic performance factors." (11) Management of expenses thus demands an examination of all costs in light of their effectiveness in benefiting the company economically.

*Cost control.* Ernest Schleusener writes as follows:

- Lower costs now—and improve earnings. It requires just as much daily attention as getting out a product.
- Make lowering costs a way of life. Controlling lost time, saving on materials and supplies, safety, and planning one's own time are all ways of controlling costs.
- Control costs through increased productivity. This should be a coordinated approach to cost analysis, cost reduction, and cost control in relation to their effect on production. Increased productivity is one of the best ways to reduce relative costs. Cost is often a percentage of production or sales, rather than a number

of dollars; therefore, when volume can be increased with little or no increase in cost, relative operating costs have been lowered.

■ Overcome resistance to the change which often occurs when reducing expenses. Lowering costs is often a matter of finding places to make improvements. Keep people informed and involved during every phase of the improvement, and resistance can be minimized.

■ Make it a habit to operate within the budget. Things go pretty smoothly when the airplane stays on course; but when it approaches danger, a sudden and jolting correction is often necessary. The same can be said regarding expense operations. Learn to use the budget constructively to make improvements to meet budget, to excel, and to show the results of management innovation.

■ Use economically and wisely the major budget items—manpower, materials, and financial resources. If the manager can save 5 to 10 percent of the cost of these resources, he may actually double earnings.

■ Organize for lower operating costs. This involves inspection to make certain that all activities are proceeding according to plan and expenses are in line with budget. Organizing for lower costs also means studying, evaluating, and controlling important cost areas. Find problems as they arise and solve them quickly, as well as developing ideas for further improvement.

■ Develop favorable and cooperative attitudes. You can't do it alone. You can't get the job done with just some of the people, some of the time—you need everyone on your team all of the time. Use your management tools of communication, motivation, and recognition to create positive attitudes.

■ Consult with others—especially your superior. Ask for his suggestions. If you are about to engage in a major cost-reduction project, it might be well to touch base with him ahead of time. (12)

Cost control has to involve a total concept approach. Although it does mean reducing expenses, it does not mean sacrificing growth and profit opportunities. It does not mean devoting strenuous effort to savings and then defeating the whole program by the careless handling of an emergency. It does not mean reduction of every expense category by 10 percent. The manager who has learned to manage production and people must also learn to manage costs with the same delicate balance of "not too much and not too little."

*Nickels and dimes.* The manager of a company insurance and employee welfare program acquired a reputation as a cost control expert. When asked how he managed to keep costs in line he replied, "I nickel-and-dime it all the way." This was his way of emphasizing that the little expenses also deserve attention. Sometimes these small but steady leaks—the unauthorized expenses—are the ones that sink the budget, the profit, and the manager.

*Business Week* reports that corporate financial managers are sharpening up all kinds of tools for making profits out of their companies' idle cash rather than letting it remain idle. (13) Perhaps this is merely a throwback to earlier generations of managers, for many of the founders of today's leading corporations had reputations for exceptional thrift. Possibly this thrift kept them from going broke because of excessive costs and, at the same time, provided the profits that led to success.

## The Professional View

Management, once more, means accountability for both profit and expense. It means applying the profit-contribution performance test to all costs. It requires research and judgment regarding short-range savings as opposed to long-range profits. It balances cost reduction against potential offsetting increases in production or other benefits to the company. Above all, it calls for keeping costs in line with budget and, at the same time, maximizing opportunities for improvement and growth even though risk is involved.

Henry Ford once said, "Businesses that grow by improvement do not die. But when a business stops making creative improvements, when it believes it has reached perfection and needs to do nothing but produce, it is done for." Most companies recognize the accuracy of this statement. With the steadily rising costs of labor and materials, they are more and more seeking improvement in the direction of profit and cost control.

It can truly be said that "profits make the world of business go round." Professional managers need never apologize for making a profit; rather, they had better be prepared to instigate changes if a profit is not being made. Just as business survival and growth are dependent on profit, so is the profession of management.

The manager should be able to equate his own personal goals with the profit goals of the enterprise of which he is a part. If the company makes a profit it can, in turn, grow and provide increased opportunities and compensation for him. As a member of management, he has a continuing responsibility for making profitable things happen and for preventing unprofitable things from happening.

In the final analysis, the executive must build economic performance into the corporate enterprise which he is responsible for helping to manage—and the criterion of economic performance is profit.

## NOTES

[1] Peter F. Drucker, *The Practice of Management*, Harper & Brothers, New York, 1954, p. 73.

[2] M. Valliant Higginson, *Management Policies I: Their Development as Corporate Guides*, AMA Research Study 76, American Management Association, New York, 1966, p. 26.

[3] *Ibid.*, p. 26.

[4] Lawrence A. Appley, "The Development of Managers Who Can Make Money," a speech delivered before various AMA top management briefings.

[5] John S. Knight, "Editor's Notebook," *The Charlotte Observer*, Charlotte, N.C., November 5, 1967.

[6] Drucker, *op. cit.*, p. 46.

[7] Jon R. Katzenbach, "A Guide for Successful Profit Planning," *Management Review*, July 1967, p. 38.

[8] *Ibid.*, pp. 41–42.

[9] *Ibid.*, p. 45.

[10] "Costs Go Under the Microscope," *Business Week*, July 8, 1967, p. 26.

[11] Wolfgang Jakobsberg, "Cost Effectiveness: What It Is and How to Use It," *Management Review*, June 1966, p. 35.

[12] Ernest Schleusener, "You've Got What It Takes," AMA *Encyclopedia of Supervisory Training*, American Management Association, New York, 1961, p. 290.

[13] "The Tactics That Win That Extra Nickel," *Business Week*, August 19, 1967, pp. 76 ff.

# ⌐ 20

# Utilizing EDP

# in the Management Process

$T$HE electronic computer has a more beneficial potential for the human race than any other invention in history." So stated Ray Eppert, president of the Burroughs Corporation, a few years ago. Although this prediction seemed fantastic at the time, today it is evident that the concepts and applications of EDP will, in the years to come, have more effect on work, physical environment, and human life than any of the major inventions of the past, including the wheel, the pulley, and the printing press.

Equally fantastic is the incredible speed with which EDP has made its impact. It took earlier inventions hundreds of years of slow evolution to make major contributions to human progress; but since the first privately owned computer was delivered, in 1954, to the General Electric appliance plant in Louisville, Kentucky, the rate of growth has exceeded the most ambitious predictions. Every year more than a billion dollars is being spent on computer installation and service, and the pace seems certain to continue. Computers, like all other machines, have to be replaced as other and still more capable hardware is developed. So the replacement factor added to the growth factor makes the computer industry, including both hardware and software, the fastest growing industry on the international business scene.

The computer age has been called a second Industrial Revolution. But can the average-size company—the one with fewer than 500 or even 50 employees—participate in this new era alongside the large corporation? The answer is an emphatic yes. The corner grocery is being serviced by electronically controlled warehousing and trucking. The local bank and the modest job-shop manufacturing concern have available to them service bureaus designed specifically to enable small businesses to enjoy the benefits of EDP through shared time. At the opposite extreme, instantaneously through the miracle of EDP, the far-flung multidivisional corporation computerizes its manpower and product inventories for immediate reference. The schoolteacher, the service station operator, the truckdriver, the plant foreman, the insurance agent, and the stockholder are directly affected by EDP.

What about top management? The retired president of a nationwide corporation warns a group of executives, "You'd better learn how to manage effectively with EDP or be prepared to move over during the next five years." In short, the company that ignores EDP in the future will be as competitively disadvantaged as the covered wagon would be if it tried to compete with trucks and planes.

## What EDP Does

Electronic data processing has been defined as "the collection of data; the subsequent sorting, analyzing, and storage of the data by means of a computer; and the summarizing and transmitting of the resultant information." (1) To state it in another way, the electronic computer is a device for ingesting, judging, and processing—or usefully modifying—knowledge.

Just as the sharpened stick, chiseled stone, and lever improved man's physical ability to produce results, the computer now enlarges his brainpower and mental capacity.

The first truly electronic computer was about 60 times faster than the mechanical calculator; but by the mid-1960's the computer was capable of performing a million transactions during the four seconds it took a man to add two short columns of figures. Thus it is able to make computations in minutes that might take a man an entire century to complete. In fact, only a computer is capable of the lightning-fast calculations required to analyze the data from a satellite or to control the flight of a missile.

In addition to speed in manipulating numbers or symbols, computers have other important abilities. They sort data; are equipped with a memory; can store information; and can assess, select, conclude, discriminate, control, and communicate. Communication can be in terms of numbers, sounds, or pictures—all of which can be transmitted electronically to remote points. It is evident, then, that the computer has become an instrument of vital concern to managerial problem solving and decision making. The manipulation of data provides the same answers as if the physical objects represented by the data had been manipulated. Through EDP, the manager has gained the advantages of incredible speed and accuracy.

The principal advantage of the computer, therefore, is that it is capable of doing a great number of little tasks very rapidly under rigidly controlled conditions. Information is reduced to computer language, and the task to be performed is then programmed into the computer. After the information has been processed, the results assembled in the form of reports help management to function more effectively.

To give the manager at least a sampling of key concepts, the following definitions are quoted from UNIVAC's *Glossary of Computer Terms*:

> *Computer:* Any device capable of accepting information, processing the information, and providing the results of these processes in acceptable form.
> *Data processing:* A generic term for all the operations carried out on data according to precise rules of procedure; a generic term for computing in general as applied to business situations.
> *Real time:* Used to describe a problem in which time requirements are particularly stringent. The term is derived from the process control field and from military applications in which the data processing must "keep up" with physical process, in a time scale of seconds or less. Other applications of real time would include reservation systems used by airlines, loading of telephone lines, the use of utilities in the electrical industry, and other areas where information on a real-time basis is absolutely necessary for adjustment and decision making. (2)

This entire *Glossary of Computer Terms* is in itself an indication of the new language that has been created by the advent of computer hardware and its applications. It defines hundreds of terms ranging from "absolute coding" to "zero suppression." As is true in every field of specialization, the general manager's first step is to gain an understanding of the language used. This is certainly true of the technical world inhabited by computer programmers, systems analysts, and the hardware and software of their trade.

## Impact on Operating Environment

The computer is changing the techniques of management drastically. When modern methods of communication are linked with EDP, managers have available for instantaneous viewing and evaluation the results of activities throughout the vast corporate network. They are no longer dependent on reports that take weeks to prepare and must filter through many minds and company levels.

With computers linked to production equipment, startling gains in output are occurring. The need for human effort is fast diminishing. Management has new means of control; results of decision making can be fed back in time for the indicated action to be effective. Whole new fields of knowledge and product development have been created.

Prior to the availability of computerized data, the information accessible to top management was often inaccurate, incomplete, and late. It did not encourage analytical reasoning. Since facts could not be relied on, management depended heavily on intuitive judgment for gauging variables and unknowns; on rules of thumb, shrewd guesses, and hunches. The computer both enables and forces the executive to think in more exacting terms, to formalize his decision making, and to base his conclusions on information that can be verified.

Computers now constitute a $5 billion world market. All over the globe they are doing new jobs—from running steel mills to planning new cities. The computer business is in fact on the way to becoming the next great international industry, ranking with oils and autos. It has been predicted that this worldwide trend will enable Western Europe as well as less developed areas to move forward rapidly in industrialization, education, transportation, and communication. Another result will be an inevitable tendency on the part of business methods everywhere to assume the same patterns. Professional management education is of course adding to this "standardization" along with the use of common types of computers and systems.

## A Continuation of Man's Search

The question is often posed: Is the computer revolution something new and unique or merely an extension of the Industrial Revolution? Most agree that it is a continuation of man's search for new tools, new sources of power, new resources of information, and better ways to produce goods and make them available to the consumer. Yet the rapid growth of EDP has certainly been unique.

Most other great inventions have flourished mainly within single industries, but this universally versatile EDP development is already indispensable in countless ways. Several thousand distinct applications have already been cataloged, and the lists are out of date before they leave the presses. Never before has a single device generated in so short a time so many technical papers, pamphlets, articles, and books. The gulf between the experts and the laymen is doubtless far greater than in the case of previous inventions. Never before has a single innovation generated such a technically sophisticated competitive, expansion-minded, and well-heeled business.

The real impact of computers on individual lives, both inside and outside business, is still only vaguely suspected. The manager of today, and even more importantly of tomorrow, cannot ignore the advantages of speed, economy, linkage, and information handling that the computer makes possible. It is the only way in which he can remain competitive.

Management must investigate realistically the contribution that the computer can make to its particular business. It must have an accurate understanding of what the computer is capable of doing and what it cannot be expected to do. It must decide where the responsibility for data processing logically belongs in the organization and how it can be fully integrated into company operations. The computer is not a toy, a gimmick, or "something that we had better get because it seems the thing to do."

Management's understanding of computer systems, it is safe to predict, will be as important to continued success as any other contributing factor.

## Basic Purposes and Applications

The Stanford Research Institute says that computer applications serve four basic purposes: To—

1. Reduce operating costs, either directly or indirectly.
2. Lower working capital requirements, thereby releasing funds for investments that yield a higher return.
3. Improve the ability of a company to serve its customers.
4. Enhance the effectiveness of activities that produce long-range improvements. (3)

Computer applications that bring about long-range improvements generally facilitate long-range planning and top-level decision making by means of the analysis of variables, simulation techniques, and better control procedures. This is where the real payoff lies. Looking at the future, a spokesman for the Research Institute of America declared:

> By the end of this decade, we predict, U.S. companies will devote their major computer-application development effort to the top management decisions of the company. These problems are typically of the broadest nature, taking into account all of the resources within the company, as well as groups outside the company such as customers, suppliers, competitors, the financial community, government agencies, and the general economic environment. (4)

An AMA survey lists the following measurable goals of EDP use as cited by participating companies:

- Improved clerical savings.
- Reduced data processing costs.
- Lower administrative or overall cost.
- Better service to customers.
- Greater timeliness of information.
- Increased speed of information.
- Improved accuracy of information.
- Greater efficiency.
- Higher contribution to profits.
- Fewer employees.
- Higher productivity. (5)

In order to accomplish these goals, computer application is used in the following areas: payroll, sales analysis, inventory control, billing and invoicing, general accounting, accounts receivable, cost accounting, accounts payable, personnel, production control, production planning, shipping and distribution, sales planning, and purchasing and ordering.

Company use of past, present, and future information prepared by computers may be divided into the following categories:

*Past information:*
- To meet legal and government requirements.
- To fulfill commitments to customers, suppliers, and the like.
- To inform employees, stockholders, and so forth.
- To analyze past conditions.
- To evaluate past performance.
- To set standards.

*Present information:*
- To measure performance against standards.
- To determine quality and quantity (materials, products, services).
- To schedule (time).
- To allocate present resources (capital and human).

*Future information:*
- To allocate future resources.
- To establish time factors.
- To forecast conditions.

It should be emphasized that EDP serves management directly in "making the right things happen and preventing the wrong things from happening." To insure a minimum of error and a maximum of certainty, the manager must have available the pertinent past, present, and future data on factors, both inside and outside the company, that will influence its course. Gathering and processing such information by computer makes it available at speeds and in forms never before possible.

## Integration and Coordination of Activities

According to Jay Forrester, "an organization is a system which has six interconnected networks of personnel, money, materials, orders, capital equipment, and information." (6) A primary use of EDP is to integrate all these systems into one coordinated, functioning whole. Although the development of information may be handled on a segregated basis, it makes its maximum contribution only when it interacts with other systems. Just as the home thermostat serves a useful purpose only when it activates the heating system and produces corrective results, sales and inventory controls are most meaningful when the resulting data provide manufacturing departments with appropriate information on product needs. In other words, computer results become valuable when they are used to activate, to make decisions, to link together, and to provide additional masses of information that have been sorted, evaluated, and distilled.

David B. Hertz declares that to integrate information successfully a management information system must—

- Be derived from the needs of the company that uses it, not from the details of a system constructed to meet external requirements.
- Take risk and uncertainty into account, and provide managers with information they need to evaluate the effects of risk and uncertainty in specific areas.
- Clearly reflect the distinction between critical factors that affect end results of the business and those that have little or no bearing on its ultimate objectives.
- Be flexible enough to accommodate increasingly sophisticated processing of the data in the storage base. (7)

The system, the information, the processing, and the end results should all be clearly oriented toward meeting specific company needs.

## EDP Influence on Management

Management may never be the same again. Because the computer directly replaces manpower and enables other machines to replace even greater numbers of employees, it is perhaps the most powerful means ever invented for increasing human productivity. It is eliminating some middle management jobs and causing drastic changes in others. Most important of all, it is steadily enlarging top management's ability, through accurate decision making, to control the activities of the company.

> The great achievement of the computer, as it affects management, is that it is enabling the executive to clear away some of the uncertainty that surrounds him, to subtract some of the variables from the circumstances that fret him, to convert many ill-structured and inherently insoluble problems into well-structured and partly soluble ones, to rely less

on hunches and intuition and more on analysis, to behave less like an artist and more like a scientist in disposing of routine matters, and to save his creativity and imagination for more important work. (8)

The following areas are especially affected by computerization.

*Organizational structure.* The first question encountered when a computer is to be purchased or rented is, what department will be in charge of the operation? And where, someone asks, will the manager be on the organizational chart? Numerous mistakes have been made in this area, principally because too little significance has been attached to EDP. Often the computer has been considered just another office machine and has therefore been assigned to the office manager or probably the financial department. A McKinsey & Company survey has revealed that most companies whose quality of management is above average place the responsibility for computer operations only one level down from the chief executive. None of these companies assigns it more than two levels down, and only those companies classed as average to below average in terms of management assign it as low as the third level down. It has become increasingly clear that the computer is a tool of top management—that the top level must support its operation, check its results, and insist that it be used for the benefit of the entire company.

Computer use has tended to flatten the organizational structure, requiring fewer levels of management and integrating activities throughout. By means of computer-processed data, each executive is able to see more clearly how his own responsibilities and functions interrelate and interact with others in the company.

*Centralization of management.* When companies were small, top management knew the status of raw materials and finished inventory, sales, equipment, and payroll at any given time. But, as companies grew in size and expanded geographically, this type of continuous personal accounting was no longer feasible. Executives began to feel they no longer had full, direct control over the company. The computer is now returning this sort of control to top management.

The chief executive can again know at all times the current state of the company—its assets, commitments, work flow, cash flow, and sales to date. To internally generated data he can add market information, the findings of customer research, and economic forecasts and so match company plans to the probable requirements of the outside environment. He can make better production decisions because he has accurate figures on production capability, present inventories, estimated and actual sales, and—very importantly—any change that is likely to occur. For example, the manufacturer of high-style ladies' garments can now program into the computer the style life of an item (possibly as short as six weeks), the percentage of sales represented by initial orders, the rate at which the item will be reordered, and the rate at which orders will decelerate. He can then proceed with greater assurance that the right number of garments, not too few or too many, will be manufactured.

*"People" problems.* Perhaps the most difficult challenge facing management in connection with EDP is not cost, staffing, or type of equipment but the necessity of dealing with human resistance to change. It is, to a large extent, the attitudes of the executive himself that will influence the climate in which EDP operates and determine whether resistance is a problem. Certainly, as an integrating device, EDP must not be allowed to become a divisive force.

Some of the changes brought about by the introduction of EDP have to do with changing levels of knowledge and skills required. Mathematicians, especially with advanced degrees, are in growing demand. Whole new specialties and job categories have been created—such as those of the computer programmer and systems analyst. Moreover, the training and development of middle and top managers is bound to accelerate. Older executives are in danger of becoming obsolete.

Employees may be required to work undesirable hours. The tremendous investment represented by the hardware of EDP means that it must often be in use around the clock. Not all individuals can or are willing to work other than "normal" hours.

Personnel administration will become more and more computerized. All record keeping—payroll, employee benefits, administration, manpower inventory, employment procedures—will be integrated into the EDP system.

The problem of "meaningful work" is likely to be intensified. As computers take over more of the strictly manual, repetitive, routine tasks, men and women will be free to engage in more interesting and meaningful work. But for some individuals work may become less meaningful and interesting, and there will be few markets for some of today's skills. Management must remain aware of the individual's need to engage in meaningful activity and of the explosive implications of large-scale dislocation of workers. With regard to EDP personnel, a new breed—with new traits—will be required.

> They expect to be paid more; they will be experts in their own special field and might know more than their boss; they will be mobile and will frequently identify more with their profession than with an individual company, and if they don't like their present job they will seek greener pastures; and they will want extras—high salaries and promotional op-

portunities, and also a sense of challenge and achievement, recognition, and continuous growth with learning. (10)

## Professional Management and EDP

It is predicted that the computer-age professional manager will require new talents. The traditional manager's ability to plan, organize, and control on the basis of his knowledge and experience alone must be modified to "(1) planning by asking the computer 'What if . . . ?' (2) organizing by choosing wisely from the many more alternatives that the computer provides; and (3) controlling by utilizing computer feedback." (11) Let's take a closer look at the computer's influence on several areas of management.

*Establishing objectives.* Factors that must be considered in establishing goals, both quantitative and qualitative, can now be programmed into the total picture much more quickly and with more certainty. Defining the philosophy of the business, assessing its immediate and future environment, and formulating business objectives to support company philosophy become more realistic with computer-processed data.

Objectives can now be established on the basis of past relevant experience, present circumstances, and future probabilities. They depend less on guesswork, judgment, and opinion and more on concrete facts and figures that can be statistically supported.

*Management planning.* Planning is the development of broad programs to achieve established objectives. This often includes resource-oriented subprograms for the full implementation of plans. Planning begins with forecasting, and predictive systems start with a forecast of demand. Computers make possible the collection, evaluation, and processing of data of all types essential to accurate forecasting and planning, including allocation of resources—manpower, financial, equipment, and so forth.

*Control.* Thomas J. Lipton, Inc., has as its objective in EDP: "To integrate related functions and provide a bank of perpetual data which will permit improved control and contribute to profit." (12) Other companies reflect their desire to achieve similar results through

- Control of manufacturing and development operations; reduction, avoidance and control of direct and indirect cost; meeting contract time and quality requirements; development of management information systems.

- Improved production planning through more efficient production controls to be accomplished through computer usage.
- Improved operating control; improved effectiveness of management control. (13)

Computers provide for immediate feedback of information concerning results. This information can be used by management to take corrective action. The advantage of the computer is that the information is available quickly and can be inclusive enough to provide management with the significant facts needed. The computer even goes a step further and predicts what the probable results will be if management takes certain action.

*Administration.* Administration is primarily concerned with getting things done. Getting things done depends on management decisions, and management decisions benefit infinitely from EDP.

If executives make incorrect decisions, the cost to the company may amount to many thousands or millions of dollars. Management decisions must be correct most of the time—in the best interests of the company from the standpoint of economic performance and opportunity for growth. Computer-processed reports based on data that are right up to the second can substantially improve the validity of the managerial decision-making function. Obviously important here is a "real time" system which will enable executives to make the best decisions they are capable of—*promptly.*

*Coordinating and communicating.* EDP is particularly beneficial in the areas of coordinating, communicating, and keeping all company systems and activities tied together. This is evidenced by the following results cited by various companies:

- More action is being taken on the information being supplied.
- Increases the tempo of the organization.
- Has encouraged management to accelerate new plans, programs, and analysis.
- The broadening of managerial concepts with respect to modernization.
- Keen analytical approach toward operating the business.
- Management has more flexibility.
- Greater discipline.
- It has provided for closer cooperation between the major departments.

- Better understanding of interdivisional and departmental problems.
- Communication has increased. (14)

*Review of results.* Management must appraise and evaluate results—comparing objectives and actual achievement. EDP provides immediate feedback on results. This profile of "what has happened" provides first an opportunity for evaluation and then a basis for future planning and forecasting.

## Going the EDP Route

How does a company decide whether EDP will pay off and, if the possibilities look good, go about installing it? First, the top executive should make a "total" investigation by checking with similar companies, by surveying the use of EDP throughout his industry, and by checking with equipment manufacturers and professional associations. Then, once the company is seriously contemplating the introduction of EDP, the first actual commitment should be the employment of an EDP expert—an individual who can provide the technical knowledge the company must have for a successful installation.

Many experts feel that an organization employing 500 or more employees can probably justify its own EDP equipment, depending on the nature of the company and what it does. Units vary in cost according to size and degree of sophistication. Larger units require a commitment in excess of $750,000.

Rather than outright purchase, many companies are renting or leasing equipment. One large national company owned its equipment for several years and then switched to leasing. Rental cost alone is now running in excess of $250,000 per month.

Smaller companies, and those that have still not taken steps to install equipment for private use, are purchasing EDP services from service bureaus and private computer companies.

The best advice that can be given regarding the relative merits of purchasing, leasing, and contracting for EDP is to investigate thoroughly. Millions of dollars have been wasted by hasty, ill-considered action: The wrong equipment has been bought, management's expectations regarding EDP have been unrealistic, and the result has been disillusionment. In many instances companies have not known what to do with the equipment they have invested in and have therefore failed to utilize its potential.

Most managers are not computer experts. However, they don't have to be technical experts or computer engineers to understand EDP and manage it more effectively. Wise management involves relying on the experts when necessary, avoiding quick decisions, and making a careful and thorough determination of total cost based on return on investment—both short-range and long-range.

Some final points for management guidance:

1. EDP does not guarantee fail-proof management.
2. It provides no substitute for management thinking, decision making, or day-to-day activities.
3. The manager must be extremely careful not to expect too much or too little from computers.
4. "Garbage in, garbage out." The computer can only process the information it receives. If unreliable, inaccurate, disorganized, and outdated information is fed into it, the same kind of information will come out.
5. One of the principal advantages of EDP lies in the discipline required to gather, systematize, and prepare data for computer processing. It is this reduction of information to common symbols or numbers that provides the basis for communication and understanding.
6. Don't expect dramatic dollar savings when switching to EDP. In many instances costs will increase, but other advantages and gains should eventually offset the additional cost.
7. If properly utilized, the computer should have a significant impact on the growth of the business through improvement in management decision making; increased speed of management response; improved control of inventories, processes, and activities; and increases in competitive edge. These benefits could prove far more important than actual dollar savings.
8. The computer can be the servant of management only if it is fully and appropriately integrated into company operations.

## Management in the Computer Age

The potential of EDP is almost beyond comprehension. Computers are now able to talk with other computers over long distances. Equipment in one part of the world is able to activate equipment elsewhere for filling orders, billing, inventorying, and printing out results for use in other systems. There is no doubt about it! Management is in the computer age.

In addition to mastering the basic skills of the professional manager, the computer-age executive must be knowledgeable in the following areas:

- The building of information systems.
- The kinds of data that will be of greatest benefit to his company.
- The best ways for utilizing the computer to make decisions, solve problems, and manage resources.
- Using computer benefits for achieving peak performance and results by putting the right people in the right jobs at the right times.
- Using the computer to look objectively at the business, evaluate its goals, and discover and implement ways of improving it.

Each chief executive, it has been suggested, should ask himself the following questions.

- Do I devote to the computer-systems effort the time and attention its cost and potential warrant, or have I backed away from my role and delegated the responsibility to the technical people three and four levels down?
- Do I see that the computer is used for more than just routine record keeping—that we are also using this resource to find new and better ways of running the business?
- Have I insisted on carefully pricing out all proposed computer applications, and do I follow up to insure that we have earned a significant tangible return?
- Have I clearly indicated to operating managers that I hold them accountable for seeing that they get the most out of computer systems in running their divisions?
- Have I provided the company with the kind of computer-systems manager needed to get the job done; and have I given him the support, stature, and staff he needs? (15)

As with all management expenditures of money and time, there must be bench marks for the evaluation of computer results in terms of the measurable gains derived by the company in return for the investments required. What tangible benefits is the computer system producing in the form of better operating information, reduced manufacturing-cycle time, improved customer service, and the like? How effective is the computer in contributing to profits? It should be making itself felt in all major areas of the business.

Management cannot realistically ignore the tremendous potential that computer systems are able to put at its disposal. EDP is taking more and more of the guesswork out of managing and replacing it with reliable data.

NOTES

[1] M. Valliant Higginson, *Managing with EDP*, Research Study 71, American Management Association, New York, 1965, p. 19.

[2] D. D. McCracken, Harold Weiss, and T. H. Lee, *Programming Business Computers*, with permission of the publishers, John Wiley & Sons, Inc., New York, 1959.

[3] Higginson, *op. cit.*, p. 45.

[4] *Ibid.*, p. 45.

[5] *Idem.*

[6] *Ibid.*, p. 37.

[7] David B. Hertz, "Developing a Computerized Management Information System," *Management Review*, April 1966, p. 63.

[8] Gilbert Burck and the editors of *Fortune*, *The Computer Age*, Harper & Row, Publishers, Inc., New York, 1965, p. 101.

[9] John T. Garrity, "Getting the Most Out of Your Computer," McKinsey & Company, Inc., New York.

[10] Donald G. Marquis, as quoted in *Personnel Management—Policies and Practices*, September 19, 1967, p. 4.

[11] John W. Cogswell, as quoted in *Personnel Management, op. cit.*, p. 5.

[12] Higginson, *op. cit.*, p. 85.

[13] *Idem.*

[14] *Ibid.*, p. 80.

[15] Garrity, *op. cit.*

# 21

# The Executive Interacts
# with the World Outside

Tʜᴇ executive and his company cannot exist as an island. They are part of a dynamic, living world community that is interacting at all times, whether by design or neglect. The business enterprise cannot ignore or be ignored by the world outside its corporate walls. Benefits ought to flow in both directions. Enterprise and external environment should function to the advantage of each.

To put it in simple terms—every modern-day manager has an undeniable responsibility to the world outside the organization. He must be prepared to cope with the powerful influences of that world on his company and himself. These influences are inevitable and decisive. They constitute an opportunity which offers potential gain for both sides.

*Changing Environmental Patterns*

The alert, responsive company's internal organizational structure is constantly changing. But even greater and more significant are the changes taking place in the external environment, thereby modifying the internal climate as well. These changes affect the manager, his functions, his job performance, and the company's economic performance. The manager has to be aware of them and react appropriately—or, preferably, participate in their design, initiation, and implementation.

What are some representative environmental changes that are influencing managerial job performance?

- *Population dynamics.* Included under this heading are the overall increase in the U.S. population (past the 200-million mark in 1967); increases in the percentages of the total population in both younger and older age brackets; the accelerating restlessness of families, customers, and employees; the worldwide population explosion in all its implications; and rising expectations, purchasing power, and political response.

- *Increased role for government.* According to a Labor Department survey, the fastest-growing segment of the labor force is to be found not in electronics or transportation but in government. This includes local, state, and national agencies. In many communities there are more employees on government payroll than on the payroll of any other single employer. Moreover, in addition to competing for talent and business, government exerts a direct influence on business as the taxing authority and as a regulator, inspector, and controller of the economy.

- *New technology.* The technological and informational revolution is drastically affecting every phase of management. The combination of the computer with automated, self-regulating machinery points to a production system of almost unlimited capacity.

- *The revolution in human rights.* Even more significant than technological change is the revolution in human rights, expectations, values, and loyalties. The manager senses this change internally almost as much as he is reminded of it by the daily news. Employees are changing, and so are their attitudes, their work habits, and their organizational involvement. New vision, new understanding, and new tolerance will be required on the part of management.

- *Mobility and communication.* There are no captive markets any longer—you can't count on the business just because you are there. Customers are mobile; they are well informed and independent. The freedom of movement created by superhighways, the ubiquitous automobile, easy credit, and increasingly quick communication mean that customers will patronize the company which best merits their business. One out of every five families moves each year. Fads, new words, new movements, new attitudes, and new ball games are being created almost overnight. Management must react in the right direction and degree.

These are only a few of the many forces outside the corporate walls that are determining, to a large extent, what must go on inside those walls. Corporate graveyards are too crowded with "bankrupt," "out of business," "acquisition," and "merger" inscriptions to ignore the realities of changing environmental patterns.

### Development of Corporate Citizenship

Management has moved from a posture of isolation, a "live and let live" philosophy and active hostility to outside influences, to direct and active involvement in the outside world. This has involved a shift from paternalism to corporate citizenship. The "profit is everything" creed has been replaced with a social concern and awareness implemented by the commitment of funds and executive talent. The companies that contribute most generously to the United Fund also furnish the volunteer leadership that insures the success of the program.

To be sure, certain standards and guides must be recognized by both parties: mutual trust, the sanctity of contracts, and general integrity in the pursuit of daily activities. Neither side should be so suspicious of the motives and practices of the other that constant policing requires a disproportionate amount of attention. At the same time, however, it is generally accepted that our free enterprise system relies on an elaborate framework of political surveillance over private affairs.

It is assumed, also, that competition serves as a regulatory control over the internal affairs of the corporation and its relationship with outsiders, that risk taking is essential to innovation and progress, and that the benefits of the economic system must be shared on a fair basis in accordance with the contribution of the individual or organization. This sharing of benefits, it is believed, must be kept in balance, thus restraining power groups from abuses of control. Investors, managers, employees, customers, and others who have a vested interest in the company and its activities all need to have their interests protected, and all have the right to associate or not associate with a given company. The traditional prerogatives of management are rapidly being modified. Government, unions, and society in general are making inroads on its right to make decisions and operate without outside regulation and inspection. Then, too, management's own concept of its role has changed steadily over the years. Early scientific management was oriented to the slide rule and stop watch; it attempted to maximize the efficiency of the work environment and work methods—with a minimum of consideration for the individuals involved. Finally, professional management emerged, combining efficiency with a concern for human lives, rewarding the individual in accordance with his contribution, providing certain job-related benefits, but leaving the management of the individual's private life largely in his own hands.

As the corporation has become less of a manipulator of lives and destinies, it has found itself increasingly at the mercy of outside forces. More and more, management has had to recognize and accept these significant and often decisive influences beyond its control and, accordingly, has taken increasing interest in initiating, shaping, and guiding those influences. This has caused executives to turn to politics and governmental affairs. For example, it has caused such business leaders as Fred Lazarus, head of Federated Stores—feeling that business can be no healthier than the community in which it operates—to urge Federated management to take as much interest in good local government, good schools, and good roads as in the affairs of the company.

The shift from isolation to direct involvement, participation, and influence is a recognition that the welfare of the company and its people is dependent on a sound educational system, honest government, and an economically sound and enlightened community.

## The Chief Executive's Changing Function

The public finds it difficult to identify with a large, impersonal corporation. Although millions are being spent by companies each year to communicate their nature, integrity, and "lovability," it is still easier and cheaper to tell the public about *individuals* in those companies—especially the principal executives. There are advantages in so doing that shed light on the changing role of the executive:

- It is easier to like a person than a mausoleum.
- People want to know about top executives, because they are the success symbols and, therefore, intrinsically glamorous.
- More influence for the boss often means more sales and status for the company.
- If the boss seems dynamic, people tend to assume that his company is, too—which improves the financial position of the company.
- Fame for the boss helps morale, discipline, and efficiency within the company. People want a leader who leads. (1)

This opportunity to become a "shining knight" also involves the possibility of becoming the "goat." The "Mr. Cleans" render a distinct service to corporate interests, but executives who become involved in unfavorable publicity can render just as much disservice. Inevitably, what the executive is and does affects the company; he cannot dissociate himself from it and contend that what he does publicly, and often privately, has no effect on it. Whether favorable or unfavorable, there will be a reaction in employees; in the company's particular section of its industry—its competing companies, its associations, its major distributors and suppliers; in shareholders and the financial community at large; in industry as a whole; in the general public; and in government.

Because of this impact, the executive will usually benefit by consulting with others about matters that concern these groups. He will often want to sound them out before deciding to run for political office, endorse or condemn proposed legislation, or change major policies involving himself or the company. It is often wise to channel the resulting announcement through one individual who is responsible for the company's public relations. When all executives do this, the company is protected against indiscriminate statements and presents a consolidated front to the public.

The chief executive in particular must come to realize that, aside from paid publicity and advertising, company executives are the company's greatest potential asset in the public arena. Through the imprint of their personality, the corporate image can be given individuality, warmth, humanity, and the stamp of progress. As long as they are in positions of leadership they personify the company, and it is only good management that they should represent it systematically, widely, and well.

## New Demands and Opportunities

A phenomenon of our day is what Daniel Lerner, of Massachusetts Institute of Technology, calls "the importance, to the participant society, of the enormous proportion of individuals who are expected to have opinions on public matters—and the corollary expectation of these people that their opinions will matter. . . ." (2) This places new demands on management.

The tide of rising expectations has reached flood stages. People associated with a company, regardless of whether they are employees, customers, stockholders, or mere neighbors, now feel entitled to a great deal from it. Employees expect to be paid fairly, receive numerous fringe benefits, have safe and comfortable working conditions, and in general meet with treatment which personifies the value and dignity of the individual. Suppliers and customers alike expect honesty, dependability, and quality. Investors expect a reasonable return on their money, and neighbors expect the best corporate foot to be forward at all times. Many of these expectations amount to "rights" that are protected by law; hence company interests are being served from both the public relations and the legal standpoint when management responds appropriately.

The changing status of the corporate institution and of the professional manager, and the relationship of both to today's world, present unique opportunities for renewal and innovation looking to a better company, a better society, and more beneficial interaction between the two. Management has the opportunity to apply its genius, its resources, and its influences toward personal affirmation, meaningful work activity, self-direction, and wholehearted contribution on the part of all individuals everywhere—not just within the company. This means encouraging good citizenship as well as good workmanship. It means measuring up to community responsibility as well as company responsibility. It means contributing fully in all phases of life.

Management's new thrust ought to be, in the words of John Gardner, "outward and upward." Management is reaching out—overflowing into all facets of community and world affairs.

## Ingredients of Company Reputation

Let's take a look at the factors that influence public regard for a company. Opinion Research Corporation, through 145,000 personal interviews and other measurements, has discovered that the individual organization is helped or hindered in moving ahead by three factors:

1. Public attitudes toward companies in general.
2. Public attitudes toward the industry of which the company is a part.
3. The individual corporate image the public holds of a company, in comparison with the image held of its competitors. (3)

These factors must be taken into consideration in devising a sound public relations program. If public attitudes favor large companies, then size should be emphasized. However, the little business often tends to arouse the sympathy of many for the "underdog." A prominent Fifth Avenue store advertises, "We are still your small, friendly, intimate place to shop."

If the industry of which the company is a part is highly regarded, then the company should identify itself with the industry. However, if the industry is regarded unfavorably, the company would do better to develop a strong individual reputation with a minium of identification with the industry.

If the public regards the company much more highly than it does the company's chief competitors, management should certainly make every effort to determine what characteristics or policies may be responsible for this preference and emphasize them consistently. However, if the public has less regard for the company than for others in the industry, or if the public's image differs markedly from management's own image of its position vis-à-vis its competitors, management knows it must change either its internal policies or its advertising and promotion methods.


## Projection of Reputation

Company image is primarily determined by how widely and how well the company is known, the degree to which people feel well disposed toward it, and the public's ideas of its main characteristics. On the other hand, the reliability of the company's products or merchandise, the experiences people have had in their dealings with it, and the composite picture of what the company is and does constitute its reputation; and this reputation must be *projected*; that is, the company must tell its story to the public.

The Galeries Orleanaises, a firm located 80 miles south of Paris, states its thinking on the projection of reputation as follows: ". . . Public relations is only a means of conveying the results of an overall public relations policy and should not be embarked on until the internal public relations policy matches the concrete facts of the firm's day-to-day existence." (4) Thus it emphasizes the importance of having "your house in order" and practicing policies that deserve projection before attempting to publicize them.

Since many companies have regarded their public as consisting primarily of customers, present or potential, they have devoted very little attention to projecting their reputation to other segments of the public. They have failed to realize how important it is to communicate with others—including the public as a whole. Today, more and more companies are realizing that they can scarcely afford to be silent; that they are operating not only in an age of easy communication but in a democratic society that expects participation. Moreover, because companies are more visible to the general public now than they were in the past, they have a responsibility to inform the public about their beliefs and policies. Frederick Kappel, as chairman of the board of AT&T, stressed that business should increase the public's understanding and confidence:

> Doing our best is not enough. We must also tell our story and tell it convincingly. We must do this in every community. We must see to it that the public really knows us, and that the public's representatives in government are directly and fully and honestly informed about what we are trying to do. If we are given treatment that we believe is wrong or shortsighted, we must say so and say why, and never stop working to get the situation corrected. When on the other hand, regulators and legislators give us the means or encouragement to step up progress, then we must work to the limit of our ability to justify their confidence and trust. (5)

The various publics have both subconscious feelings and logical opinions concerning a company because of what they know about it. If the company, because of its service, its product, its employees, its executives, or its activities, is viewed favorably, then individuals or groups have maximum identification with it. The foundation for this favorable image and identification is being right and doing right, then getting credit for it by aggressively projecting the company's story to the public.

## Concern for Social Problems

It has been relatively easy for the executive to identify his company's self-interest with good government, good highways, and enlightened educational systems. But it has been more difficult for him to concern himself and his company with the social problems and challenges of the world community.

Although management has generally been skeptical of the academicians, it is beginning to listen to the behavioral scientists whose findings are providing many of the answers to questions about why people react the way they do—both employees and the company's publics. Robert O. Carlson, of the Public Relations Department, Standard Oil Company (New Jersey), says that the alliance between the corporate manager and the social scientist has come of age—to the benefit of management. Employee opinion, public reaction to advertising campaigns, consumer attitudes toward new products—all these are in the realm of the social scientist and are of paramount concern to management.

But what is social awareness? It is a concern for people—employees, certainly, but others as well. It has a moral tone that extends to the whole of humanity. It is not the assumption of total responsibility for poverty programs, public welfare, or our entire package of social ills. It does, however, mean extra effort on the part of a big and powerful corporation to reach down and help a youngster, to rehabilitate a worker or school dropout; and it does mean extending the hand of opportunity, of a chance for honorable self-support, to those who have never learned to hope.

After the Detroit riots in the summer of 1967, Ford Motor Company employees were on strike for several weeks. During this time, some 5,000 obtained other employment and did not return to their jobs when the strike was over. Ford announced that it would replace these workers with hard-core jobless and others from Detroit's poverty areas. Carl Rowan, in his newspaper column immediately following this announcement, wrote:

> Suddenly, 5,000 ghetto-dwellers will have a meaningful stake in their city, their society, their country. That will be 5,000 more effective voices—voices more effective in the ghetto than any Negro middle-class voice—sounding hope where heretofore there was mostly despair, even self-pity. . . . We can all hope that ugly violence is not necessary to awaken other giants of American industry. Surely they will have a slightly better idea, as they watch the new Ford workers go by. (6)

The corporation's social self-interest was evident when the first Henry Ford decided to raise wages to five dollars a day. He recognized that cars could be sold only to people with earnings high enough to buy them. Today, corporations are realizing increasingly that—in addition to their moral, human and religious implications—riots, poverty, poor education, and low standards of living mean inadequate markets and unsatisfactory sources of employees. Thus they also mean an extremely unfavorable environment in which to do business. (During the 1967 riots in Milwaukee, one of the country's largest shoe manufacturers ran 40 percent behind in production because employees refused to pass through disturbance areas.) In city after city throughout the country, concern for social problems has become a very real influence on corporate life.

## How Companies Are Responding

As an increasing number of corporations see their responsibility to society in terms of the problems of poverty, lack of educational opportunity, and low cultural and living standards, they are responding in many ways:

- Funding, jointly or individually, special programs for training, counseling, and providing job opportunities for disadvantaged individuals.
- Lowering employment standards, including test cutoff scores, in order to provide job opportunities for still more individuals.
- Providing know-how and guidance for special training and employment programs such as the National Association of Manufacturers' "Solutions to Employment Problems." These programs are usually implemented through local funds and leadership resources. They offer general courses in mathematics and reading, as well as skill training.
- Establishing special programs in deprived areas. Employment interviewers go into ghetto areas and make job offers; then training facilities are set up within the company to accommodate the new recruits.
- Providing special supervision and counseling to assist the individual who lacks the discipline and background for adjusting to the job and its requirements.

Why does a corporation go to such lengths—unprofitable as they are at least for the short range? A North Carolina State University professor has said that the limiting factor on company growth in highly industrialized areas will not be lack of capital or physical facilities but lack of manpower. If people will not seek jobs, training, and improvement on their own initiative, then coorporate leadership must seek them out where they are, train them, and work to integrate them into the productive apparatus of the enterprise.

American management has demonstrated its mettle in solving production problems throughout the world. Who is better qualified than this leadership to respond to the social problems affecting the business community? The only real and lasting solution to these problems will be profit-producing employment in private enterprise, not welfare or government-subsidized programs.

## The Executive and Outside Groups

The executive must cooperate effectively with many outside groups in the discharge of his company- and community-related responsibilities. Listed here are a few of these groups and some suggestions for effective relationships with them.

*The general public.* The corporation must deserve a continuing vote of confidence from its constituent customers. The manager is responsible for initiating and guiding those activities that will earn this continuing confidence and for reinforcing it in the eyes of the public with every resource available. Too, as he interacts with the public, he learns from it and is influenced by it.

*Trade associations.* Almost every type of business has a trade association specifically organized to serve the particular needs of its industry. These associations provide information, stage workshops and meetings, publish printed material, and generally seek to offer any services required by member companies. Individual executives should take full advantage of these services.

Association leaders are knowledgeable in all areas affecting the specialized interests of its members. Often the exchange of information is the most meaningful of the services available. However, the association can share only that information which has been shared with it by member companies. Executives should work closely with such groups, make information freely available, and provide leadership and funds.

*Educational institutions.* What does education expect of business, and what has business a right to expect from education? The academic community is dependent upon the business community for financial support, leadership, direction, and the employment of its graduates. In turn, business must make its requirements known to educators. Although high schools and colleges are primarily concerned with general education, business also expects the development of special capacity and knowledge that will enhance the value of the individual to the company throughout his career.

It is doubtful that any group has a higher stake in education than does business. The increasing complexities of business, its greater intellectual demands, and the higher skill requirements of leadership are all dependent on improving the *quality* of education. Not only will the managers, professional employees, and rank-and-file workers of tomorrow be the product of today's educational institutions, but much of the research in chemistry, science, and physics on which business and industry so largely depend is carried forward on university campuses.

Educational leadership can make a direct contribution to business, and business can make a leadership contribution to education.

*Labor unions.* The influence of organized labor may of course be internal as well as external. As general working conditions become more favorable, wages rise, and enlightened self-interest continues to improve work-related benefits, the initial need for unions, in the opinion of many, has been substantially minimized. The fact remains, however, that if business and government are to be termed the two largest power blocks in the economy, organized labor must be considered a close third. Regardless of whether a particular company is unionized, the executive must remain aware of the unions' countrywide influence and their relentless attempts to increase their membership. Where unions are a factor, the executive must learn to negotiate effectively with them, live with the resulting contracts, and acknowledge the impact on employees of outside influences.

The years ahead, it has been said, "are promising ones for labor-management relations. With management becoming professionalized, and with the new generation of labor leaders concerned more with adjustment to situations of permanency than to emergency and existence, mutual problems should yield to intelligence rather than to force." (7)

*Suppliers of capital.* Very few businesses are able to grow and operate without borrowing funds from either financial institutions or investors. In the case of many small colleges and state universities, the most important function of the president is to influence suppliers of capital or financial support, and often the same thing is true of the chief corporate officer.

In fact, the availability of capital for ambitious growth plans, regardless of the source, is often decisively affected by the interaction of the entire executive group with the financial community. In other words, financing hinges on the confidence investors have in "the management" as evidenced by past profits and reputation in the community. Certain it is that "isolation management" will not be in the best interests of the company.

*Governments.* We use the plural here because every company has to deal with scores of local, state, and federal agencies, boards, inspectors, regulations, forms, and reports. The employer is told how much he must pay his employees, how many hours he may work them, and what the specifications of his product are to be. The post office tells him what size he must make his cartons; his accountant tells him how much tax he must pay; the bank tells him how much reserve he must keep in the bank—the list is endless.

It would be almost impossible to catalog all the government guides and regulations with which the average businessman must comply. Their number and complexity have necessitated the presence of large legal and accounting staffs in most companies. Although government professes a concern for the small businessman, its own requirements have made it almost impossible for him to exist if he is too small to afford the specialized staffs necessary to deal with government regulations. Just as every manager must understand the terms of the union contract, where one exists, he must also understand those government regulations that affect his managerial practices. Whether he agrees with them or not, he must attempt to comply with them to the best of his ability.

How big and how influential is the government? *Steel* magazine states:

- The federal government is the largest single customer for many companies today—when local and state governments are included, the total would amount to about 35 percent of the gross national product.
- The federal government dominates, either through financing or control, 65 percent of the outlay for research and development.
- Solutions to many major social problems call for joint efforts of industry and government at federal, state, and local levels.
- Government is rapidly emerging as the major influence in key labor negotiations and contract settlements.
- Government has become the single most important factor in determining the profit and loss of a company. In addition to taxes, consider the costs of government accounting and reporting, trade regulations, labor law, patent procedures, Washington representation, and executive time spent in preparations for and attending hearings. (8)

Joseph W. McGuire, of the University of Washington, summarizes the situation as follows: "The government has become so firmly entrenched in our business life that our economy might justly be called a mixed economy. The role of government has expanded so greatly that our economy is today dependent on it, both as a buyer and as the chief element of control over business power." (9)

The executive will be well advised to become familiar with all government requirements affecting his job activities and to know where to find the answers to the problems he will inevitably encounter. It can be safely said that government represents the largest and most powerful group outside the company with which he will have to interact.

A good executive is also a good citizen. The executive and the corporation have citizenship responsibilities both inside and outside the company. The outside interaction involves active leadership, contributions, favorable influence, initiation of beneficial programs, a response to social awareness, and the practice of good citizenship.

The executive interacts with the world outside either effectively, for the benefit of the company, or ineffectively, to its disadvantage. Any one of the many outside groups is capable of making or breaking the company. It isn't enough to do a good job internally; effective relationships must be built and maintained externally as well. Otherwise, the executive is likely to find his climb up the management ladder halted.

## Notes

[1] Eric Webster, "The Chief Executive's Role in Corporate Public Relations," *Management Review*, December 1965, pp. 4–5.

[2] Daniel Lerner, "The New Enlightenment," *Advertiser's Digest*, June 1967, p. 14.

[3] "Business and Government: A Better Understanding," *Steel*, June 13, 1966.

[4] "A French Retailer Views Public Relations," *Pick-Up* (United Parcel Service), December 1965.

[5] M. Valliant Higginson, *Management Policies I: Their Development as Corporate Guides*, AMA Research Study 76, American Management Association, New York, 1966, p. 12.

[6] Carl Rowan, "Ford Setting Admirable Example," *The Charlotte Observer*, Charlotte, N.C., November 6, 1967.

[7] Keith Davis, *Human Relations in Business*, McGraw-Hill Book Company, Inc., New York, 1957, p. 172.

[8] "Business and Government: A Better Understanding," *op. cit.*

[9] Higginson, *op. cit.*, p. 112.

*Part VI*

*Conclusion:*

*Impacts and Imperatives*

# 22

# Conclusion:

# Impacts and Imperatives

Dramatic changes have occurred since Theodore Roosevelt told us: "Far better it is to dare mighty things, to win glorious triumphs, even though checked by failure, than to take rank with those poor spirits who neither enjoy much nor suffer much, because they live in the gray twilight that knows not victory nor defeat." The "Rough Rider" could have been talking about modern management. Its ranks do not seek the poor spirits, the play-it-safers, the twilight souls, or the don't-rock-the-boaters; but they do desperately seek those who are "willing to try mighty deeds." Opportunity for both success and failure is unique in the command ranks of corporate management, which offers—all at one time—success, failure, status, reward, disappointment, personal affirmation, and excitement. The demand, the challenge, and the opportunity are there—but individual response is measured only by performance and results.

## Management Is Impact

"To have a part in a significant enterprise, to be one of its movers and managers—in industry or in government—is *not* to fill some niche each morning and leave it each night as you found it. It is to help build and shape, to plan and to execute, to measure alternatives against the horizon and act on the course that judgment and resolution commend," (1) declared Frederick R. Kappel, retired head of AT&T, during a talk at Westminster College.

Maintenance is not enough; it is not managing. Management is impact—making things happen, getting things done, motivating people, achieving results. It is not waiting for things to happen; rather, it implies creating a planned and purposeful impact upon one's environment. It means that the score on the board is higher because you've been in the game. Managers are movers. They think. They improve the way the game is played. They widen the competitive edge. Maintenance as a management philosophy or operating guide is unacceptable.

Measure the magnitude of your impact and you have a profile of your management job performance. No impact—no management. Impact can be either constructive or destructive. The quarterback can throw a pass that wins the game or suffer an interception that loses it. He can call the right plays or the wrong plays. However, he knows one thing for certain: he can't keep possession of the ball without moving it toward the goal line. The quarterback who calls more right plays, and executes them more successfully, is the quarterback whose team wins more ball games. To have an impact on team performance is the role of management leadership. To avoid it, to misuse it, or to deny it is abdication and abuse of the right to manage.

## "Some Kind of Manager"

Every supervisor and executive is "some kind of manager." He is a manager right where he is—at the level at which he is now managing. He is effective or ineffective; he is successful or unsuccessful; he is improving or failing to improve results.

One of the most difficult facts for executives and supervisors to accept is that they *are* managers. Regardless of the present scope of their responsibility, they are managers to the same degree that the first-line supervisor or the president is a manager. Managers are responsible for resource utilization and for results. Too often they say, "If I were president around here, a few things would get done. Then I would really start managing." The imperative is to manage *now*—to be the best, most effective manager at one's present level of responsibility. The results one achieves at this level serve as the criterion for present compensation and future promotion.

Are you willing to risk your future on the type of management you are providing today? How are you managing the only management opportunity you have right now? Confront and discharge every opportunity with such a high degree of competence that the consequent activity and improvement in results will merit your being singled out for still greater opportunities.

### The Management "Stretch" for Excellence

To manage is to believe in the quality of excellence. It is to work for growth and improvement as a way of life. It implies a commitment to efficiency, development, creativity, and maximum utilization of resources; and this commitment must emanate from a personal conviction that the pursuit of excellence in every work activity and human contact is the manager's most vital task.

Competence, excellence, commitment, and the satisfaction of achievement transcend corporate and material goals. They become almost spiritual in that they give both meaning and purpose to human life. The spirit is programmed to achieve, but there can be no fulfillment when the individual's own failings, his environment, or corporate leadership denies him this opportunity. Achievements and contributions that may truly be termed excellent strengthen the fabric of the individual life, the corporate structure, the quality of free enterprise, and the self-sufficiency of mankind.

John W. Gardner expressed this well:

> The importance of competence as a condition of freedom has been widely ignored. Keeping a free society free, vital, and strong is not a job for the slovenly. Free men must be competent men. In a society of free men, competence is an elementary duty. Men and women doing competently whatever job is theirs to do tone up the whole society. And the man who does a slovenly job—whether he is a janitor or a judge, surgeon, or technician—lowers the tone of the society.

> But excellence implies more than competence. It implies a striving for the highest standards in every phase of life. We need individual excel-

lence in all its forms—in every kind of creative endeavor, in political life, in education, in industry—in short, universally. (2)

Mr. Gardner's words have far-reaching implications for every manager.

## The Will and the Commitment to Excellence

The compelling facts of corporate existence dictate that competitive advantage and, hence, ultimate survival and growth in a dynamic society will be determined by achieved results. The commitment to excellence as a philosophy, an attitude, and a practiced way of life provides the surest guarantee for personal and corporate success.

In order to respond to pursue excellence as a continuing guide, individual managers must have the will to manage effectively. This pursuit of exellence does not stop with lip service; it becomes a commitment to the extent that it is subscribed to personally by every individual in the company.

The manager who reaches or "stretches" for excellence in this way is impelled to examine thoughtfully his entire philosophy of life and the degree to which he has committed himself to it as evidenced by his performance on the job. How do others see him? How do they view the way he discharges his responsibilities in the context of excellence? Are his subordinates similarly committed to excellence, and is this reflected in performance, harmonious relationships, group loyalty, and results? What is the superior willing to do to improve results by improving commitment?

## Response to Management Imperatives

It is possible to state that response to management imperatives is satisfactory when certain essential action is taking place and stated objectives are being achieved. And these imperatives are not being responded to effectively if this action is not occurring and these objectives are not being met to the maximum degree.

What are these imperatives?

*Mental competence and application.* Management is primarily a mental activity. Its daily functions are only slightly related to physical strength or stature, but they are related directly to mental activity. The results of planning, organizing, controlling, and the like are the product of mental processes. Management performance, therefore, is determined principally by mental competence and application.

If an individual is chiefly "thing"-oriented, if he is research-minded, or if he prefers quiet, unchallenging pursuits, then management is not likely to be his cup of tea. Management requires an extended mental reach. It confronts a man with daily mental challenges, moments of uncertainty, the anguish of decision making, and countless problems that are almost solely dependent on mental skills for successful solution. Make no mistake about it: Management's principal tool is the human mind. Managing is, first, thinking; second, implementing the results of thinking.

*Development and growth.* One cannot overemphasize the decisive importance of development and growth in the corporate enterprise. Management is by people—individuals whose performance and results-producing capability is dependent on their ability to grow and enlarge their competence. Gilbert H. Clee, former managing director of McKinsey & Company, feels that ". . . the basic objective is to create a working environment in which the individual has a maximum opportunity for innovation, freedom within the discipline of teamwork, and fairly rigid quality control job performance standards." (3) This whole factor of development and growth is so basic to the future of the whole enterprise that it is often called the most decisive imperative of management. Fundamental to it are the skills and knowledge on which job performance is built. But growth in management implies the development of increased competence not only in oneself but in others. It requires greater vision and understanding of total purpose and concern for broadening of individual contributions.

*Wise use of time.* The resource of time is available equally to all managers and managements. It is what they do with this resource that determines whether they will succeed or fail. The misuse of time causes as many management problems as any other factor. Most managers feel that they could get the job done, and done correctly, if only they had enough time.

Managers with heavy responsibilities are bound to run short of time if they try to give equal priority to all their activities and if they have not learned that management is "getting things done through other people." Almost every top manager needs to be reminded occasionally to "put first things first." He should review his position description and list those items in it on which successful performance is dependent. He should be discriminating in deciding between the essential and the desirable. Then he should arrange this list of activities in the order of their importance. Finally, he should decide whether others should be helping him by doing part of the job.

A good way to begin using one's time more effectively is to determine just how it is being used at present. This alone is often sufficiently shocking to demonstrate the need for change. Trying to do everything, or too many things at one time, often results in doing nothing well. Excellence can be achieved only by concentrating completely on a limited number of areas at any one time.

One of the manager's continuing responsibilities is not only to use his own time effectively, but to provide the leadership and environment that will enable his subordinates to use their time to the best advantage. Matching assignments to the abilities of the individuals will help to keep time productive. The man who is the best tax accountant, obviously, should spend more time on tax accounting and less time on customer relations if customer relations is his weak suit. And it is a principle of sales management that the man who is a brilliant supervisor and trainer of men in the field should not be required to spend hours in nonproductive paperwork. In short, it is the manager's job—beginning with himself—to steer people into those jobs and tasks that they can do best and most profitably. Used within the organizational framework, this practice can make strengths productive and weaknesses irrelevant.

### Innovation and Creativity

Creativity should not, as we have seen, be confined to the research and development department. Every man has the potential for creative contribution, and management is responsible for insuring that each has unrestricted opportunity to make his full contribution to the success of the company. It is essential that companies provide the special kind of climate that is receptive to new ideas and procedures. They must also have a realistic approach to the appraisal, reward, and use of the fruits of creativity.

Top management is the single most important factor in establishing this sort of climate. The mere fact that a company has come to recognize the need for creativity in its managers is likely to result in an atmosphere that is conducive to innovation. Modern management needs more than just "bodies"; it needs originality that improves the company's product, manufacturing methods, marketing procedures, customer relations, and economic performance.

And the more it can convince its subordinates that originality is what it wants, the more originality it will get.

## The "Professional" Label

How do your job performance and results measure up to professional management as described in this book? Does everything you do reflect a belief that management is an activity, based on known principles and subject to an organized approach, which utilizes specific skills, has available to it certain tools, and is subject to fundamental disciplines?

Remember that experience is not a satisfactory criterion for judging management effectiveness. Neither is intelligence, education, or length of service. The only valid criterion is the degree to which one assumes a professional approach to management responsibility and activity. This implies a willingness to observe professional disciplines and use professional tools and techniques for the purpose of achieving the maximum potential return.

The professional manager responds to every opportunity that comes his way. If he is a wise manager, he goes one step further and creates additional opportunities for himself. Opportunities exist in every job, and every manager has ample latitude for creating still others. "Lucky" executives are able to identify them and respond to them constructively.

It has been said that some individuals are accident-prone; that is, they have certain habits or characteristics that repeatedly involve them in accidents. The same principle applies to the executive who habitually achieves the respect of others and is able to produce results through them. The job performance of this executive can be said to be competence- and success-prone. He tends to do the right things every time, not just occasionally. And he is likely to carry this tendency with him from job to job and from one management level to the next. Competence-proneness, as evidenced by achieved results, provides the best indication that the executive will continue to be successful in future environments and responsibilities. It is the sign of a professional manager.

In summary, the principal difference between the successful and unsuccessful, or between the professional and the unprofessional, is the results produced—not in terms of total number of activities, hours worked, effort expended, and so on, but in terms of constructive achievements which benefit the enterprise. It has been said that managerial performance consists of intangibles and cannot be measured or evaluated. Much of this book will have served to disprove this theory. Actually, there are scores of specific performance indexes that provide relatively accurate yardsticks: number of customer complaints, production costs, unit costs of handling and transporting products, share of market, ratio of inventory to assets, net profit as a percentage of sales, employee turnover, equipment down time, unfilled orders, percentage of deadlines missed, performance against standards or forecasts, return on investment, and many others. What better indicators can there be of performance against established goals? What easier way of insuring that the imperatives of management are being effectively discharged?

## The Final Test

In the final analysis, performance must be reduced to financial terms. Overall company performance is implicit in the profit and loss statement given to the board of directors, to the stockholders, often to the employees, and of course to interested members of the public at large. This report is the most significant indicator of how well the company has been managed. Thus it becomes the most convenient means of evaluating the success of the chief executive and his management team.

The premise of this book has been that it is possible to design successful management and maximize individual and team effectiveness through the professional approach. This includes accepting the inevitability of a major fact of corporate life—that economic performance must be built into the operation. Managing by design provides the surest guarantee of individual and corporate achievement.

### NOTES

1 Frederick R. Kappel, from an address at Westminster College, Fulton, Missouri, 1962, as quoted in Lawrence A. Appley, "To Leave an Impact," *Management News*, October 1967.

2 John W. Gardner, *Excellence*, Harper & Row, Publishers, Inc., New York, 1961, p. 158.

3 "How McKinsey Minds Its Business," *Business Week*, November 18, 1967, p. 175.

# Additional Readings

# ⌘ Additional Readings

Louis A. Allen, "The Art of Delegation," *Management Record*, March 1965.

Lawrence A. Appley, "Management and the American Future," in General Management Series 169, American Management Association, New York, 1954.

Roger D'Aprix, "Is Group Static Jamming Company Communications?" *Machine Design*, July 20, 1967.

Glenn A. Bassett, *Management Styles in Transition*, American Management Association, New York, 1966.

———— and Roger H. Hawk, "Function and Dysfunction in the Organization," *Personnel*, September–October 1965.

J. D. Batten, *Beyond Management by Objectives*, American Management Association, New York, 1966.

John A. Beaumont, "How to Write a Job Description," Small Business Administration, Washington, D.C., February 1965.

R. R. Blake, *et al.*, "Breakthrough in Organization Development," *Harvard Business Review*, November–December 1964.

Michael G. Blansfield, "Executive Development: A Group Training Approach," *Personnel*, March 1956.

Rodney H. Brady, "The Computer's Impact on Top-Level Decision Making—Today and Tomorrow," *Harvard Business Review*, July–August 1967.

William H. Burgess, " 'Calculable Growth' Means Corporate Vitality," *Management Review*, September 1965.

Richard P. Calhoon and C. A. Kirkpatrick, *Technique of Successful Supervision*, Prentice-Hall, Inc., Englewood Cliffs, N.J., 1960.

Robert O. Carlson, "The Corporate Manager and the Social Scientist: An Alliance Comes of Age," *Management Review*, December 1966.

Leo Cherne, "The Era of the Uncommon Man," *Personnel*, November–December 1965.

George W. Crane, *Psychology Applied*, Hopkins Syndicate, Inc., Chicago, 1946.

Ernest Dale, *Organization*, American Management Association, New York, 1967.

John Dearden, "How Useful Are Real-Time Information Systems?" *Harvard Business Review*, May–June 1966.

"Describing Men to Machines," *Business Week*, June 4, 1966.

D. C. Dougherty, "The Function of Top Management Organization Planning and Control in a Manufacturing Corporation," *Personnel*, January 1954.

The Editorial Board of Business and Professional Publications, *Executive Leadership Course*, Vol. 1, Prentice-Hall, Inc., Englewood Cliffs, N.J., 1963.

Dwight D. Eisenhower, "What Is Leadership?" *Reader's Digest*, June 1965.

David W. Ewing, "Getting Corporate Planning off the Ground," *Harvard Business Review*, July–August 1967.

Robert E. Finley, editor, *The Personnel Man and His Job*, American Management Association, New York, 1962.

Guy B. Ford, *Building a Winning Employee Team*, American Management Association, New York, 1964.

Andrew Forrest, *The Manager's Guide to Setting Targets*, The Industrial Society, London, England, 1966.

Saul W. Gellerman, *Motivation and Productivity*, American Management Association, New York, 1963.

Edwin E. Ghiselli and Clarence W. Brown, *Personnel and Industrial Psychology*, McGraw-Hill Book Co., Inc., New York, 1948.

George D. Halsey, *Supervising People*, Harper & Brothers, Publishers, 1953.

Lowell D. Hamric, "Automation's Impact on Jobs and Hiring," *Administrative Management*, November 1966.

Cameron Hawley, "The Quality of Leadership," *Personnel*, May–June 1960.

Carl Heyel, *Organizing Your Job in Management*, American Management Association, New York, 1960.

Richard H. Hill, "Data Processing: How to Use Outside Programming Services," *Data Processing Magazine*, March 1966.

Robert Hoppock, "Ground Rules for Appraisal Interviewers," *Personnel*, May–June 1961.

Daniel D. Howard, "Management Is Leadership," *Advertiser's Digest*, July 1967.

Hubert H. Humphrey, "America's Great Success Story," *Reader's Digest*, December 1965.

Ray Hyman and Barry Anderson, "Guides for More Effective Problem Solving," *International Science and Technology*, September 1965.

"The Implications of the Industrial State," *Business Week*, July 8, 1967.

Frederick R. Kappel, "The Information Revolution: Every Manager in It," *Stores*, October 1966.

Marion S. Kellogg, *Closing the Performance Gap*, American Management Association, New York, 1967.

Frank X. Kiefer, editor, "Could the Secret Be Atmosphere?" *Department Store Economist*, March 1964.

John T. Kimball, "The Age of the Intuitive Manager," *Dun's Review and Modern Industry*, January 1966.

Warren E. Kirby, *Long-Range Planning: The Executive Viewpoint*, Prentice-Hall, Inc., Englewood Cliffs, N.J., 1966.

Donald A. and Eleanor C. Laird, *The Technique of Personal Analysis*, McGraw-Hill Book Co., Inc., New York, 1945.

*Leadership on the Job*, edited by the staff of *Supervisory Management*, American Management Association, New York, 1957.

Harry Levinson, "What's Happened to Loyalty?" *Think*, January–February 1966.

Douglas C. Lynch, *Leading and Managing Men*, The Ronald Press Company, New York, 1950.

"Machines Won't Take Over After All," *Business Week*, October 8, 1966.

Jennifer S. MacLeod, "The Effect of Corporate Reputation on Corporate Success," *Public Relations Journal*, August 1967.

Walter R. Mahler, "Bringing About Change in Individual Performance," in General Management Series 186, American Management Association, New York, 1957.

———, "Every Company's Problem: Managerial Obsolescence," *Personnel*, July–August 1965.

Pietro V. Marchetti and Robert L. Malone, "Understanding: A Key to Leadership?" *Personnel*, January 1956.

Alfred J. Marrow, *Behind the Executive Mask*, American Management Association, New York, 1964.

A. T. Mathews, "Keeping Tabs on 7,500 Middle Managers," *Personnel*, May–June 1966.

L. F. McCollum, "Developing Managers Who Make Things Happen," *Management Review*, May 1967.

Edward A. McCreary, "When a Decision Is a Gamble: What's Your Best Bet?" *Think,* March–April 1967.

Thomas O. McDavid, "How to Listen—Effectively," *Business Management,* 1962.

Douglas McGregor, "Do Management Control Systems Achieve Their Purpose?" *Management Review,* February 1967.

Jerrold M. Michael, "Problem Situations in Performance Counseling," *Personnel,* September–October 1965.

James Nathan Miller, "The Art of Intelligent Listening," *Empire,* July 25, 1965.

Robert B. Morton, " 'Straight from the Shoulder'—Leveling with Others on the Job," *Personnel,* November–December 1966.

William H. Newman, "Overcoming Obstacles to Effective Delegation," *Management Review,* January 1956.

William Oncken, Jr., "The Authority to Manage," *The IMC Bulletin,* May 1966.

Willard E. Parker and Robert W. Kleemeier, *Human Relations in Supervision,* McGraw-Hill Book Co., Inc., New York, 1951.

"Program for Automated Future," *Business Week,* February 5, 1966.

William Rados, "Keeping Sales Meetings on Schedule," *Sales Meetings,* March 18, 1966.

Thomas S. Roberts, "Training Managers to Make Decisions: The In-Basket Method," *Personnel,* September–October 1965.

Fred J. Schreiber, Jr. and Wesley E. Hervi, "Top Priority Need: Long-Range Planning," *Burroughs Clearing House,* July 1967.

David Joseph Schwartz, *The Magic of Thinking Big,* Prentice-Hall, Inc., Englewood Cliffs, N.J., 1963.

Harvey Sherman, "Organization Planning: How to Get Results Your People Can Live With," *Management Review,* October 1966.

William R. and William B. Spriegel and Edward Schulz, *Elements of Supervision,* John Wiley & Sons, Inc., New York, 1956.

Lynde C. Steckle, *The Man in Management,* Harper & Brothers, Publishers, New York, 1958.

George Strauss and Leonard R. Sayles, *Personnel—The Human Problems of Management,* Prentice-Hall, Inc., Englewood Cliffs, N.J., 1960.

Lydia Strong, "Do You Know How to Listen?" *Management Review,* August 1955.

Laurence J. Taylor, editor, "The Freedom to Change," *The Hillsdale College Leadership Letter,* May 1962.

Raymond F. Valentine, "Appraisal Interviewing Without Stress or Strain," *Supervisory Management,* December 1965.

————, "Laying the Groundwork for Goal Setting," *Personnel*, January–February 1966.

————, *Performance Objectives for Managers*, American Management Association, New York, 1966.

Eric Webster, "How to Mismanage Managers," *Management Review*, January 1967.

————, "Ideasmanship: What Every Manager Should Know," *Management Review*, February 1964.

————, "No. 1 Executive Problem: Finding Out What's Going On," *The Pemberton Quarterly*, No. 20, 1967.

Hensleigh C. Wedgwood, "Fewer Camels, More Horses: Where Committees Go Wrong," *Personnel*, July–August 1967.

E. F. Wells, "To Solve a Problem—Change the Problem," *Supervisory Management*, October 1966.

*What's Wrong with Work?* National Association of Manufacturers, New York, 1967.

Eugene E. Whitworth, "How to Give an Order," *Supervisory Management*, January 1966.

Edward S. Zelley, "How to Say a Few Words," *Nation's Business*, July 1966.

*Index*

# ꙮ Index

# About the Author

Ray A. Killian is vice president and director of personnel and public relations for the group of 400 Belk department stores. He received his undergraduate degree at Lenoir Rhyne College and did graduate work and special study at the University of North Carolina, George Washington University, and Harvard University Graduate School of Business Administration.

Mr. Killian was associated with the Committee on Scientific Research and Development, Washington, D.C., and was personnel director for the North Carolina Department of Revenue and later for Belk Brothers Company before assuming his present position. He has taught at Queens College, the Graduate School of the University of Virginia system, and has conducted special courses at the Harvard University Business School.

He has conducted many training programs and seminars for managers and supervisory personnel. He is a frequent speaker on management leadership subjects and has written numerous articles for national publication. His book *Managers Must Lead!* was published by the American Management Association in 1966.

Mr. Killian is active in both business and civic organizations. He has served as chapter president and national director of the Society for the Advancement of Management, three-term member of the board of directors of the National Retail Merchants Association, president of the Personnel Directors Association, and member of the training advisory committee of the Educational Foundation for Commerce and Industry for North Carolina. He is currently serving as chairman of the Charlotte Chamber of Commerce Manpower Development Committee.